A Portrait of Historic Athens & Clarke County

A Portrait of

Historic Athens & Clarke County

Frances Taliaferro Thomas

Pictorial Research by Mary Levin Koch

THE UNIVERSITY OF GEORGIA PRESS

ATHENS AND LONDON

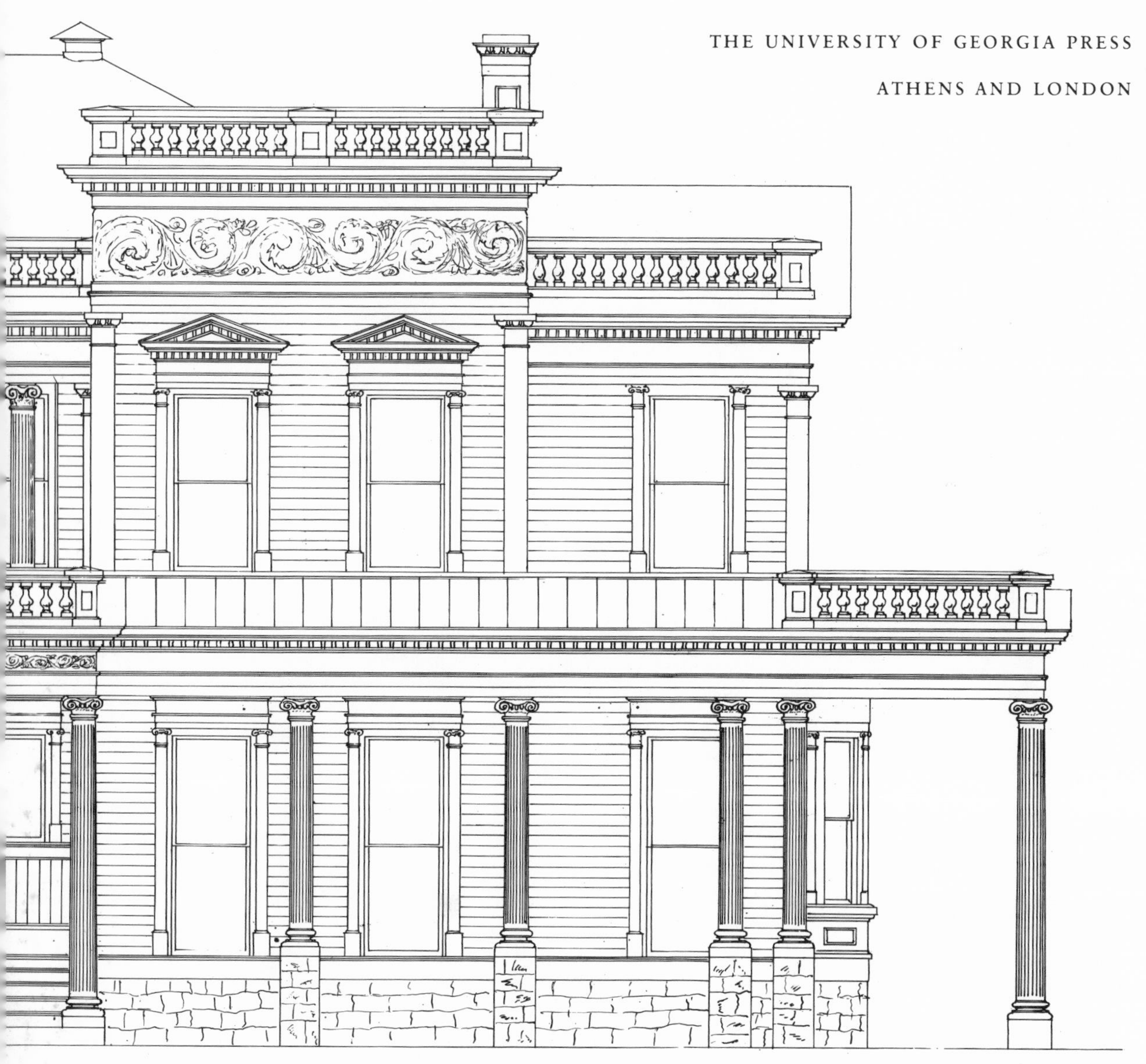

Designed by Sandra Strother Hudson
Set in Sabon by Keystone Typesetting, Inc.
Printed and bound by Thomson-Shore
The paper in this book meets the guidelines for permanence and durability of the Committee on Production Guidelines for Book Longevity of the Council on Library Resources.
Printed in the United States of America
96 95 94 93 92 c 5 4 3 2 1

Library of Congress Cataloging in Publication Data

Thomas, Frances Taliaferro.
A portrait of historic Athens and Clarke County / Frances Taliaferro Thomas : pictorial research by Mary Levin Koch.
p. cm.
Includes bibliographical references and index.
ISBN 0-8203-1356-4 (alk. paper)
1. Clarke County (Ga.)—History. 2. Athens (Ga.)—History. 3. Clarke County (Ga.)—Description and travel. 4. Athens (Ga.)—Description. I. Title.
F292.C5T46 1992
975.8'18—dc20 90-23435
CIP

British Library Cataloging in Publication Data available

For the preservation community in Athens

to John and Karen
hands-on preservationists
(see pages 200, 202, 211) and
good friends and now neighbors,
Affectionately,
Fran of Middle Cobbham

Contents

Acknowledgments *ix*

Chapter 1
Life and Times on the Oconee Frontier *1*

Chapter 2
Town and Country: The Antebellum Experience *30*

Chapter 3
The Confederate Years *70*

Chapter 4
Toward a New South: The Aftermath of War *101*

Chapter 5
Rails and Roads: The Changing Face of Clarke County *139*

Chapter 6
The Urbanization of Clarke County *185*

Chapter 7
Into the Eighties and Beyond *228*

Appendix 1
National Register of Historic Places,
Clarke County Listings *257*

Appendix 2
Chief Administrative Officers, City of Athens *261*

Bibliographic Notes: A History of the Histories *263*

Bibliography *267*

Illustration Credits *275*

Index *285*

Acknowledgments

We have been blessed with the enthusiasm and expertise of numerous individuals and organizations in compiling this history of Athens and Clarke County. Indeed, the generosity of the community and the University of Georgia in sharing many and varied resources has been overwhelming.

The author acknowledges particularly David J. Hally, professor of anthropology, and Louis DeVorsey, Jr., professor emeritus of geography at the University of Georgia, for their help in preparation of chapter 1; the late Paul Hodgson for his oral history of the period covering the Great Depression, cotton industries in Athens and Clarke County, and the massive urban renewal projects in which he played a leading role. In addition the author thanks especially Mary Anne Martin Hodgson for her insightful editing and criticism of the manuscript in all its varying forms. The Athens-Clarke Heritage Foundation has been most generous in sharing the plethora of information in their files.

We thank Thomas E. Camden and Nelson Morgan of the Hargrett Rare Book and Manuscript Library, University of Georgia Libraries, who generously opened the library's voluminous files; Sarah Lockmiller, libraries photographer of the University of Georgia; Sharon Sanderson and Mark Sorrow of Photo Express for their care in reproducing photographs; Martha Blakeslee, former registrar, Georgia Museum of Art, for her thoughtful suggestions; and the many lenders who shared with us their family collections and allowed us to reproduce their photographs for this volume.

Given the format of this volume, it is not possible to cite all sources that were helpful in recording modern events. However, the author acknowledges a great debt to a handful of local journalists, including Rufus Adair writing for the *Athens Banner-Herald* and *Daily News* and Conoly Hester, Pete McCommons, and raconteur Morgan Redwine of the *Athens Observer*. Clarke County agricultural extension agent Dan Gunnells also provided valuable information.

We extend to Karen Orchard, associate director and executive editor of the University of Georgia Press, our gratitude for her encouragement in the publication of this book. Ellen Harris has offered invaluable assistance as copyeditor.

Finally the author acknowledges Emory Morton Thomas—scholar, teacher, critic, editor, and first husband extraordinaire—for his particular brand of expertise and encouragement. A true scholar-athlete, Emory has always felt that the most significant fact about Athens, Georgia, is that it was once the home of the Hanna Bat Company. His viewpoint helped keep things in perspective.

A Portrait of Historic Athens & Clarke County

1

Life and Times on the Oconee Frontier

A dominant theme in the story of Clarke County has always been land—who wanted it, who had it, and to what purpose people planted, planned, and built upon it. In prehistoric times native Americans hunted, fished, and gathered plants here. White people founded a college and with the aid of African-American slave labor built towns here on the Georgia frontier. An era of cotton plantations and early manufacture later yielded to modern urban and academic development. Throughout its history, how and why this land along the north and middle forks of the Oconee River took shape is a fascinating study of priorities.

THE NATIVE POPULATION

The first inhabitants of present-day Clarke County were direct descendants of people who entered the New World from Asia some twenty thousand years ago. Known to archeologists as Paleo-Indians, the nomadic tribes probably arrived in Georgia and Clarke County around 10,000 B.C. These aboriginal hunters tracked now-extinct large game such as mammoths, mastodons, and ground sloths, and gathered native plants in a climate somewhat cooler than the current clime.

By 6000 B.C. Clarke County's environment more closely resembled what it is today. The Archaic Indians of this period collected a greater variety of wild foods—including hickory nuts and acorns, fish, and small game—than their Paleo-Indian ancestors. Population was increasing, and people were beginning to live in semipermanent camps. By 2000 B.C. they were cultivating some native plant species, in particular squash and sunflower, and they were making and using pottery tempered with vegetable fiber.

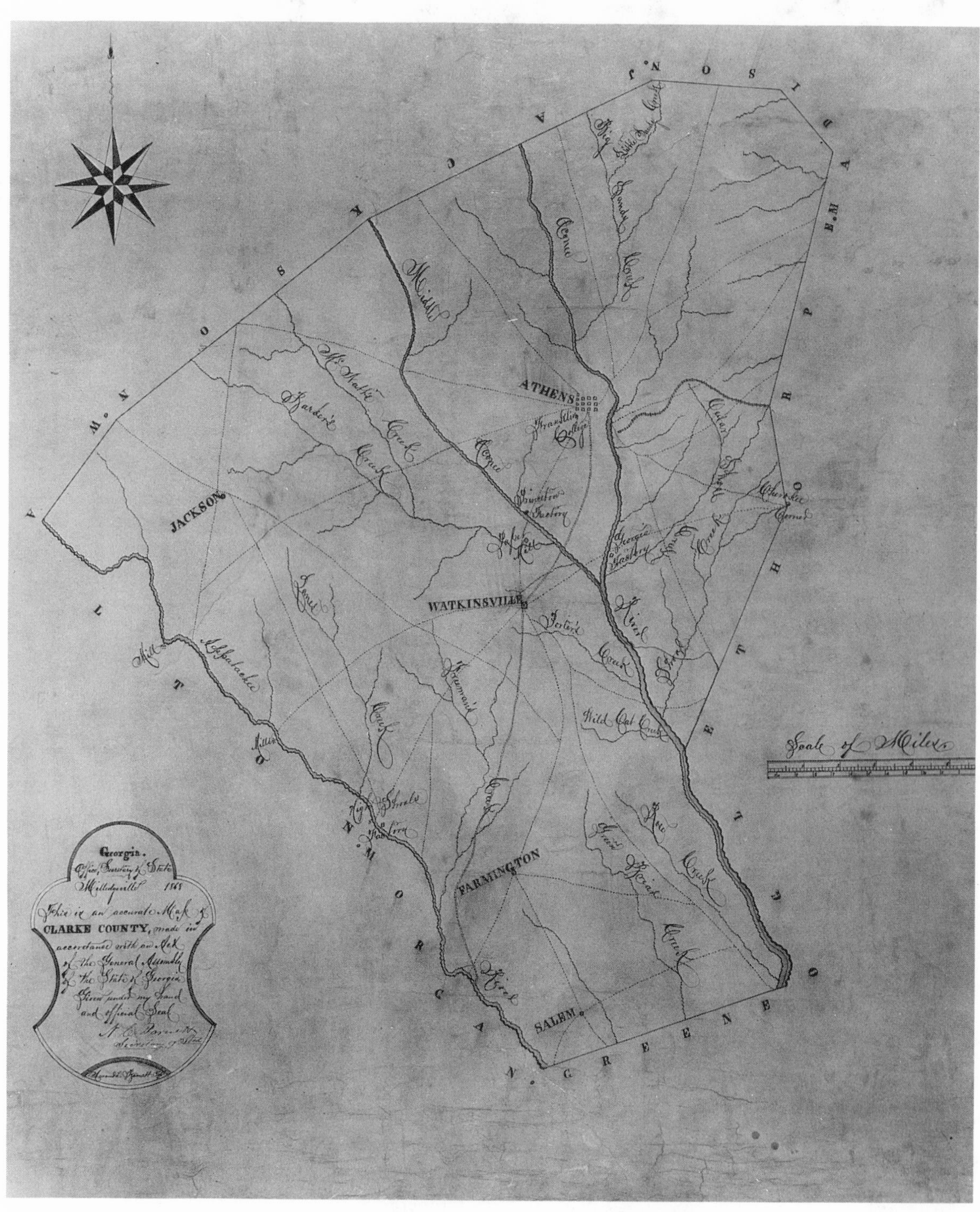
ATHENS
Franklin College
JACKSON
WATKINSVILLE
FARMINGTON
SALEM
Wild Cat Creek
Scale of Miles
Georgia.
CLARKE COUNTY,

This 1868 map is the earliest official rendering of Clarke County. Drawn by Amanda Barnett, daughter of the Georgia secretary of state, the map defines the towns of Athens, Salem, and Watkinsville, then the county seat.

During the Woodland Period (1000 B.C.–A.D. 1000) settlements grew larger and agriculture more important, especially with the introduction of maize (corn) from Mexico by 100 B.C. Still, wild animals and plants constituted the principal diet of people subsisting here.

By the Mississippi Period (A.D. 1000 to European contact), the native inhabitants of northeast Georgia were town- and hamlet-dwelling agriculturalists with an increasingly sophisticated socio-religious system. Hereditary chiefs, considered divine, ruled vast territories covering hundreds of square miles and including thousands of people.

During this period present-day Clarke County was part of a "chiefdom" that had its capital at Scull Shoals, just south of Clarke in what is now Greene County. Most citizens of this chiefdom actually lived within a few miles of the large political center. The area now Athens was probably most heavily used for hunting white-tailed deer and turkey and for gathering nuts and other wild plant foods. There were probably only a few scattered farmsteads in the Clarke County area.

About three inches long, this native American tobacco pipe from the late sixteenth century is made of finely ground clay. Archeologists recovered it from the grounds of the Navy Supply Corps School. The pipe was used with a hollow wooden stem or cane inserted into one end. The pipe's owner probably came from a settlement in nearby Greene County.

The first European to penetrate the northern portion of Georgia was Hernando de Soto. In the 1540s he led an army of five hundred soldiers northward from present-day Tallahassee, Florida, in search of gold and other wealth. His expedition likely bypassed today's Clarke County, but probably some of the people of the Scull Shoals chiefdom encountered his troops near Greensboro.

This and subsequent European penetrations into the interior of the southeastern United States proved disastrous for native populations. Without natural immunities to European illnesses like smallpox and measles, native Americans died by the thousands, and the Mississippian culture of fine crafts, sophisticated political systems, and complex religion perished. The trauma of European contact would prove historically decisive for the native inhabitants of northeast Georgia and the Southeast in general. Unable to withstand the devastation of epidemic diseases and the rapidly expanding European population, they would relinquish first their land, then their traditions, and ultimately their very existence in the Georgia Piedmont.

This small incised clay pot dates from the late sixteenth century. Probably used for storage or for serving liquids by the native Americans who hunted in the Athens area, the pot was unearthed at "Kissing Rock" on the grounds of the Navy Supply Corps School.

WHITE SETTLEMENT PATTERNS

White settlement of northeast Georgia did not occur until the last decades of the eighteenth century, when the Oconee River became the western limit of Georgia's frontier as the boundary between the United States and the Creek nation. But earlier settlement and growth patterns determined the path of coastal and Piedmont migration and the pattern of settlement of towns and counties.

King George II signed the charter of the colony of Georgia on June 9, 1732, creating the last of the thirteen original British colonies from vast lands relinquished by South Carolina. He set up a trusteeship that lasted for twenty years. The following year General James Edward Oglethorpe, member of the British Parliament, military hero, and philanthropist, began the settlement of Savannah. He established the town of Augusta at the Savannah River Falls in 1736 as a trading post with the native Americans of the interior. The Trustees returned their charter to the king in 1752, whereupon Parliament lifted early restrictions on land tenure and slavery and offered large land grants as incentive to settlers.

During Britain's colonial wars with France and Spain, coastal Georgia was slow to populate. But in time thriving plantation agriculture quickened the pace of trade and commerce and generated a growing class of wealthy landowners and a proliferation of yeoman farmers.

When Spain ceded Florida to the British in 1763, the Mississippi River became the western boundary of Georgia. With a prospering economy and a protected coastal zone, Georgia looked to the rich lands of the Piedmont, including the area now in Clarke County, for expansion.

Here below the Appalachian Mountains of northern Georgia, rolling hill country descended gradually in shelves before reaching the fall line that separated the Piedmont from the coastal plain. Run-off water from the northern mountains and upper Piedmont forms most of Georgia's rivers, including the Oconee (a native American word meaning "river") which forks into its middle and northern branches in present-day Clarke County.

The original forest in the colonial period included hardwoods mixed with pine; the fertile soil was a mixture of sandy loam and red clay blended from the disintegration of metamorphic rock. The rivers, tumbling among the foothills, were rapid and full of waterfalls and shoals favored by native Americans as sites for trading posts. The swiftly flowing streams would later generate power to turn machinery for the early mills and other manufacturing plants as Clarke County developed.

As the result of early European contact, the total native American population in Georgia was very small at the dawn of the Piedmont migration. Before white settlement of the region, present-day Clarke County was the north–south dividing line between Creek and Cherokee tribes that were often at war with one another. Trading and war paths crossed the Oconee. Here the Pickens Trail running north to south intersected the east–west Middle Cherokee Path at the present site of Athens.

During the colonial period the native Americans became deeply indebted to white traders. The royal governor, Sir James Wright, urged King George III to settle these debts in exchange for land. On July 1, 1773, at Augusta some Creek and Cherokee chiefs ceded

The Old Athens Cemetery served the town from 1801 to the 1880s. A common burial ground, the cemetery sits on part of the original tract of land purchased by John Milledge for the university. Located at the center of the cemetery is the pinkish local-granite headstone of James Espey (spelled Espy here), who died in 1834. Espey, a revolutionary soldier, was a founder of the first Presbyterian church in Clarke County at Sandy Creek, and a charter member and ruling elder of the Presbyterian congregation in Athens, organized on Christmas Day 1820.

674,000 acres along the Ogeechee, Oconee, Broad, Savannah, and Tugaloo rivers to the British. There followed an influx of white settlers not only from the coastal regions of Georgia but also from Maryland, Virginia, and the Carolinas, as many farmers migrated southward away from exhausted soils.

As the migration into the Piedmont of northeast Georgia began, the American Revolution broke out. In the backcountry the Revolutionary War was especially vicious—Tory fought Rebel; British fought colonists; Cherokee battled neutral Cherokee; Creek fought Cherokee; and white settlers engaged in riotous conflicts for various causes with shifting alliances. But with the surrender of British troops at Yorktown on October 19, 1781, and the conclusion of peace with independence from Great Britain in February 1783, Piedmont settlement began again in earnest. The Oconee territory was then the farthest frontier for the young nation.

In an early display of states' rights, the new state of Georgia signed its own treaty with the Cherokee nation on May 31, 1783, not waiting for a draft of a peace treaty between the United States and the Cherokee (which was written in November 1785 and signed into law by George Washington on August 26, 1790). In 1784 the state cleared all Cherokee debts in exchange for the territory lying about the sources of the Oconee River. The legislature divided this tract into two counties, Franklin and Washington.

The new county named for Benjamin Franklin comprised an area larger than the state of Rhode Island. As the population increased, so also did the counties multiply. Thus it came to pass in 1796 that Franklin begat Jackson County; and on December 5, 1801, Jackson begat from its southern portion the county named Clarke. In the ensuing decades a few minor shifts in boundaries occurred: Clarke added some territory from Greene County in 1807, and Clarke gave land to Oglethorpe County in 1813 and to Madison County in 1811 and 1829. After these slight alterations in its configuration, Clarke covered 311 square miles.

To entice settlers to the Oconee frontier, the state offered one thousand acres of land per family at a price of three shillings per acre. Subsequently, the legislators amended this law to require payment only for each acre exceeding one thousand per family. The

Piedmont filled rapidly as settlers cleared the forests and opened the land to agriculture.

Piedmont pioneers were a resourceful lot familiar with the dangers of the frontier. On May 10, 1793, amidst bitter controversy over partition of land between the state of Georgia and the Creeks, settlers living near the "Cedar Sholes on the Oconee" (less than a decade later the site of Athens) petitioned the governor for state

A typical vernacular country house built by the early settlers along the Oconee *frontier featured an enclosed front porch with a small room for guests. Most often the visitor would be a traveling preacher, and thus the room became known as the "prophet's chamber."*

construction of a blockhouse here "for the preservation of this settlement and the protection of a useful fishery."

On June 22, 1793, the *Augusta Chronicle* published a letter signed by an author identifying himself as an "Oconee planter." He wrote: "The forts and blockhouses cost the settlers heavy . . . but we had to build or else run away, and starve next year. Who would not be a Georgian! You see, and so the whole world may, that we stand our guard against two nations [Spain and the Creeks], on a frontier extending 300 miles."

Among these early settlers were Scotch-Irish people from the Carolinas who brought with them building methods and a hearty lifestyle derived from a close relationship with the land. Their first houses were log cabins with dirt floors, the size of rooms limited by the length of the logs. Hand-hewn timbers framed early buildings; ceilings were low; rooms were small. They adapted to the environment by using whatever materials were at hand and built simple furniture.

Early settlers on the Oconee frontier included not only yeoman farmers and traders but also wealthy planters and land speculators. But money often meant little in terms of lifestyle on the early rugged frontier. Even the wealthiest settlers lived simply in unpretentious houses whose plan evolved into a distinctive architectural mode peculiar to the Piedmont called Plain style.

A forerunner of this style was the two-room dogtrot house. Each room was a square or rectangular independent unit. Frequently these rooms were separated by an open space, roofed over to form a breezeway (called a dogtrot), which acted as a hall or outdoor living room in warm weather and through which scampered dogs, chickens, and children. Eventually most of these houses had porches front and back, and the enclosed dogtrot evolved as a central hallway. Often both ends of either or both porches were enclosed as small, self-contained rooms for visitors. Most country houses offered this "prophet's chamber" to circuit-riding frontier preachers. From the beginning Georgia Piedmont architecture of necessity emphasized a relationship with the outdoors.

Ownership of land was of utmost importance. Generally the state employed the "headright" system for land distribution. This

method, a variation on an old English system of land selection and tenure, used random metes and bounds in surveys completed before the actual granting of the land. The philosophy of the state was "Men and soil constitute the strength and wealth of nations; the faster you plant the men, the faster you can draw on both."

Revolutionary War heroes received from the grateful state huge grants of land in the new territories. Among these men was William Few, who received 1,120 acres (now part of Athens) from Governor Samuel Elbert, for whom Elberton would be named, in October

Like many heroes of the American Revolution, William Few received a land grant from the governor. Part of this grant was located along the Oconee River, at the future site of Athens. Because of ill health Few never developed this tract, choosing instead to sell it and move north. Few was one of the delegates from Georgia who signed the U.S. Constitution. He was also one of the first trustees of the University of Georgia.

1785. Few, a native of Baltimore County, Maryland, arrived in Richmond County, Georgia, in 1776. From thence he distinguished himself as a legislator, colonel in the militia, surveyor-general for the state, signer of the U.S. Constitution, and member of Congress. When his health began to fail, he sold his lands, including the future site of Athens, and moved to New York in 1799.

DANIEL EASLEY AND THE SENATUS ACADEMICUS

A settler and land speculator named Daniel Easley bought a portion of Few's grant in 1800. For $897 he purchased 693 acres bordering the west side of the north fork of the Oconee. He already owned several hundred acres along the east side of the river. Here at the spot called Cedar Shoals by the few frontiersmen who had penetrated the area, he built a race and a mill, where he ground cornmeal and flour and produced sawed wood.

An opportunist with a wily knack for striking a good land deal, Easley was among the first wave of settlers to migrate to the Oconee frontier. When the legislature created Jackson County out of Franklin in 1796, they named Easley one of five commissioners charged with finding a seat for the new county. Then they directed that the courts and elections be held at Easley's house until the commissioners found a site for a courthouse. Easley failed to move that project forward and lost his spot on the commission two years later, but by then a small community had developed around Cedar Shoals. The creation of the new county facilitated the establishment of what passed for roads along which intermittent taverns afforded rustic accommodations for road-weary travelers.

The same year that Franklin County formed, the Georgia General Assembly set aside an endowment of forty thousand acres of land for "a college or seminary of learning," and thereby initiated the concept of state-supported higher education. By this action the legislature set in motion events that led to the founding of Athens and Clarke County.

On January 27, 1785, the assembly chartered the University of Georgia, the first chartered state-supported university in the nation. Abraham Baldwin drafted the charter, which called upon the citizens of Georgia to acknowledge their obligation to educate the

Keenly interested in education, Abraham Baldwin was the author of the document establishing the first state-chartered university in America, the future University of Georgia. He served as the institution's first president from 1785 to 1801 and helped select the university's site above the Oconee River.

youth, "the rising hope of our land." Baldwin was an extrordinarily gifted individual. Born in Connecticut and educated at Yale, he was a minister, lawyer, scholar, teacher, and public servant. He moved to Georgia in 1783 and served in the state legislature; he played a critical role in drafting the U.S. Constitution and later became a U.S. senator.

From 1785 to 1801 Abraham Baldwin served as president of a university that existed only on paper. In 1801, sixteen years after adopting the charter, the legislature dispatched its "Senatus Aca-

John Milledge made many contributions to the state of Georgia. After fighting for the Patriot cause during the Revolution, he served as United States congressman, senator, and governor of Georgia. He is well remembered for his financial contribution to the university, the purchase of the initial tract of land for four thousand dollars when the state treasury was insolvent.

demicus" delegation of five men to select a site for the university in Jackson (soon to be Clarke) County and to contract for a building.

The selection committee was indeed select. Besides Baldwin it included John Milledge, a close friend of Thomas Jefferson and soon-to-be governor of Georgia; George Walton, a former Georgia governor and signer of the Declaration of Independence; John Twiggs, Revolutionary leader and brigadier general of the Georgia militia, planter, and businessman; and a prominent Georgian named Hugh Lawson.

Traveling by horseback, the committee set out in midsummer 1801 into vast Jackson County through the forests to the northwest to hilly country where the steams ran swift and clear. Here at the edge of Indian country they encountered Daniel Easley. Seizing the opportunity set before him, Easley showed them his property at Cedar Shoals. Despite the fact that the university already owned five thousand acres nearby, the committee unanimously agreed that Easley's land on a hill high above the shoals was unsurpassed as a location for a college.

They deemed its primeval forest setting and the cool, clear waters of its streams healthful; for if the college were not well situated, it could be "but an infirmary, a habitation of Diseases, rather than a seat of the Muses." Far removed from the distractions and temptations of town life, students could thrive here on clean air and fresh country produce. Historian E. Merton Coulter explained in *College Life in the Old South* that such selection criteria were common in this age. "North Carolina had already in 1793 selected much the same sort of spot [Chapel Hill] for her university, and Thomas Jefferson had expressed exactly the same sentiments [regarding a site for the University of Virginia] to Joseph Priestley in 1800." The state eventually mismanaged the disposition of, sold, or lost the nearby 5,000 acres originally set aside as a possible site for the university. John Milledge purchased 633 hilltop acres from Easley for four thousand dollars and generously donated the parcel to the trustees of the land-rich and money-poor university. Walton, then judge of the superior court, witnessed the transaction. The trustees named the place Athens after the center of classical culture in Greece.

In 1801 Josiah Meigs became the first active president—and first professor— of Franklin College. Until a classroom was erected, he often presented lectures outdoors. The curriculum included Latin and Greek, grammar, and geography, but stressed mathematics and the sciences as well. Meigs's own scientific interests included careful observation and recording of local weather conditions.

The *Augusta Chronicle* reported on the Milledge purchase on July 25, 1801:

> The river at Athens is about one hundred and fifty feet broad; its waters rapid in descent; and has no low grounds. The site of the University is on the south side, and a half a mile from the river. On one side the land is cleared; the other is woodland. On the cleared side are two ample orchards of apple and peach trees; forming artificial copses between the site and the river. . . .
>
> About two hundred yards from the site, and at least three hundred feet above the level of the river, in the midst of an extensive bed of rock, issues a copious spring of excellent water; and in its meanderings to the river, several others are discovered.

Some Georgians grumbled about the choice of this remote spot for the state university. Others applauded the site for its "sylvan glades" and "salubrious climate."

At the time of the initial visit by the Senatus Academicus committee, there were but a handful of houses in the small settlement near Cedar Shoals. A man named Stevens Thomas kept the one main tavern. Miller Easley carefully omitted from the Milledge purchase sixty acres, including riverfront property. This he subdivided and put on the market. He sold his own home to the Reverend Hope Hull and moved across river.

THE FRONTIER COLLEGE

The task of fashioning a university in the wilderness fell to Josiah Meigs. Abraham Baldwin, now a U.S. senator, had relinquished his title of president and had recommended Meigs as his successor.

Meigs, like Baldwin a Yale graduate and former tutor there, traveled south from Connecticut, left his family in Augusta, and arrived in midsummer 1801 to assume his duties. The only place to stay "in town" was Easley's home, so there he took his lodging and began to direct woodsmen in the clearing of the forest for the first crude campus buildings. Not surprisingly, Easley won the contract to build a house for the president and later a grammar school for many of the university's first students who arrived unprepared for college studies. (The state in 1800 had less than a dozen academies.)

Old College, completed in 1806, is the oldest structure in Athens. Throughout its early history the building served as a student dormitory. During the Civil War Old College housed refugees and served also as a hospital for Confederate soldiers. Some of the first graduation exercises took place on a stage erected at the side of the building. Today Old College houses university offices.

Having secured the contracts, Easley turned his home into a tavern for construction workers.

The first students arrived in September. The chronicler George White later recorded that Meigs "commenced the exercises of the University when no college buildings of any description had been erected. Recitations were often heard, and lectures delivered under the shade of the forest oaks; and for years he had almost entire instruction of the College, aided only by a tutor or some member of one of the higher classes." When his house was completed, Meigs held classes there until a log cabin twenty feet square and a story and half high was ready for the thirty or forty students he recruited.

The first graduation ceremonies took place May 31, 1804, under a brush arbor in front of the rising walls of the first permanent brick structure (later called Old College) of Franklin College. The first graduates were ten young sons of Georgia planters, politicians, and Revolutionary War heroes. On the remote campus contractors pushed to complete the first permanent college building south of Chapel Hill, North Carolina. Modeled after Connecticut Hall at Yale, the large three-story structure required three hundred thousand or more bricks molded from Georgia red clay. Writes Coulter, "Armed with $1,000 [the contractors] went to Augusta, a hundred miles away, for nails and lime. Also President Meigs called on his brother, the Indian agent at Hiawassee, Tennessee, to secure permission of the Cherokees to bring lime through their boundaries." When the building was complete in 1806, President Meigs could boast that "better accommodations for students cannot be found in any college in the United States."

The village of Athens emerged adjacent to the campus on lots sold to pay for the construction of Franklin College, as the building—and often the university—was originally called. While the original charter clearly named the institution the University of Georgia, through the nineteenth century the term Franklin College was in popular though unofficial use. As the institution grew to full university status with a number of schools and colleges, the oldest of the colleges became officially the Franklin College of Arts and Sciences.

The trustees instructed President Meigs and Hope Hull, a Methodist preacher, trustee, and early resident of Athens, to plot a thirty-

seven-acre "square of the University" and to lay out the first lots for the town. These had as their bounds Foundry Street on the east, Front (later Broad) on the south, Pulaski on the west, and Market (later Washington) Street on the north.

By late 1803 President Meigs could report that three homes, three stores, and a number of other buildings faced Front Street, and that there were contracts for others and applications for more lots than were then surveyed. Among the early structures were two hotels, at least two general stores, a blacksmith, and a tailor shop. Soon the trustees hired a professional surveyor to lay out additional lots north of Washington Street and west of Franklin College square on a street eventually named Lumpkin.

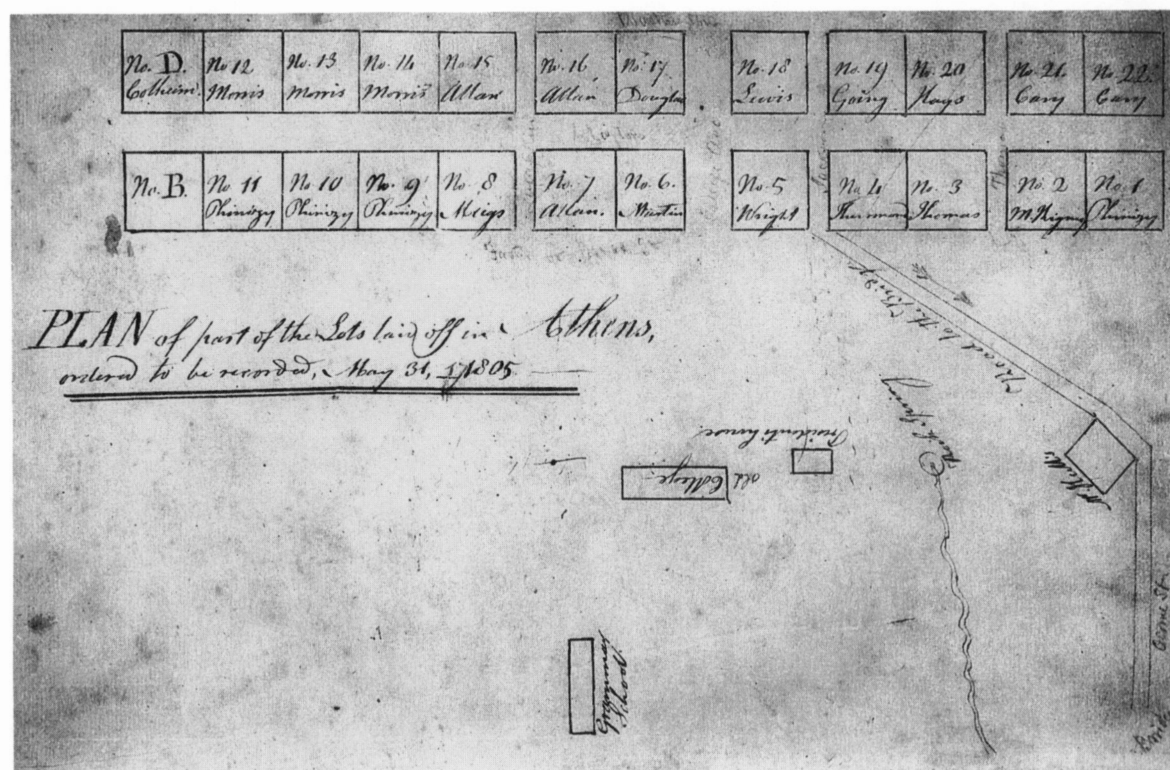

This 1805 plan of Athens appeared in the official Minutes of the University Trustees. At the center are the college buildings; facing them are numbered downtown lots bearing the names of Phinizy, Thomas, Hays, Cary, and other early townspeople.

By early 1806 the town could boast an estimated seventeen families, ten framed dwellings, and four stores. In December 1806 the legislature incorporated the town and established a commission form of government naming William Malone, Stevens Thomas (proprietor of the main hotel in the early settlement), and Hope Hull the first Athens commissioners.

The fledgling college and town seemed secure when in 1808 President Meigs wrote to Governor John Milledge, "Your institution has taken strong root, and will flourish; and I feel some degree of pride in reflecting that a century hence, when this nascent village shall embosom a thousand Georgian youths, pursuing the paths of science, it will now and then be said that you gave this land, and I was the one forlorn hope."

With the birth of the University of Georgia and the founding of the town of Athens had come the creation of Clarke County. The legislature had approved an act establishing Clarke County on December 5, 1801. They named the new county after the Revolutionary War hero and frontier adventurer Elijah Clarke. In carving Clarke from Jackson County, the legislature set these boundaries: "The line dividing the said county of Clarke, from the county of Jackson, shall begin on the Appalachee River, at the mouth of Marbury's Creek, thence a direct line to Richard Easley's Mill, on the middle fork of the Oconee River, from thence a direct line to where the Oglethorpe Line crosses the north fork of Brush Creek, thence down the Oglethorpe Line to the Oconee River, thence up the said River to the beginning." This configuration included some 250 square miles, about twice the land area of present-day Clarke County.

ELIJAH CLARKE

In many ways Elijah Clarke (sometimes spelled Clark) seems an unlikely patron for the county which bears his name. It is ironic that the county that came into being as a seat of learning took its name from a rough-and-ready frontiersman whom most historians deem a near-illiterate "cracker." But many admired Clarke for his states' rights sentiments and his exploits as an Indian fighter, agent, and negotiator. Born in North Carolina, he was living with his family on Clark's Creek in the newly ceded lands of Georgia's northwestern Indian frontier by 1773. He married Hannah Arrington (circa 1765), and they had nine children. He joined the American cause early and became a captain in the militia. He was wounded in battle with the Cherokees in 1776. The next year he battled Creek war parties. As a lieutenant colonel, he led state troops in a charge at Alligator Bridge in East Florida during an unsuccessful invasion of the British and again sustained wounds. As lieutenant colonel of the Wilkes County militia, he became a hero at the Battle of Kettle Creek (February 14, 1779) with the defeat of six hundred Loyalists.

When all of Georgia and most of South Carolina fell to the

British, Clarke led some followers back up into the Carolinas and for a time conducted guerrilla warfare between bands of patriots and the Tories. A fearsome fighter, he again suffered numerous wounds.

Clarke relocated his family after his home was destroyed and his wife and small children robbed and forced into the wilderness. He conducted several hundred men, women, and children to safety in present-day Tennessee and then returned to lead his troops in the final recovery of Augusta in June 1781.

After the war the grateful state of Georgia rewarded their victorious hero with the gift of a Wilkes County plantation, spoils of war recovered from Loyalist ownership. To this land Clarke added several thousand acres from bounty certificates. He served in the state legislature most of the years between 1781 and 1790. His frontier adventures continued. As brigadier general of the Wilkes County militia, he defeated the Creeks in a decisive battle at Jack's Creek in Walton County in 1787. He instigated a series of campaigns against the Spanish in which he schemed to enlist Creeks and Cherokees against a mutual foe.

The ever-versatile Clarke was a representative to the state constitutional convention in 1789, and he served as a commissioner for most of Georgia's treaties with the native peoples. In 1793, three years after the Creeks agreed to the Treaty of New York, George Washington reduced military aid to the frontier and canceled a planned invasion of the Creek nation. Clarke resigned from the militia and charted an independent course of action on the frontier.

He and other land-hungry Georgians created the Trans-Oconee Republic. With their families they marched into disputed Oconee territory; they laid out towns, built forts, created a council of safety, and established an independent government. President Washington ordered the state to break up the republic. Faced with a blockade by state troops and desertion by many of his followers, Clarke surrendered in the fall of 1794.

Caught in changing times on the Georgia frontier, Clarke wrote that he was "disgusted with the state of Georgia." Broken in spirit and broke financially, Clarke and others found themselves fined for drunken brawling and violent behavior once deemed acceptable on

Elijah Clarke is credited with the Patriots' 1779 victory at the Battle of Kettle Creek in Wilkes County. After the Revolution he successfully battled with the Creeks in Walton County but failed in an attempted invasion of Spanish-held eastern Florida. The Georgia legislature honored him in 1801 by naming the new county that would house the state university after this adventuresome war hero.

the frontier. He died in Richmond County in 1799, leaving only his eleven-hundred-acre plantation, Woodburn, in Wilkes County for his family. There he was buried. His reinterred remains now rest at Elijah Clarke State Park on Clark Hill Lake in Lincoln County. The Elijah Clarke Chapter of the Daughters of the American Revolution erected a monument in his memory, which now stands in the middle of Broad Street in Athens in the county of Clarke, a tribute to the spirit of adventure and daring on the frontier.

THE COUNTY SEAT AT WATKINSVILLE

The act to create the county also appointed a commission consisting of William Hopkins, William Strong, Daniel Bankston, John Hart, and John Cobb to locate the site for the county seat and to contract for the construction of a courthouse. By January 1, 1802, they had picked a site near the center of the county seven miles southwest of Athens on Call Creek at a place called Big Spring. The commissioners named the county seat Watkinsville, most likely after Robert Watkins, an Augusta attorney deemed "eminently distinguished by genius and a high order of eloquence."

The original incorporation of Watkinsville was on land granted to Roderick Easley and Josiah Woods by Edward Telfair in 1791. John Cobb agreed to add to that "a certain portion of land for a town for the use of the public or county including eight lots, six of which are to front the public square, and two back lots, and one acre for building the courthouse and jail and five or six acres for a common."

The commissioners contracted with a colorful character named Micaiga Bing to build the courthouse and jail. Until the facilities could be completed, the affairs of the county were carried out at the home of Isaac Hill. The first meeting of the Clarke County Superior Court took place there on March 22, 1802. The appointed justices elected a clerk (John Smith) and appointed several justices of the peace.

A matter that came before their second session at the Hill home was an indictment against Micaiga Bing for profane language and for bidding his Maker to "damn the legislature for passing the law that the verdict of any damn fool jury of a justice court should be final." Order on the heretofore untamed frontier came slowly. Among frequent offenses that concerned early grand juries were not only profanity but also larceny, horse stealing, perjury, assault, adultery, and even murder.

Nonetheless, Bing finished his commissioned buildings. The first court held in the new Clarke County Courthouse met in Watkinsville on October 6, 1802, with Judge Thomas Peter Carnes (for whom the nearby town of Carnesville was later named) presiding.

Early Clarke County settlers often owned freestanding corner cupboards. These massive pieces usually had a tall two-door upper section and a shorter two-door base. This handsome Georgia Piedmont cupboard is made of walnut and southern yellow pine. The vine-and-flower inlay strung across the top is maple.

This cellaret, or liquor stand, a characteristically southern piece, is made primarily of walnut, the preferred wood of Georgia Piedmont cabinetmakers. The long legs are typical of cellarets made south of Maryland. The storage area is divided into twelve sections to hold a variety of liquors or wines.

GROWING PAINS

One of Carnes's major concerns for the frontier county was the condition of the roads. Roads, bridges, and ferries remained crucial issues throughout the county's first decades. In the early years, many county roads opened—including a post road between Watkinsville and Athens in 1804—but most were often quagmires. By the 1820s a new road over less rough terrain would connect the two towns. But inclement weather and ubiquitous grime generally rendered travel—by coach, carriage, horseback, or on foot—an ordeal.

Bridges often washed out, and they were costly to rebuild. A small bridge across Barber's Creek on the Athens–Watkinsville road, for example, cost about seventy-five dollars to build, while one across the Oconee near Athens cost five hundred dollars. Completed by the mid-1820s, the two structures stayed in constant need of repair. Roads were always a hot topic, because everyone cared about mail delivery, and Athenians had to travel to Watkinsville to vote and conduct county affairs.

In April 1806, three years after the Louisiana Purchase opened up new territory, U.S. Postmaster Gideon Granger issued an order to Benjamin Hawkins, a veteran Indian agent, to lay out a horse path from Athens to Fort Stoddard on a route to New Orleans. In addition to travel within Clarke County, settlers were moving through the county to the new western frontier, and President Jefferson was eager to facilitate the westward movement. Hawkins's

William A. Carr, an early citizen of Athens, married Cynthia Walker in 1817. The Carrs built their house on top of the hill above Trail Creek along the Oconee River. This view of the Old Stagecoach Road from Carr's Hill recalls the unpaved, heavily wooded roads that Clarke County residents carved out during the early part of the nineteenth century.

William A. and Cynthia Walker Carr began building their house shortly after their marriage in 1817. A fire in 1897 destroyed all but the two front rooms. A wealthy landowner, Carr once owned the parcels where the Athens Factory and the Georgia Railroad Depot were built. Pictured here are Miss Florida Carr, a descendant of the original owners, and Judge Robert C. Orr outside the home in 1890.

instructions were to lay the road four to six feet wide, "trees to be fallen across the water courses so to enable the mail carrier to pass the waters upon them carrying the mail secure from the water and swimming his horse by his side." After lengthy negotiations with the Creeks, Hawkins completed the task by November 1811, and the road became safe and well traveled.

Despite westward migration, Clarke County experienced steady growth in the years immediately following the 1806 incorporations of its two towns. The number of county merchants increased, and a modicum of small-scale industry began. Baptists, Presbyterians, and Methodists all had churches in the county. The university's first chapel opened in 1808. The chapel was the first religious edifice in town (although many secular activities took place there as well); most of the townspeople who were interested in going to church still attended services in the country during Athens's early years.

Agriculture dominated life in Clarke County in the first decade of the nineteenth century. By 1810 there were 2,500 slaves among the

Many nineteenth-century Georgia households had freestanding furniture used for storing books. Mounted atop a desk, the piece enabled its owner to read and write on the same surface. This surviving example, made primarily of walnut, came down to its present owners from Mrs. Hamilton McWhorter and has remained in the family for four generations.

In the 1820s the Morton family moved into Clarke County. William M. Morton became a leading businessman, and his brother, Joseph F. Morton, established one of the largest cotton farms in eastern Clarke County. Pictured here is Pleasant Grove, Joseph's Federal-style country home, which had two rooms up and two rooms down; the veranda is a later addition. Morton, like other large-scale farmers, erected a school and a commissary on his property for his tenants and slaves.

county's 7,628 inhabitants. Even within Athens there were 134 slaves out of 273 townspeople. The number of planters (a term generally defined in early tax digests as persons owning twenty or more slaves) doubled between 1802 and 1810, although the total remained small. Among that number (thirteen listed between 1802 and 1810) were Daniel and Roderick Easley, William and Richard Billups, William Strong, Sr., and his son William.

The county's growth and development slowed considerably during the War of 1812. Economic dislocation in the nation and souring university politics briefly combined to deter progress.

President Meigs inclined toward the sciences. When Thomas Jefferson wrote Meigs a congratulatory letter upon his assuming the presidency of "The College of Georgia," he reminded Meigs that the South's hope of enlightenment lay in the sciences "unshackled by the clerical chains of New England."

At first Meigs was quite successful as president of the college. In

1806 the five-year-old Franklin College boasted seventy students and the precollege academy forty more. Two years later the college enrollment fell to twenty-five and the grammar school to fifteen. Meigs was at quiet war with conservative Federalist trustees who resisted a curriculum that included the sciences. As early as 1803 Meigs had observed, "The Crown of the President of a College is indeed a crown of thorns." He resigned from the presidency in 1810 but remained as professor of natural philosophy, mathematics, and chemistry. Amid financial difficulties the university suspended classes briefly in 1811, and although classes soon resumed, by 1818 the college shut down.

Meigs said of the period, "I have always believed that knowledge pure and unveiled . . . was the true basis of the happiness of individuals or nations. . . . I have . . . been a target for the shafts of those who dread the true light of science." It fell to Moses Waddel, appointed in 1819 as the fifth president of the infant institution, to chart a new course and stabilize the university.

Despite troubles in academe, Clarke County continued to grow in its first two decades. By 1818 the county could boast a third incor-

The Church-Waddel-Brumby House dates from around 1820. The Federal-style house, built for Alonzo Church, was originally located on East Hancock Avenue. Successive owners altered the original white frame two-story home. This picture, for example, shows the long veranda that replaced a small porch.

The Hoyt House in its earliest form was a two-rooms-up and two-rooms-down structure built circa 1826–29 for Mrs. Catherine Baldwin. Originally located on the ridge at the northern edge of downtown, the Hoyt House is now part of the History Village complex. The house is named for its second owner, Nathan Hoyt, minister of the First Presbyterian Church.

porated town, one that would prosper for a time and then, in the waning decades of the century, virtually disappear. The town of Salem emerged as a thriving farming community in the western corner of the county. Located eleven miles southwest of Watkinsville and three miles east of the Appalachee River, Salem became the site of two excellent male and female academies. For a time Salem rivaled Watkinsville in population growth.

By 1819 the Indian boundary had moved further west (from fifteen to fifty miles away from the county border), and the area became still safer for settlement. "Savage Creeks and gallant Cherokees," as some defined them, continued a part of the scene, according to the historian E. Merton Coulter, who chronicled the friendship between Cherokees and Athenians. In *College Life in the Old*

The doorway on the west side of the Cobb-Jackson-Ward-Erwin-McFeely house probably dates from the late 1820s. According to family tradition the dwelling once faced Finley Street, but Malthus Ward, the third owner, turned it or relocated the chimneys so the house would face Dearing Street.

South he wrote, "Indian squaws came down out of the mountains trudging along with loads of moccasins, deerskins, jerked venison, and cane baskets, and struck bargains with students when they were not reciting Homer or measuring the rise of the Pleiades."

With peace—with England in 1814, with the native peoples in 1819, and within the university soon thereafter—came prosperity. Agriculture continued to dominate the economy of the county as the number of slaves continued to increase disproportionately to the number of whites. The growth of Watkinsville and Salem and the resurgence of the university in Athens set the stage for a new boom in the 1820s.

2

Town and Country: The Antebellum Experience

During the decades preceding the outbreak of the Civil War, the growing significance of the university in the state attracted a variety of people to Athens and Clarke County. As the population grew, commerce and industry prospered in a thriving cotton economy. Cotton mills processed the rich harvests of adjacent plantations and farms, and for a time Athens—a pioneer in the South for cotton manufacture—could claim the sobriquet "Manchester of the South." The extension of rail lines to Athens tied the county to major cities of the South. Planters and industrialists built fine town houses in Athens in an era characterized by a rich cultural life coupled with a thriving and diversified economy—all made possible by the natural resource of the Oconee River and the unnatural resource of slave labor.

Despite the remarkable growth of Athens and the vitality of Watkinsville, Salem, and smaller communities, Clarke was an overwhelmingly rural and agricultural county, and the increasing slave population was a major factor in the local economy. In the early decades of the antebellum period, whites outnumbered blacks by ever-decreasing percentages. By 1850 Clarke had joined the Black Belt of the South, with slaves outnumbering the free population. The county's first census in 1810 recorded a county population of 7,628; slaves numbered one-third of that total. By 1860, fifty years later, there were 5,660 slaves in a county of 11,218 people. Even in the towns of Athens and Watkinsville whites outnumbered blacks by a very slim margin.

Despite the number of slaves within the county, only about 10 percent of the whites were slaveholders; less than 2 percent of the white population were "planters." Clarke County had five planters

This wood engraving of Franklin College dates from about 1844. This particular view of the campus appeared on a mantel clock manufactured in New York at this time and showed up ten years later in Gleason's Pictorial Magazine. *Old College is visible in the center. To the right of Old College are the Chapel, Demosthenian Hall, the Ivy Building, and the corner of the Presbyterian church. At the left is Phi Kappa Hall. In the 1850s a cast iron fence replaced the wooden fence pictured in this engraving.*

in 1802, ten in 1810, twenty in 1820, and sixty by the early 1830s. By 1860 there were seventy planters; only 544 whites (out of 5,500 countywide) owned any slaves at all.

What had developed by the 1840s, wrote Ernest Hynds in his history of Athens, was a "fairly well-defined class system at the top and half the population living in slavery at the bottom."

"Between the whites and slaves in the social structure were a few free Negroes. Clarke County never had more than a handful of persons in this group," according to Hynds, "although one or two of them did quite well in business. Such persons were in a sense displaced in the South; they were free, yet their race caused them to be grouped with slaves."

Slaves worked on farms and plantations; in homes and in the fields; in industry, business, and trade. In slack seasons county farmers hired out slaves for cash; many labored side by side with

STAND FAST
0
10
20
©

The home of the president of the university is one of the finest surviving examples of Greek Revival architecture in Georgia. The mansion was built in 1857–58 for John T. Grant, a contractor for many of Georgia's first railroads. The original formal gardens were splendid and included varieties of jasmine, lilacs, roses, yucca, cassinas, flowering quince, and forsythia. A row of cherry laurel and crape myrtle secured the family's privacy.

whites in the burgeoning cotton-textile factories, where about half of the factory workers in Athens were slaves.

In class structure, next to the planters came the vast majority of urban and rural white citizens. Not only planters but also small farmers arrived in a steady stream during the 1820s and 1830s, attracted by the then-fertile topsoil and gray sand of the Oconee region in the northern part of the Cotton Crescent. Cotton was their principal crop, but tobacco, corn, wheat, and a few livestock provided some additional income. On many small farms family members supplied the only labor; on others a small number of slaves worked side by side with their masters, weeding and thinning long rows of cotton with a hoe—the main tool for slave and small farmer alike. Few farmers practiced good soil maintenance, and by 1850 soil erosion and exhaustion took their toll on the land, production of cotton, and the rural population.

SALEM AND WATKINSVILLE

Urban Athens seemed little affected by the vagaries of rural life, for the town continued to attract newcomers. Although from the outset Athens established a position of leadership in the county, antebellum Watkinsville and Salem also continued to grow. The two towns extended one-half mile in all directions from their centers, and for a short time Salem rivaled the county seat in size and population. In 1827 Salem could boast twenty-one houses, two stores, three offices, seven shops, a male and female academy, a Methodist meeting house, and an impressive tannery. But the relatively isolated town relied almost completely on the prosperous surrounding farm community for its well-being. The population reached one hundred in the 1840s but leveled off there; in 1860 Salem, "a village of thirty houses," stopped growing.

Watkinsville was both the county seat and the junction of mail routes, stage runs, and rudimentary roads to Athens from Greensboro and Madison in Morgan County. Until 1831 all voting in Clarke County took place in Watkinsville, and Athenians had to brave seven miles of abominably kept roads, fords, and bridges to cast a ballot or transact legal affairs there.

Abijah Conger, originally from New Jersey, came to Athens in 1831, after working as a missionary among the Cherokees in Tennessee. Soon thereafter he built this farmhouse in the northern section of Clarke County for his son, David. The original, or central, part of the house, with its relatively small rooms grouped around a large central chimney, is unusual for the area.

Grinding mills dotted the countryside throughout the nineteenth century. Old McRee-Crawford's Mill near Watkinsville operated from around 1840 to 1958. This picture shows the second mill building, circa 1880. The miller hauled the grain to the top window and fed it into the hoppers from which it flowed down into the grinding stones. Old McRee-Crawford's Mill ground wheat into graham flour.

Tradition has it that the Eagle Tavern first served as a frontier blockhouse. The oldest part is constructed of logs covered at a later date with wide boards. Eagle Tavern was one of the earliest stopping places for travelers going to and from Milledgeville and Athens. This photo, circa 1936, shows the building before its restoration.

By 1837 stages departed from Milledgeville bound for Athens via Watkinsville three times a week, and traffic on county roads increased to a steady stream of wagons, sulkies, carts, and travelers on horseback or on foot. The Eagle Tavern, a handsome two-rooms-up-and-two-down Plain-style building (probably constructed circa 1820), and the Watkinsville Hotel (completed in 1829) vied for customers and competed as centers for political and social life. Professional wagoners were the tavernkeepers' steady customers. When a stage approached, the number of blasts the driver sounded on the deerhorn told the innkeeper how many guests to expect. The innkeeper prepared sleeping arrangements and set the tavern tables accordingly. At Eagle Tavern wagoners and foot travelers slept on pallets on the barroom floor in exchange for dollars spent on whiskey. Stage passengers slept upstairs two or three to a bed. Occasionally these rooms accommodated a judge and sequestered jurors guarded mid-trial by a bailiff who bedded down on a cot in the hall to prevent infringements of rules of the court.

There was little love lost between Watkinsville and Athens. Athenians unanimously agreed that the university town should have been the seat of Clarke County in the first place. Athens attorney

Emory Speer grumbled, "The woodpecker would continue to beat his monotonous tattoo upon a dead limb in the town of Watkinsville for many a day before she aroused from her lethargy." At times the courthouse town of Watkinsville had a rough-and-tumble reputation for fights on the common and gypsies dancing in the streets, but in 1849 White's *Statistics of Georgia* stated that "very obliging and kind people reside in the village" distinguished by a "good brick courthouse," jail, two churches, two taverns, two schools, two stores, three groceries, one billiard room; a carpenter, a tailor, two shoe shops, two blacksmiths, two tanyards, two wagonmakers, one saddler, two lawyers, one doctor, and one minister. By 1860 there were 467 free whites and 426 slaves living in the town.

Despite the presence of the courthouse and county offices in Watkinsville, most people only traveled through the county seat on their way to and from Athens. The Classic City from birth had the advantage of the university.

FRANKLIN COLLEGE

Franklin College stabilized under the steady leadership of Moses Waddel, a graduate of Hampden-Sydney College in Virginia, an ordained Presbyterian minister, and a highly respected educator. In his ten years as president, from 1819 to 1829, Waddel raised enrollment from seven students to a steady one hundred. A strict disciplinarian, he injected stern Presbyterianism into daily student life, insisted upon high academic standards, and coaxed more funding out of the state legislature.

When Waddel resigned the presidency to return to the ministry in 1829, a New Englander named Alonzo Church took his place. Church was another staunch Presbyterian. He came to the university to teach mathematics in 1819, married a planter's daughter, and served as pastor to the Athens Presbyterian congregation for ten years before assuming the presidency of the college. Church, a graduate of Middlebury College in his native state of Vermont, remained president for the next thirty years, a record tenure still unbroken. Throughout these decades Franklin College was a liberal arts school with about one hundred students and six faculty members—elite, all-male, and decidedly church-related.

Alonzo Church moved to Athens in 1819 from Vermont. As president of the university, he was an extremely conservative disciplinarian who conflicted with faculty and students. Still, during his tenure two literary societies flourished, and the campus acquired several handsome new buildings.

During the Waddel-Church era, the sylvan campus began to assume an air of permanency with the construction of handsome buildings reflecting Georgian, Federal, and Greek Revival architectural styles. Rival literary societies debated one another in Demosthenian Hall (built in the Federal style in 1824) and Phi Kappa Hall, a Greek Revival structure which, by 1836, faced Demosthenean across the common green. These two sites became training grounds for many future orators, statesmen, and jurists.

Philosophical Hall, completed in 1821, for a time housed books and scientific equipment until the construction of a new library (soon called the Ivy Building) in 1831. In 1862 the library moved

This handsome Federal building houses the Demosthenian Literary Society. Organized in 1803, the society functioned as a social club and Demosthenian Hall as a repository for books. Demosthenians engaged in lively debates with members of the rival society, Phi Kappa.

Phi Kappa Hall, built in 1836, is on North Campus directly across from Demosthenian Hall. Both of these secret literary societies sponsored animated debates and public lectures, providing a diversion from the rigid academic routine. World War II brought an end to the Phi Kappa Literary Society. The building then became the office and library of the well-known university historian E. Merton Coulter.

again, this time to a new building next door. (Later the two were joined to one another by an elaborate Corinthian colonnade to form the present Academic Building).

In 1830 New College, a dormitory and classroom building constructed in 1823, burned to the ground. Trustees contracted with two "brick masons," James R. Carlton and Ross Crane, to reconstruct the building. These two talented artists moved to Athens, prospered in business, married cousins, and brought up large families.

Ross Crane won the contract to design and build a permanent chapel for the university. Completed in 1832 at a cost of fifteen thousand dollars, the Chapel was one of the first Greek Revival structures in Athens. Featuring a temple form and six fluted Doric columns supporting an entablature and pediment, the beautiful and well-proportioned building met widespread approval; trustees found the massive portico "apparently correct in its proportions." Indeed, building forms borrowed from the Acropolis seemed academically correct and architecturally appropriate for an American Athens. The classical style and the architect quickly gained great popularity among wealthy planters and others eager to build fine houses on town lots nearby.

When the University Chapel was constructed, students attended religious exercises here daily. The bell tower (removed in 1913) was also in constant use to call students to chapel, announce the beginning and end of classes, and notify the citizens of Athens of an emergency. Located today atop a wooden tower behind the chapel, the bell is rung by freshmen to hail athletic victories!

Robert Taylor moved to Athens from Savannah to educate his sons at the university. Around 1845 he built this imposing Greek Revival mansion distinguished by its thirteen Doric columns, said to represent the original colonies. Owning 247 slaves, according to the 1840s tax digests, Taylor was the largest slaveholder ever in Clarke County.

This unique outbuilding, originally built as a pigeon cote, is located on the grounds of the Taylor-Grady House. Birds flew into the holes below the molding and roosted inside. An 1870 plat indicates that the building later was a kitchen.

Over the ensuing decades, Crane built a number of Greek Revival and Italianate mansions along Athens's newest streets. His own elegant house now anchors the west end of the downtown historic district, having served as the chapter house for Sigman Alpha Epsilon fraternity since 1929. Another downtown landmark, First Presbyterian Church, is a Greek Revival temple-form Crane completed in 1856.

The Athens version of the national phase of architectural Neoclassicism proved eminently suitable to the southern climate. Most houses were on piers one to five feet above ground, allowing air to circulate. High ceilings, tall porches, large-scale windows on at least two sides of every room, and doorways opening on spacious central hallways all facilitated comfort and welcomed summer breezes. Louvered shutters offered shade while admitting air in good weather, and central chimneys warmed the interior in colder weather. Large residential lots balanced the massiveness of temple-style houses and accommodated various outbuildings including kitchens and privies, smokehouses and slave quarters, stables and barns. Fences enclosed vegetables, flowers, and formal boxwoods in varying garden settings.

All but vanished today is the university's first Botanical Garden, established in 1833 by Dr. Malthus Ward, professor of natural history and a native of Salem, Massachusetts. Located just west of campus and north of Broad, the extensive garden included several acres of the original Milledge land grant and extended above Tanyard Creek to Finley Hill. Today specimen magnolia, ginkgo, elm, and other trees of the original garden still stand in the side yard of Ward's house, now at the corner of Dearing and the cobblestoned street named Finley.

Once begun, the garden expanded to include many rare and exotic plants contributed by well-traveled and well-connected antebellum Athenians; soon it became a showplace, the town's greatest attraction. For example, William H. Crawford (Georgia legislator, judge, secretary of war and secretary of the treasury in the cabinet of President James Monroe, and university trustee) donated a cutting from the weeping willow at Napoleon's grave on St. Helena, a specimen presented to Crawford when he served as minister to

France. Two naval officers donated plants from the Cape of Good Hope, and offshoots from the Washington Elm on Cambridge Commons (where Washington had taken command of the Continental Army on July 3, 1775) and the Charter Oak (a tree in Hartford where colonialists in Connecticut hid their charter from the British in 1687) graced the garden and honored the young nation. E. Merton Coulter wrote of these acres as "a veritable Garden of Eden with hills and valleys, two sparkling brooks, a lake containing 'a few perch and a harmless alligator' and over two hundred plants, shrubs, and trees from all over the globe."

Designed as a laboratory for the study of botany, the garden also provided a peaceful and romantic setting as the town's first and only park. But as it grew in size, the garden became too costly to maintain on the modest budget allotted the university by the legislature. Despite the efforts of Alonzo Church to raise an endowment for the garden, the trustees sold this beautiful acreage in 1856 for one thousand dollars. Thus at a time when the pioneer landscape architect Frederick Law Olmsted was designing New York's Central Park, Athens lost forever an urban botanical garden that might well have rivaled other great city parks of America.

In 1858 the trustees used proceeds from the sale to plant more trees on campus and replace a wooden fence around the perimeter of the campus green to keep out stock and other domestic animals, which roamed free throughout the town. The new fence and gateway of cast iron produced in an Athens factory were decorative as well as utilitarian. Patterned after the Great Seal of Georgia, with three columns representing wisdom, justice, and moderation, the Arch (no longer gated) remains today the literal and figurative main point of entry to the university. It is perhaps the most symbolic object in Athens.

Within these fences antebellum students led prescribed lives. President Church was a tough taskmaster. Students could miss neither weekday chapel nor Sunday services. Attendance at all classes and proper recitation therein were mandatory. Forbidden were drinking, cursing, fighting, gambling, playing cards or billiards, masquerading as women, going to the circus, or breaking any state or local laws. Outlawed on campus were women, dogs, horses, other pets, and slave bodyservants.

In recognition of his long service to the university, the citizens of Athens presented Alonzo Church with a silver tea service in 1856. Asaph K. Childs, a local silversmith, decorated and engraved the service in his Franklin House shop. After the Civil War Childs turned his interests elsewhere. He helped organize the Lucy Cobb Institute and establish the National Bank of Athens, where he served as president from 1881 to 1900.

Many students were only sixteen years old when they entered the university. Most had enjoyed considerable freedom in their middle- and upper-class homes, and they often resisted the rigors President Church imposed. Church went too far when he required faculty members to spy on students to enforce his stringent rules. His unbending attitudes on discipline and curriculum eventually resulted in the loss of several faculty members—most notably the LeConte brothers.

Joseph LeConte joined his brother John on the faculty in 1853 as professor of geology and chemistry. The brothers, both graduates of the university, belonged to a new breed of academicians who warred with the classicist Church and the conservative trustees when the administration de-emphasized the sciences and demanded rigid faculty control over students' behavior. The LeContes resigned from the faculty to teach at the University of South Carolina. John LeConte left in 1855, and Joseph was gone a year later. After the Civil War the brothers founded the University of California, where John became president and Joseph a "beloved idol" among students

and faculty alike. Bearing the name LeConte are a glacier in Alaska, a Sierra mountain and one in the Smokies, numerous fossils, and academic buildings and streets in South Carolina, California, and Georgia (including Athens).

Despite the loss of the LeContes and their colleagues and however repressive the Church administration, the university managed nonetheless to nurture and educate an astounding number of accomplished men in the antebellum era. Among them was Crawford W. Long, who entered the university at age fourteen and shared a room in Old College with Alexander Hamilton Stephens. After graduation in 1835, Long studied medicine and later enjoyed a distin-

This brick building, completed in 1849, was the university chancellor's home until 1926. Thereafter it housed the art and music departments, the University Press, and sophomore women, who used it as a dormitory. The house was demolished in 1950, and the Dunlap Library now stands on the site. As artist-in-residence at the university in the early 1940s, John Held, Jr., drew this picture of the building where he worked.

guished career as a physician. He is credited with the discovery of ether anesthesia. Stephens became a Whig leader in the U.S. House of Representatives and later vice-president of the Confederacy. He was re-elected to Congress and in 1882 became governor of Georgia. Statues of the two roommates now stand in Statuary Hall in the United States Capitol, the only two Georgians thus honored.

Crawford W. Long and Alexander H. Stephens were but two among a number of antebellum graduates destined to achieve greatness. According to Robert Preston Brooks in his history of the university, among the men graduating from the University of Georgia between 1821 and 1844 were an associate justice of the U.S. Supreme Court, eleven justices of the state supreme court in Georgia and other states, two U.S. senators, eleven members of the Congress and a speaker of the House, a cabinet member, seven governors, and many prominent professionals.

When Augustin S. Clayton, a member of the first class to graduate from the University of Georgia, founded the Alumni Society thirty years later in 1834, he established a club composed of his peers, men of influence and power. After his marriage to Julia Carnes, the daughter of Judge Thomas Carnes, Clayton moved to Athens from Franklin County in 1808. He remained in Athens for the rest of his life and became one of the town's leading citizens. As a successful young lawyer, he became a member of the university's board of trustees. Clayton served in the Georgia House of Representatives and the Georgia Senate. Later he was named superior court judge for the newly designated western circuit in the rapidly growing upcountry. He served two terms in the Congress of the United States before retiring to his home in Athens in poor health in 1835. Clayton was not only a highly respected attorney and legislator; he was a wealthy farmer (the 1820 census listed him as the owner of sixteen slaves) and one of Athens's first industrialists as well. Despite all his accomplishments, Clayton considered his service to the university as one of the major accomplishments of his life. Certainly he was the ideal person to initiate alumni support. And when alumni returned to their alma mater annually for a Commencement Week round of parties, frivolities, and political strategy sessions, the town of Athens assumed a special role as a center for influence and power brokering in the state.

John Addison Cobb moved to Athens to educate his sons at the university. A gentleman farmer, businessman, and land speculator, Cobb owned property in northwest Athens along Prince Avenue, between Barber Street on the east and Hill Street on the south. In 1834 he subdivided this tract into eighty lots and offered them for sale. The area soon became known as the village of Cobbham, the first suburb in Athens. Although in somewhat deteriorated condition, this portrait and one of Cobb's wife (facing page) hang today in the Cobbham home of Cobb descendants.

THE COBBS OF ATHENS

Athens developed an urban character distinct from the surrounding country. Among early transplants to Athens, drawn by urban allure and educational opportunities, were the Cobbs of Jefferson County.

About one year after the April 10, 1823, birth of their second son, Thomas Reade Rootes Cobb, Colonel John Addison Cobb and his wife Sarah left 150 slaves and their six-thousand-acre farm in Jefferson County in the hands of an overseer and moved with their new baby, their nine-year-old son, Howell, and their daughters, Laura and Mildred, to Athens. The Cobbs were destined to figure significantly in almost every aspect of the economic, cultural, and political future of the town and county.

William B. McCash, biographer of T. R. R. Cobb, concludes that viewed from almost any perspective, the Cobbs' decision to "take up town life" made sense. In describing Athens in this era, he wrote that the "population increased, businesses of every description multiplied, a lucrative upcountry wagon trade developed, a rail connection with other points in Georgia was established, rival newspapers competed to shape public opinion, male and female academies sprang up, Franklin College . . . grew in size and prestige, churches flourished . . . and a complex and highly differentiated occupational structure evolved."

John A. Cobb had inherited a fortune. He owned plantations in Jefferson and Jackson counties as well as farms at Trail Creek and near Athens in Clarke County. According to Clarke County tax digests, Colonel Cobb was one of only two men who reported ownership of two hundred or more slaves at any time in the antebellum period. (The other was General Robert Taylor of the Georgia militia.) Cobb joined other wealthy planters who educated their children, built fine town houses, and invested their considerable fortunes in Athens and Clarke County in a number of profit-making ventures that ranged from land development to industry, banking, and railroads.

By 1828 the population of Athens had reached 1,100 (583 whites and 517 blacks). There were twenty-six four-wheeled carriages—along with gigs and sulkeys—and twenty-six windows; a tailor

Sarah Robinson Rootes Cobb grew up at Federal Hill in Fredericksburg, Virginia. She was a member of the Athens gentry and a charter member of Athens Baptist Church (organized 1830). Among her seven children were Howell and Thomas, who became political leaders and prominent Confederates.

shop and a bakery; a blacksmith and several contractors. Town limits extended to present-day Lumpkin Street, and three springs supplied citizens with water.

The Cobbs contributed to the population growth, adding three more children to the family in their early years in Athens. While the Cobbs were adapting easily and comfortably to Athens society, the townscape and the local economy were taking some lively turns encouraged by the reign of King Cotton and the entrepreneurial spirit of eager investors.

EARLY TEXTILE INDUSTRIES IN CLARKE COUNTY

Three cotton mills powered by the Oconee River and capitalized for the most part by large-scale planters and slaveholders opened near Athens between 1829 and 1833. The first of these was the Athens Manufacturing Company (soon called the Georgia Factory) located about five miles south of town on the lower end of a half-mile-long shoals on the north fork of the Oconee River. Investors in this early venture were wealthy Athens or Clarke County citizens: William Dearing, John Nisbet, Abraham Walker, Judge Augustin S. Clayton, and one man from Massachusetts named John Johnson. Johnson brought to the enterprise technical and managerial skills gleaned from New England manufacture. Indeed, newspaper accounts reported he had "gone north" in 1829 to purchase machinery. The original factory opened in 1830 with one thousand spindles and thirty looms.

An Irish textile expert, John White, a native of county Antrim, arrived in 1837 to take over management of the factory. He quickly acquired ownership and lent his family name to the factory-owned mill village of Whitehall, which developed there. His son, John Richards White, born in 1847, eventually took over his father's interests. The son prospered in industry and banking, and the Whites figured prominently in the history of Athens and Clarke County in the ensuing decades.

By 1849 the average daily production of the factory's seventy laborers was 140 bundles of yarn and 800 yards of cloth. A true industrial complex, which included factory, houses, stores, and

John White was one of the wealthiest and most prominent men in Athens. Soon after his arrival in Athens to manage the failing Georgia Factory, he became full owner and turned the textile plant into a profitable concern. White was also a founding director of the National Bank of Athens. His original investment totaled forty thousand dollars, or two-fifths of the stock.

other facilities for the labor force, grew along the river banks and adjacent to the dams, gates, and races of the factory.

After the sale of the Georgia Factory to John White, three of the original investors—Dearing, Nisbet, and Clayton—joined Abraham Walker to finance Clarke County's second largest textile plant, the Athens Cotton and Wool Factory. They paid eight thousand dollars for a fifty-five-acre tract near the center of Athens at the same shoals (Cedar) where Daniel Easley was operating flour, grist, and saw mills when the Senatus Academicus first encountered him in 1801. The Athens Cotton and Wool Factory opened in the fall of 1834, and investors experienced a series of profits and losses during the ensuing years. In 1835 fire destroyed the sophisticated new carding machinery and much of the plant. Then came the Harrison Freshet of 1840, a disastrous flood named for William Henry Harrison, who had just won election as president of the United States. Torrents of rushing waters washed out most of the bridges in Clarke County and both of the bridges in Athens. The freshet virtually destroyed the factory at Cedar Shoals. After another fire in 1857, the seemingly undaunted investors again rebuilt and reopened the Athens Cotton and Wool Factory for production of osnaburgs (a coarse cloth for sacks and work clothes), stripes, bed ticking, linsey-woolsey and other textiles.

The third original Athens-Clarke water-powered textile factory was incorporated in 1833. The *Southern Banner* reported that "a Company of Gentlemen belonging to our town have bargained for the mill seat of Mr. [Noah] Prince, situated within 2-1/2 miles of [Athens], where they intend erecting another [factory]. We will have then three distinct branches of the 'American System,' or as John Q. Adams would say, 'Palaces of the Poor,' located in our immediate vicinity, Old England has her Manchester—New England her Lowell, and why should not Georgia boast her Athens?" Apparently, not all Athenians were enthusiastic about this local manifestation of the Industrial Revolution and its effects on their quiet college community.

The new factory, originally called Camak Manufacturing Company, soon became Princeton Factory in honor of Noah Prince, a former Revolutionary soldier who had operated a mill on the Mid-

The Princeton Factory operated for more than a century. The mill building, which burned in 1973, was a large two-story brick structure where workers produced cotton and woolen textiles. A mill community including houses and a store, seen on the right in this drawing, grew up near the factory above the banks of the Oconee several miles south of Athens.

dle Oconee. Investors included James Camak, Asbury Hull, William Lumpkin, Daniel Grant, and Elizur L. Newton. The factory produced cotton and woolen textile products. The factory president, William Williams, boasted in 1838 of his "Georgia Nankeens" (a durable brownish yellow cotton fabric originally woven by hand in China), "a large supply of cotton yarns, spun from prime white cotton, and put up in Bales of 240 lbs," and "carding of wool for county customers . . . in the best manner, and with promptness and dispatch."

The Princeton Factory sold to Dr. James Hamilton in 1845 and later to James White. Like Whitehall, Princeton was enough distant from town (close to the present bridge over the Oconee on the Macon Highway) to necessitate the construction of houses and other amenities for workers at the site. The British author and world traveler James Silk Buckingham recorded that white families "live in loghuts clustered about the establishment on the river's banks, and the negroes repair to the huts allowed them by their owners when they are near, or stay at the mill, when their master's plantation is far off."

The whites, Buckingham said, "looked miserably pale and unhealthy . . . said to be very short-lived . . . fevers and dysenteries . . .

In the 1890s workers at Bobbin Mill made bobbins, that were sold to textile plants throughout Georgia.

sweeping numbers of them off by death." He decried the factory system, particularly in a "heated temperature" and wrote, "I do not wonder that the most humane members of the community deplore the introduction of factories in the South, and wish that the labours of the people should be confined to agriculture, leaving manufactures to Europe or to the States of the North."

Princeton Factory, the Georgia Factory at Whitehall, and the Athens Manufacturing Company continued in more or less constant operation into the mid-twentieth century. A paper mill began at McNutt Creek (near today's Macon Highway crossing) in the antebellum period. Later, Star Thread Mill operated at Barnett's Shoals (at today's Oconee and Clarke County line). Both supported mill-village settlements.

At Bobbin Mill (now an aboretum and bird sanctuary at the scenic intersection of West Lake Drive and Milledge Circle) workers made bobbins from the hard, dense wood of local dogwood trees to supply the growing textile industry throughout the South. The mill, which at one time also fashioned wagon spokes, stayed in operation until the 1920s.

James Camak was the driving force behind the state's first successful railroad. At a meeting in Camak's Athens home, the Georgia Railroad Corporation was organized.

Thanks to the establishment of the first three major factories, Athens and Clarke County were second only to Savannah and Chatham County in capital invested in manufacture by the 1840s. By then cotton planters and manufacturers were pressing for better transportation. Athenians became heavily involved in the development of a state-owned system of railroads.

RAILROADS AND ROADWAYS

James Camak was a leader in the organization of the Georgia Railroad. A native of South Carolina, he originally came to Athens in 1817 as a professor of mathematics. Camak married the daughter of the third president of the university, Robert Finley, and moved for a time to the state capital at Milledgeville, where he owned and edited the influential local paper, the *Georgia Journal.*

He returned to Athens in 1833 as one of the founders of Clarke County's third textile mill and began construction of a handsome Federal-style brick mansion dominating a hilltop overlooking the town—a spot technically at the time in Cherokee territory. Here on March 10, 1834, Camak convened the organizational meeting of the Georgia Railroad, bringing together a group of entrepreneurs who elected Asbury Hull chairman and Camak president of the company. Camak then toured the state to solicit support and sell stock in the railroad. The same year he became a director of the Branch Bank of the State of Georgia, and when the Georgia General Assembly extended banking powers to the Georgia Railroad in 1835, Camak became the first president of the Georgia Railroad and Banking Company. Later he served as cashier, and William Dearing became president.

Like Camak, other Georgia cotton manufacturers were eager to facilitate transportation of their goods via Augusta and Savannah. While South Carolina forged ahead with the completion of 136 miles of track from Charleston to Hamburg (opposite Augusta) in 1833—at that time the longest rail line in the world—transport wagons in Georgia continued to bog down in mud. Most "highways" were little more than country trails. Maintenance consisted mostly of cutting back low-hanging branches, hacking away underbrush, and shoveling earth into mud holes. And for passengers, stagecoach travel was an endurance contest.

Early in 1838 the Augusta line extended to Crawfordville, transporting passengers and cotton. Four-horse post coaches met the train and relayed passengers to Athens and Gainesville via Washington, and to Athens via Greensboro, Dr. Poullain's Bridge, and Watkinsville, according to the *Southern Banner.*

By spring 1839 rail lines extended eighty-four miles from Augusta to Greensboro. The trip (including stops for breakfast, firewood, and water) took seven hours. From there Athens-bound passengers endured another eight hours by stage. Rail travel was twice as fast as stagecoach and cost half as much at five cents a mile. A traveler leaving Augusta at 5 A.M. arrived in Athens after 10 P.M.

The railroad did not extend to Athens until 1841, and then, to the

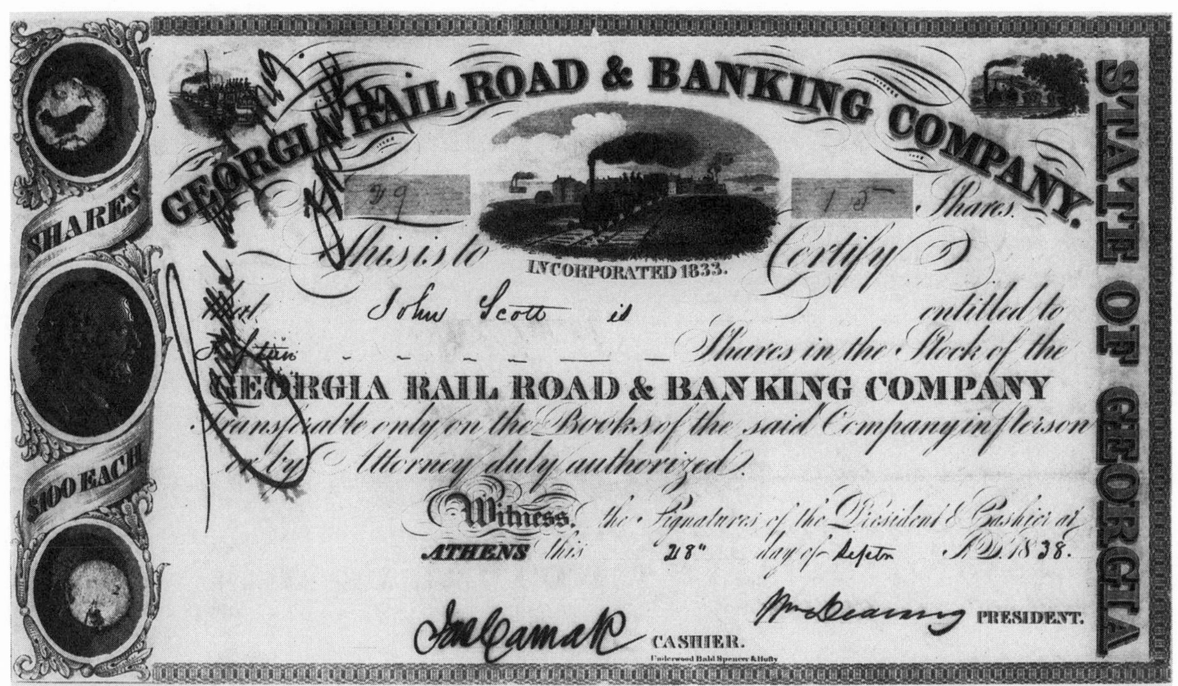
GEORGIA RAIL ROAD & BANKING COMPANY.

STATE OF GEORGIA

SHARES

$100 EACH

49 15 Shares.

INCORPORATED 1833.

This is to Certify that John Scott is entitled to Fifteen - - - - - Shares in the Stock of the GEORGIA RAIL ROAD & BANKING COMPANY Transferable only on the Books of the said Company in Person or by Attorney duly authorized.

Witness, the Signatures of the President & Cashier at ATHENS this "28" day of Septr A.D. 1838.

PRESIDENT.

CASHIER.

Underwood Bald Spencer & Hufty

The Georgia Railroad and Banking Company was formed in 1835. Subscribers quickly invested two million dollars' worth of stock. The bank had offices in both Athens and Augusta until 1842, when the Athens office closed.

consternation of merchant and traveler alike, the tracks stopped at Carr's Hill on the far side of the Oconee River from the town. Carr's Hill remained the Athens terminus for the next forty years, before the construction of a railroad bridge across the river. University students and others who came to Athens by train faced, by necessity, a tedious trek into town by cart or carriage, on foot, or on horseback. Augustus Longstreet Hull wrote in his *Annals of Athens,* "There no doubt lingers in the memory of many a traveler the horrors of the long ride between the depot and the hotel, as he was pitched about in Saulter's old omnibus, splashed with mud or suffocated with dust, according to the season of the year."

For the first few years of service, the Athens rail branch from Union Point (a town forty miles to the southeast) was horse powered; later three small locomotives, each weighing about three and a half tons, pulled freight and passenger cars. By September 1842 freight moved between Athens and Augusta twice a week, and passengers traveled by train every day except Sunday.

Elizabeth Hodgson, her daughter Ann, and two sons were among the passengers on the very first train to arrive at the Carr's Hill

When the Georgia Railroad reached Athens in 1841, the tracks stopped on Carr's Hill on the far side of the Oconee River. To get into town travelers hired a carriage, rented a horse, or walked. George Cooke's painting, executed in 1845, illustrates how difficult this situation was for all concerned. Forty years later a bridge finally connected the line to downtown Athens.

ATHENS.

Proprietors of the Franklin House hosted visitors to Athens from the late 1840s until the end of the Civil War. Antebellum hotels were notoriously unclean and offered little privacy. Indoor plumbing was not yet available, and boarders used either chamber pots or an outdoor privy. The Athens Hardware Company, shown in this late 1930s photograph, occupied the three-story brick structure until 1972.

terminus. Mrs. Hodgson was the widow of a British coach and carriage manufacturer whose changing fortunes had landed his family in America (originally in Troy, New York). Their son Edward Reginald Hodgson, ailing with asthma, came south for his health and arrived in Athens in 1839 via Georgia Railway to Greensboro and stagecoach from there to Athens. Soon his letters implored the rest of the family to join him in Athens.

In 1842 the three Hodgson brothers (Edward, William, and Robert) established one of the first carriage, coach, and wagon factories in the South when they opened E. R. Hodgson and Brothers in Athens. Edward and William established a stagecoach line between Athens and Gainesville to transport mail and passengers in 1845.

TOWN LIFE: BUSINESS AND FINANCE

Life in Athens centered around the new Town Hall, completed in 1847 facing Lumpkin Street. The first floor doubled as space for the town market and the local calaboose, while the second floor featured a hall for town meetings, political debates, concerts, and minstrel shows.

The Southern Mutual Insurance Company, chartered in Griffin, Georgia, in 1847, moved to Athens in 1848, thanks to the number of local investors led by Judge Young L. G. Harris. The Pioneer Paper Mill, begun in the 1840s by Albon Chase and John S. Linton, incorporated in Athens in 1852 as the lucrative and successful Pioneer Paper Manufacturing Company. The Athens Steam Company incorporated in 1850, telegraph lines extended to town in 1852, and in 1856 the Bank of Athens opened.

While business, commerce, and transport flourished, the county's several hotels, including the Franklin House, Planter's, Central, the Newton House, and the Eagle, became well known. Early in 1839 James Silk Buckingham stayed in the Planter's and thought it the best available at that time, despite the "incessant and uninterrupted chorus kept up every night by the dogs, cows, and hogs that seemed to divide among them the undisputed possession of the streets at night."

On the same visit Buckingham recorded the "elegant manners" of the citizens of Athens and the charm and beauty of the town:

> The mansions are almost all detached buildings, constructed of wood, with porticos, pediments, and piazzas, surrounded with spacious and well planted gardens; and as all the houses are painted white, with green venetian blinds, they afford a striking relief to the deep-green foliage in which they are embosomed. There is but one regular street of business, in which houses are continuous; and [as] this is as yet built on one side only, the rest of the dwellings are scattered like separate villas, and the surface being greatly undulated, and the wood or forest trees approaching close to their borders, the whole appearance of the village is picturesque and romantic.

Wilson Lumpkin completed his "Rock House" in 1844 on a hill overlooking the university. It remains intact today in the center of South Campus. As governor from 1831 to 1835, and later as Indian commissioner and U.S. senator, Wilson Lumpkin played a major role in Georgia history.

By the time Buckingham visited, Athens had its first "suburb." In 1833 the trustees of the university surveyed a large area west of town, which they divided into lots and offered for sale. In July 1834 John A. Cobb subdivided his farm adjacent to these new town limits and offered eighty lots for sale "immediately lying on both sides of the main road (now Prince Avenue) leading through Jefferson and Gainesville to the Gold Region." His suburb assumed a separate identity as the "Village of Cobbham," a pastoral setting for Greek Revival mansions and their dependencies on full-block lots, some as large as four acres. Soon Gothic Revival style houses were also in evidence along the shady dirt streets in the Cobbham forest.

THE LUMPKINS

Shortly after Cobbham lots west of town went on the market, Georgia Governor Wilson Lumpkin purchased the first parcel of what became an almost one-thousand-acre plantation south of town on the "road to Watkinsville" at a site Sylvanus Morris called "one of the most commanding situations in this part of the state." In 1835 Governor Lumpkin wrote, "I procured me a delightful situation, in the margin of town, in full view of the state university, together with six or seven hundred acres of good, productive land, finely timbered and watered, bounded on one side by the Oconee River. My design was to make this my permanent home, and live by the cultivation of the land."

This mahogany-veneer sideboard belonged to Governor Wilson Lumpkin. Made for him in nearby Lexington, Georgia, the sideboard stood in Lumpkin's Rock House in Athens. The sideboard traveled around the world with Lumpkin's granddaughter and her husband, Nathaniel Stewart, when he was in the consular service. It has returned to Athens and belongs to a Lumpkin descendant.

By 1842 Lumpkin's farm was actually in the Athens town limits. That year he designed his residence (now South Campus's Rock House) of native stone dressed on the site. When he completed the house two years later, he wrote, "I have endeavored to put a piece of my character in its stone walls . . . and until this building falls down, or is destroyed, there I stand to be praised or lampooned, as the work may be thought, to be good or bad, by the beholder."

In the first years of his "retirement" Lumpkin had little time for farming. As Indian commissioner he enforced the removal of the Cherokees from their remaining lands in Georgia under a treaty

that passed one month after his term expired in 1835. Elected to the U.S. Senate in 1837, Lumpkin resisted all Senate efforts to overturn the treaty. He regarded the Cherokee removal of 1838 "the capstone" on his life's work. Retiring from the Senate in 1841, Lumpkin administered the construction of the state-owned Western and Atlantic Railroad, facilitating its successful completion in 1851. Thereafter, he lived the life of a gentleman farmer on his Athens plantation.

Wilson Lumpkin died in 1870 at the age of eighty-seven. Gradually his heirs sold the plantation lands for use by the growing university and town that by then extended beyond Tanyard Creek to consume the "delightful situation." His daughter Martha Compton, for whom Marthasville (the railroad town earlier called Terminus and later Atlanta) was named, sold Lumpkin's Rock House and the few remaining acres to the university in 1907 with the provision that her father's dream house never be destroyed.

If Wilson Lumpkin was a consummate politician, his younger brother Joseph Henry Lumpkin was the pivotal figure in the world of Georgia jurisprudence. Like his brother before him, Joseph moved to Athens from Oglethorpe County in the 1840s. Joseph married Callender Cunningham Grieve; the two had eleven children. Educated at the University of Georgia and then at Princeton, Joseph became one of the outstanding jurists of the nineteenth century. He helped frame the Penal Code of 1833 and served briefly in the Georgia General Assembly. He was a "lawyer's lawyer": eloquent, well reasoned, and solid in his knowledge of the law. Chief Justice Logan Bleckley once said of the handsome and impressive jurist, "Those who never saw or heard him cannot be made to realize what a great master he was."

When the Georgia General Assembly created the first state supreme court, the legislators chose Hiram Warner, Eugenius A. Nisbet, and Joseph Henry Lumpkin as the first judges in 1845. Warner and Nisbet named Lumpkin the presiding judge; he became the first chief justice of the court upon the creation of that office in 1863.

During his years on the court and until his death in 1867 Lumpkin lived in a Greek Revival mansion on Prince Avenue. In 1844 his

John Maier painted this portrait of Joseph Henry Lumpkin in 1860. At the time, Lumpkin was a member of the Georgia Supreme Court; three years later he would become its first chief justice. As a resident of Athens and a Franklin College alumnus, Lumpkin took great interest in the university and laid the foundation for the school that today bears his name: the Joseph Henry Lumpkin School of Law.

daughter Marion married T. R. R. Cobb. As a wedding gift, Lumpkin gave his son-in-law a Greek Revival mansion on the crest of a hill adjacent to his own home. In a tiny law office they shared on the property, father and son-in-law, with William Hope Hull, founded the law school of the University of Georgia in 1859. There in the 1810 clapboard structure (at the present site of Saint Joseph's Catholic Church) they taught the first classes of a school that would produce many of the state's political leaders.

WOMEN IN ANTEBELLUM ATHENS AND CLARKE COUNTY

Marion Lumpkin Cobb possessed no real property in her own name, for not until the state constitution changed in 1869 could a married woman hold property in her own right in Georgia. Nonetheless, she and many of her contemporaries by necessity possessed multiple management skills. Antebellum white women managed vast estates or small farms or kept house in town. Many confronted numerous pregnancies and illnesses and often deaths among their children while supervising and caring for slaves under their charge. Some studied at academies in Athens or Salem or Watkinsville; some attended schools in the North; others intermittently attended "field schools" with their brothers when their struggling parents could spare them from farm labor. Life styles among antebellum Clarke County women were as diverse as the women themselves.

Sarah Cobb, for example, led a pious life. "Church and family were the most vital elements in [her] life," wrote William McCash. She expected proper Christian conduct of all her children. "Once, in 1847, upon hearing that her daughter Mary Willis had attended the theatre, she expressed marked disapproval and implored her 'not to do what is unbecoming a Christian and bringing disgrace upon the cause of her Master,'" McCash continued.

Hull in his *Annals of Athens* described another woman, the wife of Edward R. Ware, a prominent physician who came to Athens in 1829, as "full of life, loving the company of old and young, rich and poor, hospitable to lavishness, never too sick to go to a 'party,' and never too tired to give one, she was universally popular and retained . . . that youthful vivacity and unfeigned cordiality which, added to the other attractions of her elegant home [today the Lyndon House, the city-owned art center], made it one of the centers of social life in Athens."

Hull recalled the daily routine of his own mother: "She was out in the morning before breakfast giving instructions for pruning fruit trees or planting seeds, or cultivating or gathering vegetables each in its season. After breakfast work was cut out for the seamstresses, an interview with the cook was held, the work of the household inspected, or arrangements were made for pickling and preserving or putting up meat for the year. . . . The young girls must be taught to sew, and the plantation hands must be provided with clothes." The housewife was "dispenser of food, clothing, and medicine for a large family or dependents whose claims and duties absorbed her waking hours."

At the Hull homeplace adjacent to the college campus in Athens were four families totaling sixteen slaves. Among the women were two cooks, a laundress, three seamstresses, and a housemaid. One male was a carriage driver, another a "utility man," and there were "a lot of children." In addition, Hull's sister had a maid, and his brother a valet. "Four negroes were hired out," and two carpenters were "hired in."

Hull described the family plantation, where "each family of negroes had its own home" as a community unto itself. "Nearly all supplies were made on the place; wheat, corn syrup, and tobacco for man and ample grain and forage for beast." Though the slave family worked from "sun up to sun down," the mothers "cooked and made the clothes for the family, they ate together at their own table and had personal belongings."

Hull was describing only one Clarke County plantation and the lives of women and men slaves there. Obviously, treatment and tasks varied throughout town and country. Almost all the county's slaves remained illiterate. Georgia statutes prohibited teaching slaves (and free blacks) to read or write.

SCHOOLING IN THE ANTEBELLUM COUNTY

From the outset Clarke County more than held its own in education of white children when compared to other counties in Georgia. With the growth of the university came an increasing number of grammar schools and academies (high schools) for both sexes in Athens, Salem, Watkinsville, and other county communities. According to U.S. Census figures, a dozen or more schools were in operation in Clarke County throughout the period; enrollment of schoolchildren exceeded four hundred. After 1858 the number of county children attending school increased significantly.

Still, many prosperous parents felt they must send their daughters north for the best education. In 1854 an anonymous mother wrote a letter to the editor of the *Southern Banner* entitled "Female Education in Athens." The author was in fact Laura Cobb Rutherford (daughter of Sarah Cobb), and she pled for the establishment of a fine high school for young ladies of the community. "The female mind is susceptible to the highest state of cultivation," she wrote. She urged Athenians to facilitate higher education for young women in the South. The anonymous letter moved Laura's brother T. R. R. Cobb to action as the school's principal supporter. So prodigious was he in seeking funding from his peers that, according to Hull's *Annals*, "When a citizen was backwards in subscribing he subscribed for them and said, 'if you don't pay, I will.' "

Trustees for the female academy purchased eight acres in the Cobbham area in 1856. In January 1859 the Lucy Cobb Institute opened in a building 135 feet long, 60 feet wide, and three stories high. Seventy-seven young women, many from distant places, formed the first student body. The school was named in memory of the young daughter of T. R. R. and Marion Lumpkin Cobb. Lucy Cobb died of scarlet fever at age thirteen while the school her father championed was under construction. The Lucy Cobb Institute soon ranked among the finest girls' schools in the nation.

LIFE, DEATH, AND RELIGION

To the south of the Lucy Cobb campus, lovely new homes, many built in the Italianate style, emerged on large lots along the avenue newly named Milledge for the town and university benefactor. In 1859, for reasons both prideful and practical, an appointed committee named forty-six Athens streets, including Lumpkin, Clayton, Hancock, Prince, Thomas, and Baldwin. Until that time no street names were official, and many streets had no names at all. That year the city contracted with the Athens Gas Light Company (incorporated in 1856) to install lamps on College and Broad streets. Evidence of further city planning came with the opening of the Oconee Hill Cemetery in 1856 to replace the crowded old burying ground on Jackson Street.

During the antebellum years residents of Athens lacked a proper high school for their daughters. Thomas Reade Rootes Cobb succeeded in organizing a group of backers who purchased property for a girls' school on Milledge Avenue. The institution opened in 1859 with seventy-five girls in attendance and educated young women until 1931. This picture appeared in an 1899 school announcement.

In contemplating burial and life after death, many in antebellum Clarke County had a firm foundation in religion. Indeed, some of the earliest settlements in the county were communities begun along the Oconee River by denominations. Methodists settled Watkinsville and the area between the forks of the Oconee River. Baptists (the most numerous in the early history of the county) established churches and built homes at Trail Creek (the largest Baptist community and church), Barber's Creek (site of Mars Hill Church), and Barnett Shoals. The Trail Creek Church later helped start Athens Baptist Church (now First Baptist). Presbyterians predominated at Sandy Creek. Later, in 1830, the Disciples of Christ settled at Scull Shoals. Augustus Longstreet Hull noted "a manifest disinclination on the part of all denominations to interfere with the religious faith of a neighborhood lest they should 'build on another man's foundation,'" a distinction that separated the county into various denominational regions and communities.

Surprisingly, churches in Athens were slower to organize than those in rural settlements in the county. Although ministers of various denominations held services on the campus from the earliest days of the town's founding, Presbyterians were the first actually to start a church in Athens, in 1820. The Methodists did not found a town church until 1825, when they built the first church building of any denomination in Athens. The Baptists formed a church in 1830, and the Episcopalians followed in 1843.

Hope Hull, one of the original settlers of Athens and an early trustee, was a beloved minister some called the "Father of Methodism in Georgia." Hull held services in the environs of Athens as early as 1804 in a log cabin that was the first Methodist meeting house west of the Oconee River, and he preached on the campus until his death in 1818. When he was president of the university, Robert Finley held Bible classes for a group that became, with the support of his successor, Moses Waddel, the nucleus of the First Presbyterian Church in Athens. Elizabeth Stockton Moore, who came to Athens in 1835 as the bride of Dr. Richard Dudley Moore, began meetings in the parlor of her home on Dougherty Street that led to the founding of the Episcopal church in Athens. Stephen Elliot, the first bishop of the Diocese of Georgia (created in 1841) encouraged William Bacon Stevens, a medical doctor in Savannah and one of the founders of the Georgia Historical Society, to enter the ministry. Stevens, attracted to Athens on a visit as a newly appointed member of the university's Board of Visitors, agreed. Ordained a deacon in 1843, he came to Athens to become the first rector of Emmanuel Church. Later he became the bishop of the Diocese of Pennsylvania.

The university gave these denominations land for their first churches. The original Methodist church was a small (forty-foot-square) frame building with seats for whites in the middle and galleries for slaves on three sides. In 1828 the Presbyterians built a church on campus (where the north wing of the Academic Building now stands). The Baptists constructed a small frame structure on a corner of the campus, at Lumpkin and Broad streets. And the Episcopalians in the next decade built their first church on a lot now occupied by the Citizens and Southern Bank.

According to Ernest Hynds in his book *Antebellum Athens and Clarke County,* as late as 1831 "a vast majority of Georgians, possibly nine-tenths of them, did not belong to any church." But by 1850 there were twenty-one churches for five denominations in Clarke County. The Methodists built a new brick church downtown in 1852; the Presbyterians consecrated their Greek Revival sanctuary in 1856; and the Baptists moved to their new brick

The First Presbyterian Church of Athens was organized under the leadership of Moses Waddel. From 1830 to 1866 Nathan Hoyt (photographed here around 1847) served as minister. Under his leadership the present building, designed by Ross Crane, was erected on Hancock Avenue. Augustus Longstreet Hull, who knew Hoyt, called him a sound theologian, a good speaker, and a man who could recognize a good horse on sight!

structure on Washington Street in 1858. By 1859 the Methodist church was so crowded they were turning people away each Sunday. A revival in 1844–45 had netted the Methodists 163 new white members and 97 new black members. According to Hynds, "The increase in Negro membership was so great that the Negro members soon asked for a separate church and pastor. The Reverend John M. Bonnell, a white man, was named to the job." For a time some blacks in Athens worshiped separately in the little church on campus the Baptists had vacated. While many black Christians in town worshiped in white churches with segregated seating, separate black

congregations, for the most part, operated under the supervision of sponsoring white denominational churches. In George White's *Statistics* he noted "two churches for colored people in 1849."

In 1858 a huge revival in the spring brought many new members, black and white, into the fold. According to Hynds, "More than one hundred finally joined the Negro Methodist congregation, and the numbers added to the white churches were impressive. The Methodists added ninety; Presbyterians, fifty; Baptists, forty-one; and Episcopalians, eleven."

Throughout the 1850s a moral atmosphere seemed pervasive. The number of rural churches increased; the Temperance Society

By 1853 the old burial ground on Jackson Street was nearly full. Two years later town council members selected a seventeen-acre site along the Oconee River, across from present-day Sanford Stadium, for the new Oconee Hill Cemetery. The lots, offered for sale in 1856, sold in three price ranges. The cemetery plan included free spaces for paupers and a separate section for blacks. Dr. James Camak was responsible for laying out the cemetery; his family plot is pictured here.

activated to thwart "demon rum"; regular noonday prayer meetings in the law offices of W. W. Lumpkin drew steady attenders; Sunday school attendance in all churches soared; and in March 1857 the Athens branch of the Young Men's Christian Association formed under the leadership of Young L. G. Harris. The first YMCA officers included Harris, a Methodist; Professor Williams Rutherford, a Baptist; Dr. Richard Moore, an Episcopalian; T. R. R. Cobb, a Presbyterian; and Peyton E. Moore, a Disciple of Christ. Hynds concludes that despite this moral atmosphere and spirit of revival, "unfortunately, neither the churches nor the other institutions of society were able to solve the major social and moral challenge presented by slavery."

Thus on the eve of disunion and a war that would change the lives of every citizen—black and white—Athens and Clarke County could offer white citizens multiple advantages. But more than half the people of the county, illiterate and enslaved, had no personal share in the prosperity their labors produced and little hope for the future.

3

The Confederate Years

By the presidential election year of 1860 Athens was the center of industry and intellect not only within the county of Clarke but in larger arenas as well. "No place surpasses it in refinement, morals, splendid residences, good society, and learned men," wrote Adeil Sherwood in the 1860 edition of the *Gazetteer of Georgia.* "As Greece was enlightened by a city after which this town was named, so Georgia for years regarded this place. She gave laws to fashion and literature; and frequently from her college chapel politics sent forth its decree—who should be Governor, Members of Congress, and sustain the highest offices."

Clearly the city had outstripped the rest of the county in size and influence. The population had increased steadily from 2,500 in 1840 to 3,000 in 1850 to almost 4,000 (half white, half black) in 1860. The county grew at a lesser rate, from 10,522 in 1840 to 11,218 in 1860. Capital invested in Athens exceeded $430,000, an amount more than the tax digest of all the rest of Clarke County put together. The town limits of Athens extended by 1860 in a two-mile radius from the University Chapel at the epicenter, but its political influence reached far beyond these perimeters.

In the election of 1860 both town and county were sharply divided in support of moderate and secessionist candidates, and the two weekly newspapers fanned the flames of debate. The *Southern Watchman,* edited by John Christy, was the old Whig paper which now favored sectional compromise. The *Southern Banner,* edited by James Sledge and Anderson Reese and controlled by Democrat Howell Cobb, championed secession. The *Watchman* endorsed John Bell, a moderate from Tennessee; the *Banner* supported John Breckinridge, a southern-rights Democrat from Kentucky. On November 6 the voters in Athens (white and male) cast 383 votes for Bell, 335 for Breckinridge, and 41 for Stephen A. Douglas, a moder-

An elaborate iron veranda surrounds the Milledge Avenue Italianate house designed by Ross Crane for Dr. James S. Hamilton and his family. Ordered from Philadelphia, the ironwork arrived in 1861, just before commerce ceased between northern and southern states. The Hamilton family lived in the home until 1900, after which it was purchased by the Edward Hodgsons. Today it is the Alpha Delta Pi sorority house.

ate Democrat from Illinois. In Clarke County the vote was 695 for Bell, 451 for Breckinridge, and 51 for Douglas. "The educational and cultural center of Georgia," wrote E. Merton Coulter in *College Life in the Old South,* "was, thus, for peace, and the surrounding county was even more pronouncedly for the same course." In town and county Abraham Lincoln received not one vote.

Professor Coulter concluded, "Lincoln meant to Athenians the triumph of John Brown of Harpers Ferry infamy, and there was a fear as devastating as it was unwarranted that a servile insurrection would take place if heroic measures were not adopted." Already, in October 1860 a vigilance committee gave a white man, a "miserable Yankee" accused of "inciting our negroes to cut our throats," one week in which to leave Athens. On November 10, a week after Lincoln's election, a mass town meeting of white citizens organized volunteers to patrol every ward in the city and warned Clarke County planters to be on guard against slave insurrection. Many prominent citizens, including Thomas R. R. Cobb, Wilson Lumpkin, James Camak, and W. S. Grady, agreed to serve on a vigilance committee. According to the *Watchman,* the meeting condemned the election of "Black Republicans to Presidential offices" and stated its "determination never to submit to their rule, if our state will authorize us to resist."

THE POLITICS OF SECESSION

Tom Cobb was at the time thirty-six years old. He was tall and erect, devout, and devoted to his family. He possessed a keen intellect but a melancholy nature exacerbated by the untimely deaths of two infant sons and his beloved thirteen-year-old daughter, Lucy. Tom had graduated first in his class from Franklin College, where he earned the highest grade point average in the history of the school at that time. His codification of the laws of Georgia garnered for him statewide recognition, and he enjoyed a large and successful law practice.

In anticipation of the results of the presidential election of 1860, Tom Cobb gathered his young family before the altar in their man-

Antebellum Athens was the center of intellectual life in northeast Georgia. In this building at the corner of Pulaski and Prince were the law offices for three of Georgia's renowned jurists: Joseph Henry Lumpkin, Thomas R. R. Cobb, and William H. Hull. Here they established a school that became the University of Georgia School of Law. The state supreme court conducted its opening session here. Later, from 1873 to 1913, the building housed the city's first Catholic church.

sion on Prince Avenue to pray for the preservation of the Union and the defeat of Lincoln. He remained on his knees until dawn, when news of Lincoln's overwhelming victory reached Athens via telegraph wire. That day Tom heard an inner voice urge, "Be free! Be free!" According to the Athens physician and historian John F. Stegeman in his book *These Men She Gave,* Cobb interpreted these words as "a summons from above to help liberate his people from the shackles of a government to which his state could no longer honorably belong."

On the night of November 12 Cobb addressed a special joint session of the legislature at the state capitol in Milledgeville. With rumors of slave insurrection running rampant and news of a slave rebellion within seven miles of the capital the topic of the hour, Cobb played upon the mood of the tense legislators, delivering remarks that Clarence L. Mohr labeled in his book *On the Threshold of Freedom: Masters and Slaves in the Civil War* as "the type of

At the outbreak of the Civil War T. R. R. Cobb was a successful lawyer. Cobb was a leader of the secessionist movement in Georgia and a major contributor to the Confederate constitution. As an officer in the Confederate army, he fought mostly in Virginia, where he died in battle near Fredericksburg on December 13, 1862.

racial soliloquy which would become the stock-in-trade of a later generation of Southern politicians."

Cobb declared, "Our slaves are the most happy and contented . . . laboring population in the world. . . . But a discontented few, here and there, will become the incendiary or the prisoner . . . and . . . your home or your family may be the first to greet your returning footsteps in ashes or in death." Cobb concluded, "My voice is for immediate unconditional secession!" Deafening shouts of approval rose from the floor.

Howell Cobb served in Congress from 1842 to 1850, aligning himself with the moderate wing of the Democratic party. As Speaker of the House he played a key role in the adoption of the Compromise of 1850. In 1851 he was elected governor of Georgia, and in 1857 he joined President James Buchanan's cabinet as secretary of the treasury, resigning when Abraham Lincoln was elected president. A staunch secessionist, Cobb rose to the rank of major general in the Confederate States Army, in command of the Georgia reserve forces.

On December 8 Tom's brother Howell, then forty-five years old, resigned his post as secretary of the treasury in the cabinet of President James Buchanan. In late November he had sent his family home to Georgia, and now, despite his desire to remain loyal to the last to his friend Buchanan (whose term of office extended to March 4, 1861), Cobb could no longer postpone responding to the urgent requests of his constituents in Georgia to help turn the political tide toward secession. In a letter to his brother-in-law John B. Lamar, Cobb wrote that he now had "no hope or wish to save the union." By December 10 he was a private citizen who returned, at least temporarily, to his Cobbham home in Athens.

Howell Cobb was a graduate of Franklin College. In 1835 he married seventeen-year-old Mary Ann Lamar, the daughter of a wealthy middle Georgia planter family. Cobb entered the practice of law and in 1842 won election to Congress. He became Speaker of the U.S. House of Representatives in 1849 but returned to Georgia for election as governor on the ticket of the newly formed Union party. Although he rejoined the Democratic party in 1853 and resumed his congressional seat two years later, he earned for himself political enemies who denied him a possible bid for the presidency in 1860. Nonetheless, he was a state and national figure of considerable influence who played a key role in the politics of secession and the formation of the Confederacy.

When word reached Athens that South Carolina had seceded from the Union on December 20, 1860, Athens secessionists fired a fifteen-gun salute to hail the event. Students led a torchlight parade through streets lined with "illuminated" houses, and many citizens applauded orations at Town Hall in praise of what many thought was the bright and independent future for the South.

Clarke County elected Asbury Hull, a moderate, and secessionists Tom Cobb and Jefferson Jennings to represent the county at the state convention in Milledgeville on January 16, 1861. The three had defeated unionists M. S. Durham and Isaac Vincent of Watkinsville. Although not a delegate, Howell Cobb held an honorary seat at the convention.

In the debates that rang from the state capitol, the principal speakers on both sides were former Franklin College men well

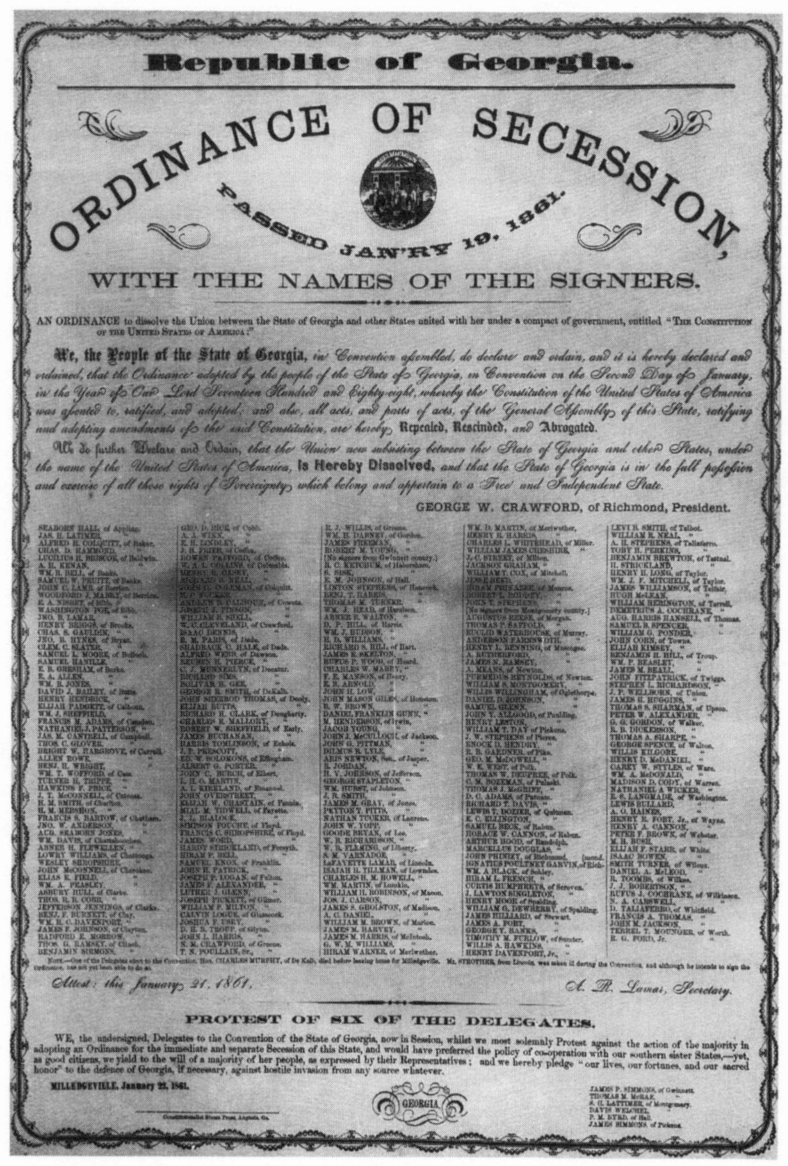

Republic of Georgia.

ORDINANCE OF SECESSION,

PASSED JAN'RY 19, 1861,

WITH THE NAMES OF THE SIGNERS.

AN ORDINANCE to dissolve the Union between the State of Georgia and other States united with her under a compact of government, entitled "THE CONSTITUTION OF THE UNITED STATES OF AMERICA:"

We, the People of the State of Georgia, *in Convention assembled, do declare and ordain, and it is hereby declared and ordained, that the Ordinance adopted by the people of the State of Georgia, in Convention on the Second Day of January, in the Year of Our Lord Seventeen Hundred and Eighty-eight, whereby the Constitution of the United States of America was assented to, ratified, and adopted; and also, all acts, and parts of acts, of the General Assembly of this State, ratifying and adopting amendments of the said Constitution, are hereby* **Repealed, Rescinded,** *and* **Abrogated.**

We do further Declare and Ordain, *that the Union now subsisting between the State of Georgia and other States, under the name of the United States of America,* **Is Hereby Dissolved,** *and that the State of Georgia is in the full possession and exercise of all those rights of Sovereignty which belong and appertain to a Free and Independent State.*

GEORGE W. CRAWFORD, of Richmond, President.

Attest: this January 21, 1861. *A. R. Lamar, Secretary.*

PROTEST OF SIX OF THE DELEGATES.

WE, the undersigned, Delegates to the Convention of the State of Georgia, now in Session, whilst we most solemnly Protest against the action of the majority in adopting an Ordinance for the immediate and separate Secession of this State, and would have preferred the policy of co-operation with our southern sister States,—yet, as good citizens, we yield to the will of a majority of her people, as expressed by their Representatives; and we hereby pledge "our lives, our fortunes, and our sacred honor" to the defence of Georgia, if necessary, against hostile invasion from any source whatever.

MILLEDGEVILLE, January 22, 1861.

GEORGIA

JAMES P. SIMMONS, of Gwinnett.
THOMAS M. McRAE, "
S. H. LATTIMER, of Montgomery.
DAVIS WELCHEL, "
P. M. BYRD, of Hall.
JAMES SIMMONS, of Pickens.

Of those who signed the Ordinance of Secession, Asbury Hull, Thomas R. R. Cobb, and Jefferson Jennings were from Clarke County.

Music played such an important role in the Civil War that this unknown Confederate chose to be photographed with his cornet. Regimental bands for both sides regularly entertained in the evening, playing sentimental songs, waltzes, and polkas. By day the troops marched to battle singing stirring hymns like "Dixie." Robert E. Lee underscored the significance of music when he commented that without music there would be no army.

schooled in oratorical skills. Alexander Stephens, Herschel V. Johnson, and Benjamin Hill urged delay; Tom Cobb, Robert Toombs, Eugenius A. Nisbet, and Francis Bartow argued for immediate secession. The Ordinance of Secession passed 208 to 89 on January 19, 1861. Georgia declared itself out of the Union.

Athenians celebrated Georgia's declaration of secession with parades and a hundred-gun salute by the Troup Artillery, Clarke County's militia unit. Students hung U.S. Commanding General Winfield Scott in effigy and launched a balloon bearing the names of each of the seceded states. Not everyone rejoiced in disunion, but

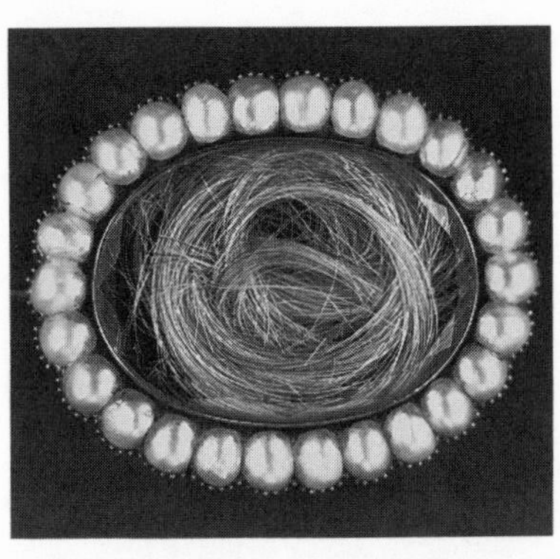

Around 1887 Eleanor Tschudi of Athens wrote to Mrs. Jefferson Davis requesting a lock of hair from the head of the former president of the Confederacy. Miss Tschudi kept her cherished memento in a pearl-studded brooch.

even John Christy, editor of the *Watchman,* conceded, "It now becomes the duty of all to cheerfully and loyally sustain the old Commonwealth in her present attitude."

Tom Cobb received a hero's welcome when a crowd greeted his return at the Carr's Hill depot and escorted him across the bridge over the Oconee to his home on Prince Avenue. There he addressed the assemblage and reportedly invited everyone inside for dinner.

On February 2 Tom departed from Carr's Hill en route to the Alabama capital, Montgomery, to join his brother Howell and the other Georgia delegates to the convention that fashioned the Confederate States of America. Of the ten Georgia delegates to the convention, eight had attended Franklin College. Howell Cobb was elected president of the convention by acclamation.

On February 18, before a crowd of ten thousand people, Howell Cobb administered the oath of office to Jefferson Davis, installing the Mississippian as president of the new nation. Tom Cobb played an important role in the drafting of the Confederate constitution; Robert Toombs became Davis's first secretary of state; Howell Cobb became the first Speaker of the Provisional Congress; and (ironically) the antisecessionist Alexander Stephens became the vice-president of the Confederacy. The convention displayed "a maudlin disposition to conciliate the Union men," wrote Tom to his wife, Marion. "So is the world: the man who had fought against our rights and liberty is selected to wear the laurels of our victory."

WAGING WAR: RECRUITING WARRIORS

Young Howell Cobb, Jr., awoke on a Sunday morning in April to an "unearthly noise" in the street outside the home of his friends Pope and Tom Barrow. Looking out of the window, he saw Captain A. A. Franklin Hill "driving a one horse buggy and braying like a Jack" at the "top of his voice" with news of the fall of Fort Sumter. Confederate guns had opened fire on the Federal garrison at Charleston on April 12, 1861, and Athens had waited anxiously for word of the outcome. With telegraph lines down (so often the case in Athens), it fell to Robert Bloomfield of the Athens Factory to

During the Civil War Confederate anthems such as "God Save the South" stimulated patriotism at home and comforted soldiers at the front. Athenians purchased their sheet music at William N. White's bookstore. White also sold stationery with the Confederate flag imprint.

When war broke out Rufus Reaves was a partner in the dry-goods and grocery business of Nicholson Reaves and Wynn. He became a private in the Athens Guards, attached to the Third Regiment, Georgia Volunteer Infantry, Company K. After Lee's surrender at Appomattox Reaves returned home to his business and entered politics; he served as alderman and then as mayor of Athens in 1886.

journey to Union Point and return next day by special train with news of the beginning of war.

Almost immediately some local men and boys prepared to depart from Athens. In Clarke County, as elsewhere throughout the South, existing state militia units grew in size. In some cases, prominent individuals petitioned the governor for permission to raise a company (one hundred men) or a regiment (about one thousand men). Advertising in newspapers or by word of mouth, they raised troops that in turn became Georgia units in the Confederate States Army.

With the passage of the Conscription Act in spring 1862, every white male between the ages of eighteen and thirty-five became liable for service. Early volunteers remained in service, while many others hastened to join the army before the draft in order to select the unit in which they would fight. Eventually the Confederate Congress raised the age of conscription to forty-five. Older men and boys served in the home guard as citizen soldiers, along with men exempted from the draft by virtue of their occupations.

The first unit to leave Athens for active duty was the Troup Artillery. Twelve days after the firing on Fort Sumter, the town gave them an emotional send-off. John Stegeman wrote, "Across the bridge and up the slope, in orderly procession, marched half the citizens of the town. A band led the way, followed by the Oconee Cavalry, behind which rolled an open barouche carrying the orator, Chancellor Andrew Lipscomb. The Troop Artillery itself marched next, sixty-nine strong, smartly dressed in green uniforms trimmed in red." There followed "the Athens Guards, the Fire Department, the Law School cadets, students from the college, and finally two thousand men, women, and children, on foot and in carriages."

The Troup Artillery held a special place in the hearts of the people of Athens and Clarke County. Captain Franklin Hill, a naval physician, editor, lawyer, and town favorite, had organized the company (soon renamed for George M. Troup, a former governor) as the National Artillery in 1859. Later Captain Marcellus Stanley of Salem in Clarke County took command. Among his young officers were Henry H. Carlton, an Athens physician; Pope Barrow, an attorney and the son of the highly respected landholder David Crenshaw Barrow, Sr.; Edward P. Lumpkin, son of the chief justice; and Franklin Pope, whose father, General Burwell Pope, had fought in the War of 1812. Stegeman concluded, "No other unit was quite so identified with the town as that vanguard of young artillerymen."

The Troup Artillery left for training in Savannah before going on to Virginia. Within days the Banks County Guards passed through town en route to the depot. After breakfast at the Lumpkin House and an address by Tom Cobb, the troops received a gift of $250 from the townspeople, who accompanied them to the depot with attendant and by now practiced fanfare.

On April 29 the Athens Guards, an infantry company organized

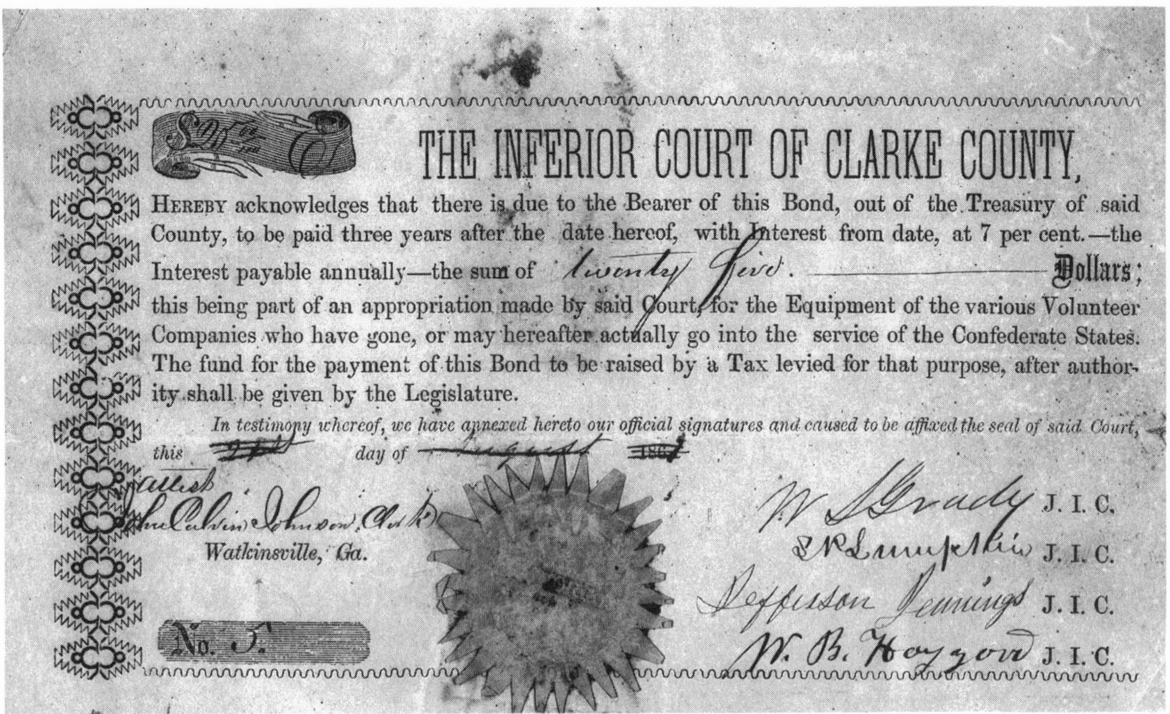
THE INFERIOR COURT OF CLARKE COUNTY,

HEREBY acknowledges that there is due to the Bearer of this Bond, out of the Treasury of said County, to be paid three years after the date hereof, with Interest from date, at 7 per cent.—the Interest payable annually—the sum of twenty five. Dollars; this being part of an appropriation made by said Court, for the Equipment of the various Volunteer Companies who have gone, or may hereafter actually go into the service of the Confederate States. The fund for the payment of this Bond to be raised by a Tax levied for that purpose, after authority shall be given by the Legislature.

In testimony whereof, we have annexed hereto our official signatures and caused to be affixed the seal of said Court, this day of 186

Attest John Calvin Johnson, Clerk
Watkinsville, Ga.

No. 5.

W. S. Grady J. I. C.
J. R. Lumpkin J. I. C.
Jefferson Jennings J. I. C.
W. B. Hazzard J. I. C.

In 1861 the county government printed bonds to raise funds for military equipment. When the state legislature failed to levy the necessary taxes to cover the 7 percent interest, the bonds were recalled.

in 1854, marched with loving accompaniment to the depot, where they boarded flower-bedecked railroad cars to begin their journey to Virginia. "As the train moved out," wrote Stegeman, "a great cheer arose from those who had come to say goodbye. When the train disappeared in the distance, the citizens once more returned to their lonely and shrinking neighborhoods."

Indeed, outward good spirits belied the inward dread of reality that faced wartime Clarke County families. By May 1, 1861, Chief Justice Lumpkin had four sons, two sons-in-law, two grandsons, and six nephews in the service of the Confederacy; Howell Cobb had three soldier sons, including young Howell, Jr., who served in the Troup Artillery. Over one hundred young Athens men had already gone to war. By the fall of 1861 Clarke County had furnished five companies, totaling about five hundred men.

One of their number was William G. Deloney, first honor graduate of the class of 1846, a handsome, successful lawyer and a devoted family man who had just won election to the state legislature when war broke out. Deloney was, according to the *Banner,* "as gallant a man as ever bestrode a horse." In April and May 1861 he scouted Clarke, Jackson, Madison, and Hall counties for men and mounts to organize the Georgia Troopers, a cavalry troop that soon rode off to Virginia. Deloney led his men in fifty fights or skirmishes. He received multiple wounds and rose to the rank of colonel. In October 1862 Tom Cobb wrote his wife, Marion, that he and Colonel Deloney, encamped at Martinsburg, West Virginia, after the Battle of Antietam, lay on the grass in the moonlight and "talked about home and the dear ones there and the hopes of peace and our plans and wishes for a quiet life by our firesides. You would have concluded that we were sick of war."

Almost a year later (September 5, 1863) Deloney wrote to his wife, Rosa, in Athens, "Strange as it may appear to one at home, there is a fascination in danger which allures a soldier, and perhaps it is well that it is so to those who are soldiers from necessity and a sense of duty. It serves to render tolerable many of the discomforts and burdens of our life." Seventeen days later a minie ball tore through his thigh during a skirmish at Orange Court House in Virginia. Deloney lingered a time in a prison hospital in Washington, and there in early October he died.

Another Athenian to raise troops was a Baptist minister and university vice-chancellor (and later chancellor), Patrick Mell. Mell resigned from the faculty to organize the Mell Rifles. Family illness forced him to remain home, but his son, Benjamin Mell, enlisted in his father's unit, now under the command of Captain Thomas U. Camak. Benjamin was the first honor graduate in the university's class of 1861. All twenty-two members of the class went to war; seven never returned. In his history of the University of Georgia, F. N. Boney wrote: "Young Mell, a fine soldier, quickly made sergeant. Tough and confident, he marched with Lee's army as it swept into Maryland in the fall of 1862, and he was cut down by rifle fire in the Battle of Compton's Gap. All told, nearly a hundred University of Georgia men died for the South."

In May 1861 Captain Isaac S. Vincent organized the Clarke Rifles among men on the Watkinsville side of the Oconee River. The

Patrick Hues Mell left his position as vice-chancellor of the university when the Civil War broke out to lead a local unit. Within a month, because of his wife's death, Mell resigned this post, but he re-entered military service shortly thereafter to lead a student-faculty unit stationed in Rome and Savannah. In 1863 Mell became president of the Southern Baptist Convention, a position he held until his death in 1888. Mell also served as the university chancellor from 1878 to 1888.

In July 1858, with a recommendation from Congressman Alexander H. Stephens of Georgia, James Barrow entered the military academy at West Point. When the South seceded from the Union, Barrow received an honorable discharge and returned to Athens to join the Confederate army. He fell on February 20, 1864, at the Battle of Olustee in north Florida, while leading a unit which fought to cut off supplies of cattle from northern troops.

political jealousy that had long separated the two sections of the county carried over into military affairs as well. Even in wartime, long-term local rivalries prevailed. Vincent, a former unionist and a personal enemy of the Cobbs, took pride in drawing his troops from the south side of the Oconee River.

In June 1861 William Sammons Grady, the prosperous owner of an Athens general store, a sawmill, and (with his brother-in-law John W. Nicholson) the city's first gas works, began raising men for the Highland Guard in Athens, surrounding counties, and the mountains of North Carolina, where Grady had lived originally. Often his eleven-year-old son, Henry Woodfin Grady, accompanied him on trips to recruit men to fight in Virginia. While on leave in Athens in 1863, Captain Grady purchased a handsome Greek Re-

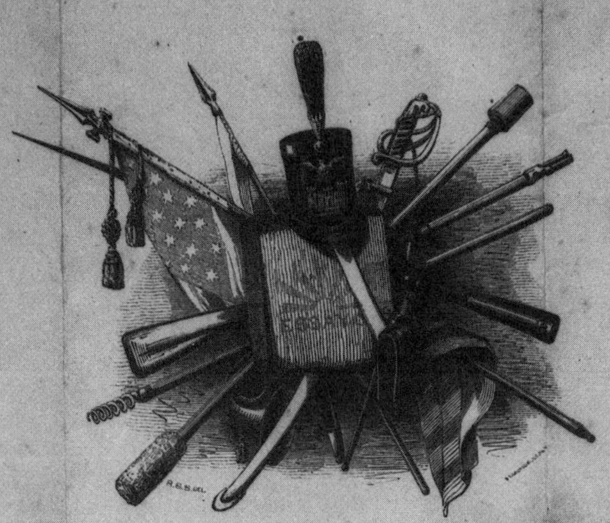

BE IT KNOWN, That *James Barrow*, appointed a CADET in the ARMY of the UNITED STATES, on the *First* day of *July* 1858, having served at the Military Academy to this date, now desires the acceptance of his RESIGNATION.

The said *James Barrow*, was appointed from the State of *Georgia* and is *nineteen* $\frac{10}{12}$ years of age.

During the period of his service he was proficient in the following branches of instruction and military exercises:

Mathematics
English Studies and Literature
French
Infantry Tactics. - School of the Soldier, Company & Battalion by practical drill.
Artillery Tactics. - School of the Piece by practical drill
Use of Small Arms. - Fencing & Bayonet Exercise.

And made progress in.

Natural & Experimental Philosophy.
Spanish
Drawing
Cavalry Tactics. school of the Trooper mounted by practical drill.

Given at the MILITARY ACADEMY, WEST POINT, State of New-York, this *Second* day of *February* 1861

Recorded page *108* Miscellaneous Book.

S. B. Holabird
1st Lieut. 1st Infy. U.S.A.
Adjutant *Mily. Acady.*

Richd. Delafield
Colonel ~~Corps~~ of Engineers,
Superintendent U. S. Military Academy.

vival mansion on Prince Avenue in Cobbham. By the time the Highland Guard entered Petersburg in 1864, Grady was the only company commander among the seven that had left Athens in 1861 still with his men. He too met his death, sustaining a mortal wound at the Battle of the Crater. He left the house and a handsome estate to his young family. His son Henry was destined to play a significant role after the war in the formation of the New South.

Tom and Howell Cobb rose highest among Athenians in the military hierarchy. When war broke out, Howell was president of the Provisional Congress, and he attended both sessions. Then he raised a regiment and saw combat in the Peninsular Campaign of 1862. On his staff were James Barrow (staff sergeant) and Cobb's sons John A. and Lamar (aides-de-camp). In 1863 he returned to Georgia and commanded state and Confederate reserve forces to the war's end, rising in rank to brigadier general.

Tom Cobb also served in the Provisional Congress. While still a legislator, he raised a regiment, the Georgia Legion, composed of artillery, infantry, and cavalry companies and received his commission as colonel in the Confederate army on August 28, 1861. In October 1862 Cobb assumed command of his brother's former brigade and on November 6 earned promotion to brigadier general.

Tom received word of his promotion from his men while camped in Culpeper, Virginia, en route with Lee's Army of Northern Virginia to Fredericksburg. The new Brigadier General Cobb walked to Fredericksburg, while sick and injured soldiers shared his horse. Atop Marye's Heights on a ridge above Fredericksburg's Sunken Road, Tom wrote to his wife in Athens, "Tell Ma my camp is now on the hills immediately in the rear of 'Federal Hill.' I can see the house plainly, there being a level plain between it and my headquarters." Federal Hill was the girlhood home of Sarah Rootes and the site of her marriage to John A. Cobb. Sarah wrote from Athens, "Oh my dear son, when I read your letter to your dear wife and about your removal to dear Fredericksburg and your camping place it almost broke my heart. . . . God I hope in mercy will prevent your having to fight over my . . . mothers, sisters, grandmothers, and nieces graves, for tho the old place is sadly changed, yet it is dear to my heart."

Thomas R. R. Cobb's funeral service and the procession to the cemetery attracted a large crowd of dignitaries and local citizens. For weeks after the funeral, local newspapers carried tributes, including one by Robert E. Lee, who called Cobb a patriot and soldier whose death left a gap in the army that was hard to fill.

On December 13, 1862, Tom Cobb died defending the stone wall beneath the heights facing Federal Hill. His brothers-in-law Charley and Ed Lumpkin, nephew Johnny Rutherford, and body servant Jesse (Athenians all) accompanied his casket from Richmond to Athens by train. Arriving too late to connect with the Georgia Railway train to Athens, Cobb's remains lay in state in Augusta overnight in city council chambers. When the night train pulled into the Carr's Hill depot on December 18, T. R. R. Cobb made his last trip across the lower bridge, through the town, and out to his stately home on Prince Avenue. The Reverend Nathan Hoyt conducted the funeral service at 10 A.M. the next morning at First Presbyterian Church, followed by burial in Oconee Hill Cemetery. The *Watchman* reported, "Never in the history of the town was such a funeral seen. All the citizens, old and young, mother and father, black and white—aging sires and prattling children—all, all, followed the honored remains of the Christian hero to their last resting place. . . . Never did any community more sincerely mourn the loss of any citizen."

THE HOME FRONT

Change was a constant in wartime Clarke County, with furloughed soldiers, refugees, and new recruits continually passing through, injured sons returning home, conscription ages rising, and casualty reports mounting. From the war's beginning Athens was the collection point for volunteers from the surrounding counties. During the early war years it was not unusual to see companies marching through the dirt streets of town. At first those left at home looked forward to news from the front, gathering on Broad Street at five o'clock to hear the latest dispatches newly arrived by afternoon train.

Almost from the start Athens became a haven for refugees from active theaters of war, including places as distant as Mississippi. In November 1861 Mary Ann Cobb reported that Georgians from Savannah and Brunswick were forwarding their valuables for deposit in the bank in Athens, and women and children were arriving daily from the coast. "Refugees rented and bought houses, lived in

hotels, and boarded in private homes," wrote Professor Kenneth Coleman in his book *Confederate Athens*. "By the spring of 1862 good accommodations were becoming hard to find."

Athens Fire Company No. 1 organized as a home guard. Another volunteer home guard formed on the Watkinsville side of the Oconee. From early 1863 there was usually an army unit of regimental size stationed nearby as well.

Patriotism ran high, and optimism prevailed despite the ever-mounting casualty reports. Citizens organized to aid the needy families of Clarke County volunteers. Women in Athens and Watkinsville formed the Ladies Aid Society, initially providing food and clothing for departing troops. When the Georgia Troopers left Athens in August 1861, the women supplied three hundred pounds of ham and five hundred biscuits to feed the traveling soldiers. Early

This Gothic Revival house, built around the time the Civil War broke out, probably first belonged to James A. Sledge, editor of the Southern Banner, *who generally supported the views of Howell Cobb and the Democratic party. The second owners were Lamar and Ann Olivia Newton Cobb, who was the first president of the Ladies Garden Club. Although Mrs. Cobb's front garden is gone, the house has been meticulously restored by its present owners.*

The daughter of a wealthy Maconite, Mary Ann Lamar considered Athens her home after marrying Howell Cobb in 1835. This portrait probably was painted when the Cobbs were living in Washington just before the Civil War. When Lincoln was elected to the presidency, they returned to Athens. During the war Mary Ann Cobb was active in the Ladies Aid Society, whose members sewed garments for soldiers and raised funds for a wayside home to accommodate soldiers in transit.

Founded in 1856, the Bank of Athens paid quarterly dividends through 1863. Assets declined thereafter, and there is no record of dividends in the latter stages of the war. When a coin shortage occurred during wartime, the bank issued paper money for amounts under one dollar. This currency could be exchanged for Confederate notes once the bearer accumulated five dollars' worth.

in the war the inferior court appropriated fifteen thousand dollars to outfit military volunteers. A pattern emerged whereby the county bought the cloth, local tailors at county expense cut the uniforms, and members of the Ladies Aid Society, with the help of their servants, made the garments in their homes at no charge.

"Business as usual lasted as long as possible," wrote Coleman, "modified by new activities to aid the war, a decline of agricultural activity caused by the absence of men who had gone off to war, changes in agriculture caused by declining cotton production and increased food production, and increased shortages brought on by lack of imported goods." Home manufacture could scarcely meet local demand, as many locally manufactured products were shipped out to support the war effort.

Concerts and other entertainments helped raise money for the cause. Lucy Cobb students collected $120 for the Confederacy, and Franklin College faculty "cheerfully agreed to remit twenty-two percent of their salaries in consequence of reduced receipts of their institution." As prices inflated, textile factories allowed families of soldiers to buy cloth at reduced rates. The town made every effort to provide free transportation for soldiers and refugees from the depot

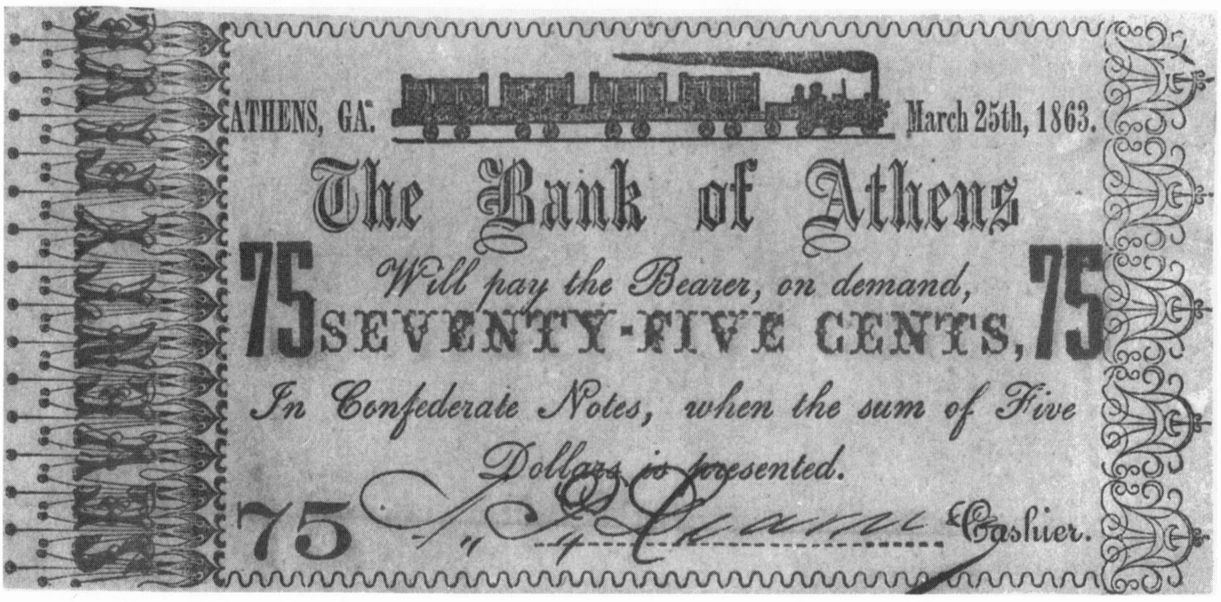

Chancellor Andrew A. Lipscomb struggled to keep the university open when war broke out. Though loyal to the southern cause, Lipscomb was a moderate who opposed lawlessness and lynching during these turbulent years. When the university reopened and former veterans antagonized occupying troops, Lipscomb's reasoning voice cooled the local hotheads.

on Carr's Hill into the city and did what it could to aid the sick and wounded at home and at the front.

The university continued to operate during 1860 and 1861 with an enrollment of about 120 students each year, but in September 1863, with about 40 students on the rolls, Chancellor Andrew Lipscomb suspended classes. The "temporary interruption" he anticipated lasted until January 3, 1866.

The Confederate government requisitioned all of the buildings on the campus at one time or another. By October the college buildings—especially Old College and New College—housed refugees. Other buildings, including the Chapel, became part of an army hospital specializing in treatment of wounds of the eye.

The most significant new industry begun in Athens during the war was Cook and Brother Armory. When war broke out, two British brothers named Ferdinand and Francis Cook owned and operated a small armory in New Orleans. In April 1862 they had contracted with the Confederate government to produce thirty thousand Enfield rifles (thirty dollars each with sabre-bayonet, sheath, and frog or fastener). Almost immediately New Orleans fell to the Federals, and the brothers were forced to flee the port city, traveling with most of their machinery on a Mississippi barge to Vicksburg. From there they hauled machines, iron, and steel overland to Selma, Alabama, and thence on to Athens, where they hoped to find relative safety for small munitions production for the Confederacy.

Here on Christmas Day 1862 the brothers opened their new Confederate armory at the foot of Broad Street on the east bank of the Oconee River in renovated mill buildings. Cook and Brother manufactured infantry rifles, artillery rifles, and carbines. At peak production the factory produced six hundred guns of each class per month. The armory also manufactured cavalry horseshoes, agricultural machinery, and bayonets and repaired small arms. The main building of the factory complex was large (300 by 150 feet), a three-story structure with a shot tower in the center. Outbuildings included a blacksmith shop, smokehouse, saw and planing mill, and wood-finishing room.

The armory could employ two hundred people, but manpower was at a premium and skilled labor scarce. Cook and Brother

Ferdinand and Francis Cook's Athens armory manufactured about four thousand Enfield-model rifles. The Confederate flag was stamped on the lockplate of each gun.

The double-barreled cannon that stands outside City Hall is an Athens landmark. John Gilleland, a local house builder, designed the cannon, which was manufactured at the Athens Foundry. Two balls loaded into the gun and connected by a chain were intended to sweep evenly across the battlefield upon firing. In repeated testing the balls traveled unpredictably, so the cannon was never used.

employed women, recruited workers from Atlanta, and used slave labor as well. To ward off conscription and to protect this vital wartime industry, the Cook brothers got permission to organize the male workers into a reserve battalion with Ferdinand as major and Francis as captain. They built breastworks all around and obtained a cannon, a single gun they transported in drills between fortifications on Carr's Hill and the hill north of the armory.

In August 1864 the University Chapel temporarily housed 431 Yankee cavalry prisoners. Captured near Jug Tavern (called Winder after 1894), they were part of the dreaded Stoneman Raiders. Two brigades of raiders under the command of Colonel Horace Capron and Colonel Adams had escaped capture when General Stoneman on July 31 near Macon surrendered part of his command to the Confederates. On August 1 the two brigades passed through Madison, setting fires and destroying commissary supplies. At midnight they halted their march just below Watkinsville. The next day the troops ransacked the village of Watkinsville, taking horses, mules, and provisions, while Colonels Capron and Adams laid plans to enter Athens and "destroy the armory and other government works" there.

Adams's brigade advanced toward Athens along what is now Highway 441. The "Mitchell Thunderbolts" (the Athens home guard) and Captain Ed Lumpkin's battery (along with Athens's double-barreled cannon forged at the armory) were well entrenched at the outer defenses of Athens on a hill above the paper mill on Barber's Creek. A few well-placed shots from Lumpkin's artillery reportedly killed a lieutenant, wounded several soldiers, and sent the remaining troops fleeing upriver in the direction of Jefferson. Capron's battalion, having remained behind at Watkinsville, got word of the strength of the Athens fortification, set out to rejoin Adams, and promptly became lost between Watkinsville and Athens.

Another battery of Lumpkin's men exchanged gunfire with a group of Yankees estimated at eighty out Mitchell's Road about sunset the same day. Again Lumpkin's batteries scattered the raid-

ers. These skirmishes were the only fighting that took place in Clarke County during the war years.

A contingent from Major Cook's Armory Battalion Cavalry, men of the Sixteenth Georgia Cavalry, and a regiment of Kentucky Infantry routed Capron's brigade near Jug Tavern and rounded up about three hundred men. Around three o'clock in the afternoon on August 3, 1864, the first Union prisoners arrived in Athens for processing on the field near Old College and internment in the Chapel. For the next few days Confederate troops rounded up other prisoners in the woods surrounding the battlefield and sent them to the Athens campus prison under guard by the Thunderbolts.

Mary Ann Cobb wrote to her husband, "Our ladies went to the campus and talked with the prisoners. . . . With the excuse of going to the prayer meeting, crowds of women gathered in the campus. . . . What sort of people are we?"

After a few days, the Thunderbolts escorted the prisoners to the depot for shipment to Camp Sumter, near the Georgia village of Andersonville. Federal troops would again briefly occupy university buildings. In the summer of 1865 they came as victors.

News of General Lee's surrender to Grant on April 9, 1865, did not appear in the Athens papers until April 26. The first Federal troops, men from the Thirteenth Tennessee Regiment, arrived in town on May 4 and immediately began to pillage homes and rob citizens. Soon another Federal force (under the command of Brigadier General William J. Palmer, who was leading a mission to intercept the fleeing Jefferson Davis) swept into town and put a stop to the looting. General Palmer's troops remained for several days, while great numbers of paroled Confederate troops came through Athens on their way home.

On May 29 an occupation garrison arrived in Athens under the command of Captain Alfred B. Cree of the Twenty-second Iowa Volunteers. He set up a provost-marshal government headquartered in Phi Kappa Hall on the campus and instituted the "Watch on the Oconee." He ordered all nonresident paroled Confederate officers and soldiers to leave town within twenty-four hours and discouraged the wearing of Confederate uniforms except when civilian clothes were not available to returning veterans.

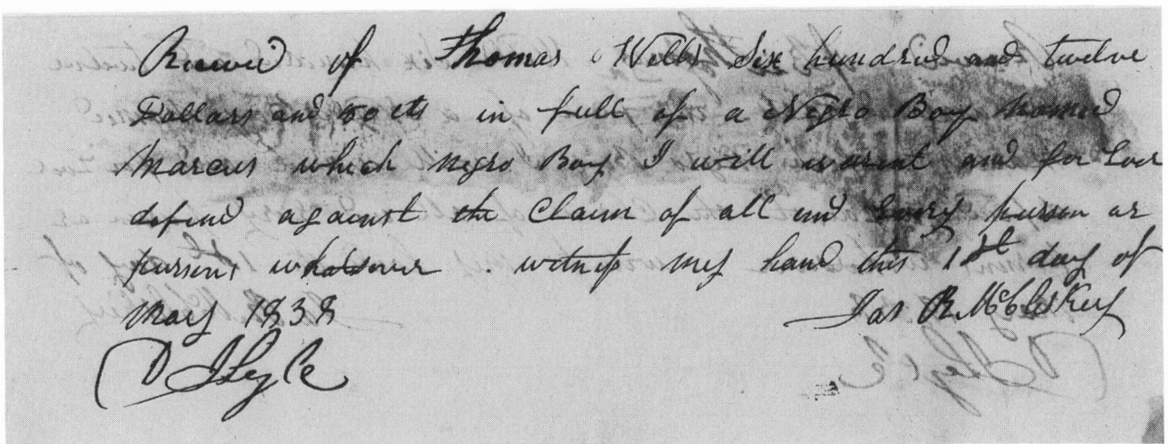

Received of Thomas Wells Six hundred and twelve Dollars and 50 cts in full of a Negro Boy named Marcus which negro Boy I will warrant and for Ever defend against the Claim of all and Every person or persons whatsoever. witness my hand this 1st day of May 1838

Jas R. McCleskey

[illegible]

By 1860 slaves constituted nearly half the population of Clarke County. Although only about 10 percent of the white inhabitants actually owned slaves, slaves constituted a valuable resource in a county dependent on cotton farming. When Thomas Wells bought Marcus in 1838 for $612.50, Wells received a written guarantee that the slave was legally the property of the seller and was not a runaway.

Formal military occupation of Athens ended before the year was out. When Lieutenant Colonel H. B. Sprague accepted an appointment as agent for the Freedmen's Bureau, a new era had begun.

The pragmatist editor Christy wrote in the *Watchman* on May 17, 1865, "We are aware that it is very difficult for human nature to forgive and forget such wrongs as have been inflicted upon us during this cruel war—it requires time to forget such things."

THE SLAVE EXPERIENCE

More than one-third of the people of Clarke County lived in Athens when war broke out, including 1,892 slaves and one free black. During the war the urban slave population increased dramatically as planters allowed their servants to "live out" (to earn wages for the master away from the plantation) or independently hire themselves out in Athens. Reportedly, a majority of the free blacks within the county moved to Athens in wartime as well.

Some urban slaves lived in quasi emancipation. For example, when Mary Ann Cobb went to live on her family's plantation near Macon, she left four to six servants, including a literate slave named Aggie, behind at her Cobbham home. She wrote to her husband on November 11, 1861, "They have to work to buy their meal and wood. Aggie takes in sewing. Ben works out by day and Vickey was to go out as a washerwoman by the day. All they can save from their support is their own. All I required of them was to take care of the house and lot—and cow and calf and make me a garden in the spring." She had left them with a small amount of food and a large supply of autonomy.

The city council granted licenses for free blacks and slaves to live off the premises of their guardians and owners but imposed an initial tax of five to twenty-five dollars to discourage the practice. For example, Alonzo Church, former president of the university, paid ten dollars each for his women slaves Caroline and Ann to live out in 1861. During that year between thirty and forty slaves lived out. Throughout the war these taxes increased drastically, though collecting fees from masters (many now soldiers) was often impossible.

Control of the black population was a constant concern of the town fathers, and they went to extraordinary lengths to pass laws to guard against insurrection or unrest. New ordinances continually restricted the blacks' mobility and their ability to earn wages. Curfew for blacks was 9 P.M. Only a few industries employed slaves, and finding employment for them became increasingly difficult. The vast majority of slaves in Athens continued to be household servants.

Occasionally the city hired slaves. For example, Athens hired a slave to keep the unpaved streets passable with a city-owned mule, cart, and a few necessary tools. The council employed Tom Cobb's slave Joe at $130 a year (an amount that increased nearer the end of the war) to work the streets and care for the mule. His successor, "Boy Lige," in January 1865 received a bonus of $50 from the council "for his faithfulness."

By 1864 at least fifty-six slaves and free blacks lived apart from their owners and guardians; fees ran as high as a hundred dollars for each. Black laborers helped sustain nearly all aspects of the war effort and at one time made up almost half the work force at Cook and Brother Armory. Some local slaves did not remain at home during the war; they went to the front with their masters as bodyservants. Still, many black Athenians were forced to roam the town endlessly in search of menial labor; many were idle; and some stole food in order to survive.

Weapons manufacturers often hired skilled black slaves during the war. Augustus Thompson, a trained blacksmith, moved to Athens, where he worked for a short time at the Cook and Brother Armory making guns. After the war and freedom Thompson eventually settled in Atlanta and opened his own business. He was also active in community affairs there as a founder of Georgia's first lodge of Odd Fellows for black men.

When slaves found employment in buying and selling foods and other farm and garden products, the council passed an ordinance against the practice. Offenders faced a fine of twenty dollars or whipping or imprisonment. Some slaves acquired vehicles and draught animals and hauled freight and passengers to and from the depot. Their enterprise competed with whites, and so the council imposed a fifty-dollar fine and a punishment of twenty lashes to slaves breaking a new ordinance that took away their right to transport customers and goods to and from the depot. Few policemen were on hand to enforce these ordinances, however, and in-

Typical rural slave homes in the interior sections of Georgia were square or rectangular buildings constructed of logs with dirt floors. Each structure commonly housed a single family who slept, cooked, ate, and lived in one room. Some houses included a sleeping loft for children.

fringements often went unpunished. Often the city seemed long on passing ordinances and short on enforcing the new laws.

Slaves learned news of the war in various ways. A literate black woman owned by an Athenian named John Crawford, according to her granddaughter, often stole newspapers and read up about the war. "She kept the other slaves posted as to how the war was progressing."

Most slaves were actively religious. Clarence Mohr wrote, "By affirming their faith in God, blacks were in reality affirming their own moral worth as human beings." In Athens Joseph Williams, a black Presbyterian preacher who had ministered to Georgia slaves since the 1840s, was a great source of inspiration to local blacks. In 1860 he was assigned to the white Presbyterian church. According to Mohr, within six months the Reverend Williams had gathered a sizable black congregation that met in the basement of the church in Athens on Sunday evenings and at "separate" black churches three miles from town on varying weeknights. "Williams's faith," wrote Mohr, "possessed a quality of enduring steadfastness which strengthened but did not immobilize. Such a faith gave black people the courage to act and the calmness not to act foolishly."

The Slave Code of all southern states after the 1830s forbade slaves to have separate religious services unless supervised by whites, but apparently in Clarke County the code was ofttimes ignored by black and white. The black services led by the Reverend Joseph Williams offer one example of an unspoken overlooking of the Confederate code.

At times blacks were allowed to congregate for recreation. On one such occasion they enjoyed hearing the black slave musician Blind Tom, who played the piano "exclusively for servants," after his performance in 1864 before an all-white Athens audience.

In January 1862 a group of fifty to one hundred blacks gathered to demonstrate their joy at the defeat of a candidate for the marshalship "by throwing up their caps and hurrahing at the very top of their lungs" in an assemblage that violated town ordinances and severely alarmed the white populace. Later in the year a lynching occurred about a mile from Athens. A slave from a nearby plantation awaiting trial for an alleged assault on the wife of an overseer was snatched from his cell by an enraged mob of white men, who marched him down Broad Street and hanged him from a pine tree near the Georgia Railroad track. This was the only recorded lynching in Clarke County during the war, and even John Christy, whose racially biased comments appeared regularly in his columns, opposed "the *manner* of his execution." "There can be no rational liberty which is not regulated by law," he wrote. "A deep and abiding respect for, and a rigid enforcement of the laws of the land, are, therefore, the greatest safeguard of freedom."

Lincoln's Emancipation Proclamation of January 1, 1863, had no immediate effect in Athens. Indeed, city council, even after the war ended, continued to charge a fee to Athenians whose slaves lived off their lots.

Near the war's end, in accord with President Jefferson Davis's plan to arm the slaves and free them, Howell Cobb (who opposed

Shortly after the end of the Civil War, the Ladies Memorial Association began to raise funds for a Confederate monument. In May 1871 they laid the cornerstone at the intersection of College Avenue and Washington Street. Dedication ceremonies were held the following June. The monument was moved twice: first to a spot in front of City Hall (above) and then to its present location on Broad Street across from North Campus.

the idea) declared himself willing to raise a regiment of black troops. But the war ended before black Confederate soldiers were ready for the field.

When Federal troops under General Palmer occupied Athens in May 1865 at war's end, freedmen from Clarke and surrounding counties flocked to Athens to join local blacks in celebrating emancipation. Soon many returned to their masters or built shanty towns on the edge of the city. The urban experience for many had been an all but autonomous existence, and, despite considerable physical hardship and legal restraint, they had learned to survive.

4

Toward a New South: The Aftermath of War

Clarke County had escaped the extensive, physical devastation suffered throughout much of the rest of Georgia during the Civil War. In many ways the county's postwar experiences, including the process of Reconstruction, were far less traumatic than those in most other areas of the South.

Nonetheless, the towns and county to which ragged veterans returned in 1865 bore the marks of wartime deprivation and neglect. Eroded streets and washed-out bridges made travel difficult. Fences awaited mending; houses needed painting and repair; store shelves offered scant merchandise; and factory machinery needed replacing. Crowding the town were refugee aristocrats, wounded veterans, children and widowed women, Union troops, transient soldiers (an estimated five hundred ex-Confederates encamped in and around Athens), and free and often idle former slaves.

Clarke County had lost more than 300 men and boys (out of a total white population of 2,660). One hundred University of Georgia students and alumni had died in battle, and the economy of the South lay in ruins. Slaves had gained emancipation but had before them the difficult task of survival as freedmen in a new order.

Federal occupation of Athens continued until early 1866 and was, all things considered, rather benign. Authority rested with the military provost marshal, whose duties included preserving order, protecting private property, paroling Confederate soldiers, administering the oath of allegiance to the United States, and assisting municipal government. Local ladies might and did cross muddy streets to avoid speaking to Yankees. But the newly reinstated town council credited the Thirteenth Connecticut Volunteers with saving the Town Hall from destruction by fire on November 18, 1865, and

offered each of the Connecticut Yankees a cash award in gratitude for their efforts on behalf of the town. And when the federal garrison moved off campus (to Rock College) to accommodate Chancellor Lipscomb's efforts to prepare the university to reopen in January 1866, tensions eased considerably.

Restrictions, however, continued to rankle local citizens. In order to mail or receive letters or parcels, local citizens, including merchants dependent upon shipments for their livelihood, had to sign an oath of allegiance to the United States. A number of wealthy and prominent citizens received presidential pardon in lieu of that requirement. Among these were Albin P. Dearing, Joseph Henry Lumpkin, John T. Grant, John W. Nicholson, and Ferdinand Phinizy.

This is the way Athens looked in 1866, just after the Civil War. No battles occurred within the town's boundaries, and only minor skirmishes took place in the surrounding countryside. At the left are the Methodist and Presbyterian churches, with the town hall, built in 1845, directly in front. This public building, with a market on the ground floor and large hall above, was the center of town life.

CHANGING FORTUNES

Ferdinand Phinizy had built a fortune on land, cotton, and slaves. At the outbreak of the Civil War he was forty-one. Phinizy became a broker for the Confederate government, accumulating cotton and running it through the Federal blockade, and floating large amounts of Confederate bonds. With his fortune depleted by war's end, he moved to Athens from Augusta and began to build yet another fortune based on banking, insurance, and railroads. Not only did he offer an example of adaptability to the new order in the New South, but he also contributed to the prosperity of the community in which he lived. Jack Spalding, editor of the *Atlanta Constitution,* would write of his great-grandfather as "a modest man of simple tastes . . . something of a patriarch" who "kept open house for his friends and family in his home in the Cobbham section of Athens."

Phinizy owned an extension of Cobbham which developed as Lynwood Park and maintained a country home and large farm beyond his town properties. A large Colonial Revival home called Wahroonga (aboriginal for "our home") stands today on the site of Phinizy's barn. Just beyond the house surrounded by a handsome wrought-iron fence is an aged vertical tombstone that reads:

Erected
In Memory Of
Fed Yarborough
aged about 80 years
a former slave of
McKeans, Hays, Bowdre
and Ferdinand Phinizy
Honest and Faithful

When Ferdinand Phinizy died in Athens at the age of seventy, he was buried in Oconee Hill Cemetery next to his first wife, Harriet Hays Bowdre. The editorial page of the *Atlanta Constitution* noted that Phinizy was "probably the wealthiest man in Georgia."

With an infusion of locally available capital—for not all Athenians had lost their fortunes during the war—banking and insurance recovered with remarkable ease. A successor to the recently deceased Bank of Athens opened in March 1866 as the National

The Whites were one of the families whose fortunes rose during the Civil War. John Richards White, son of John White, became one of the most influential men in Athens during the last quarter of the nineteenth century. He served as director of numerous companies, including the Whitehall Manufacturing Company, the Athens Foundry and Machine Works, and the National Bank of Athens.

Bank of Athens, financed largely by the sixty-five-year-old Irishman and Georgia Cotton Factory president John White of Whitehall. At the outbreak of war White had transferred his considerable personal fortune to an Irish bank. At war's end he financed the new Athens bank by putting up forty thousand dollars. Led by Young L. G. Harris, half a dozen other Athens businessmen invested capital in the new venture, and by October the value of the bank stock had doubled.

Young Harris, a wealthy former representative from Clarke County to the state legislature, was prominent in the development of the Southern Mutual Insurance Company and instrumental in moving the company headquarters to Athens from Griffin in 1848. One of the first firms to write insurance in Georgia, Southern Mutual began boldly by issuing many different kinds of policies including life, fire, and marine insurance as well as insurance on the lives and health of slaves. Some early Southern Mutual policies covered cotton in transit via steamboats, slaves (at an agreed-upon value) purchased and en route to the owner's plantation, and cotton and lumber stacked along riverbanks awaiting shipment to market. Despite the loss of half its assets invested in Confederate bonds, Southern Mutual was able to declare a 40 percent dividend in June 1866. This highly successful company, led by some of Athens's most prominent citizens, continued to figure prominently in the prosperity of the town and county.

One boost to the economy was the stockpile of cotton that had accumulated behind Federal lines and which now brought the princely sum of forty-three cents per pound. Augustus Longstreet Hull called the cotton "a mine of gold for the owners and an alluring temptation to the speculators. . . . Fortunately it brought ready money enough into the community to set the wheels of trade and manufacture in motion again." The town of Athens issued five thousand dollars in promissory notes to meet its own expenses, and, after some initial stagnation caused in part by two years of drought and poor cotton crops, industry hummed once more.

A prime example of postwar success was Athens's oldest business, the Athens Manufacturing Company, which had earned wartime profits through the production of Confederate uniforms. According

John R. White built White Hall, as his family's residence in 1891. This imposing mansion remains one of the outstanding examples of Victorian Romanesque architecture in Georgia. White located this home near his manufacturing plant and the company village that served his many employees. In 1936 the Board of Regents of the University System acquired White Hall and its adjacent forests. In 1978 the School of Forest Resources completed restoration of the house, now listed on the National Register of Historic Places.

to a 1951 booklet produced by the Athens mayor and council, "When it looked like the Confederates would lose, . . . the company's money was exchanged for gold and given to the British consulate for safe keeping." By 1867 the mill had purchased Cook and Brother Armory (closed after the war) and had greatly expanded its textile production.

Yankee ingenuity helped Asaph King Childs (a native of Springfield, Massachusetts, who was a prominent local banker and a Confederate veteran) and another New Englander, Reuben Nickerson, proprietor of the Athens Foundry, form a new partnership in Athens Hardware. Two music shops and a photography studio, groceries and clothiers, and numerous other new ventures began. By the fall of 1866 Athens had twice as many businesses as before the war.

Many citizens, however, faced financial hardship. In January 1865 the Inferior Court of Clarke County had appropriated twelve thousand dollars in bonds to ward off starvation among destitute families of Confederate veterans, and doubtless their deprivations

The Southern Mutual Insurance Company is the oldest business still in operation in Athens. Stockholders moved the home office from Griffin to Athens in 1848, a year after the company's incorporation. This handsome building on Clayton Street and College Avenue housed the company headquarters from 1876 to 1906. When company directors decided to construct a new "skyscraper" on this site, the older building was moved brick by brick two blocks away to Hancock Street, where it housed the Athens Railway and Electric Company.

After the Civil War spokesmen for the New South cried out for more local industries like the Athens Manufacturing Company to revive the southern economy. In this textile plant on the Oconee River, 375 operators worked to produce cotton yarns, ginghams, and jeans. This Sanborn Fire Insurance Map of 1893 diagrams the plant's sixty-nine thousand square feet, almost equally divided between spinning and weaving operations.

endured well beyond the war years. Fannie Atkinson, a struggling young teacher out of work in the fall of 1866, wrote to a friend, "Blessed is he who is a cotton holder or a factory stockholder. Want does not seem to tarry at their thresholds."

Outward appearances, at least, had improved by September 1867, when the naturalist John Muir, on his famous one-thousand-mile walk from Kentucky to Florida, passed through Athens. His diary entry records: "Reached Athens in the afternoon, a remarkably beautiful and aristocratic town, containing many classic and magnificent mansions. . . . Unmistakable marks of culture and refinement, as well as wealth were everywhere apparent. This is the most beautiful town I have seen on the journey so far, and the only one in the South that I would like to revisit."

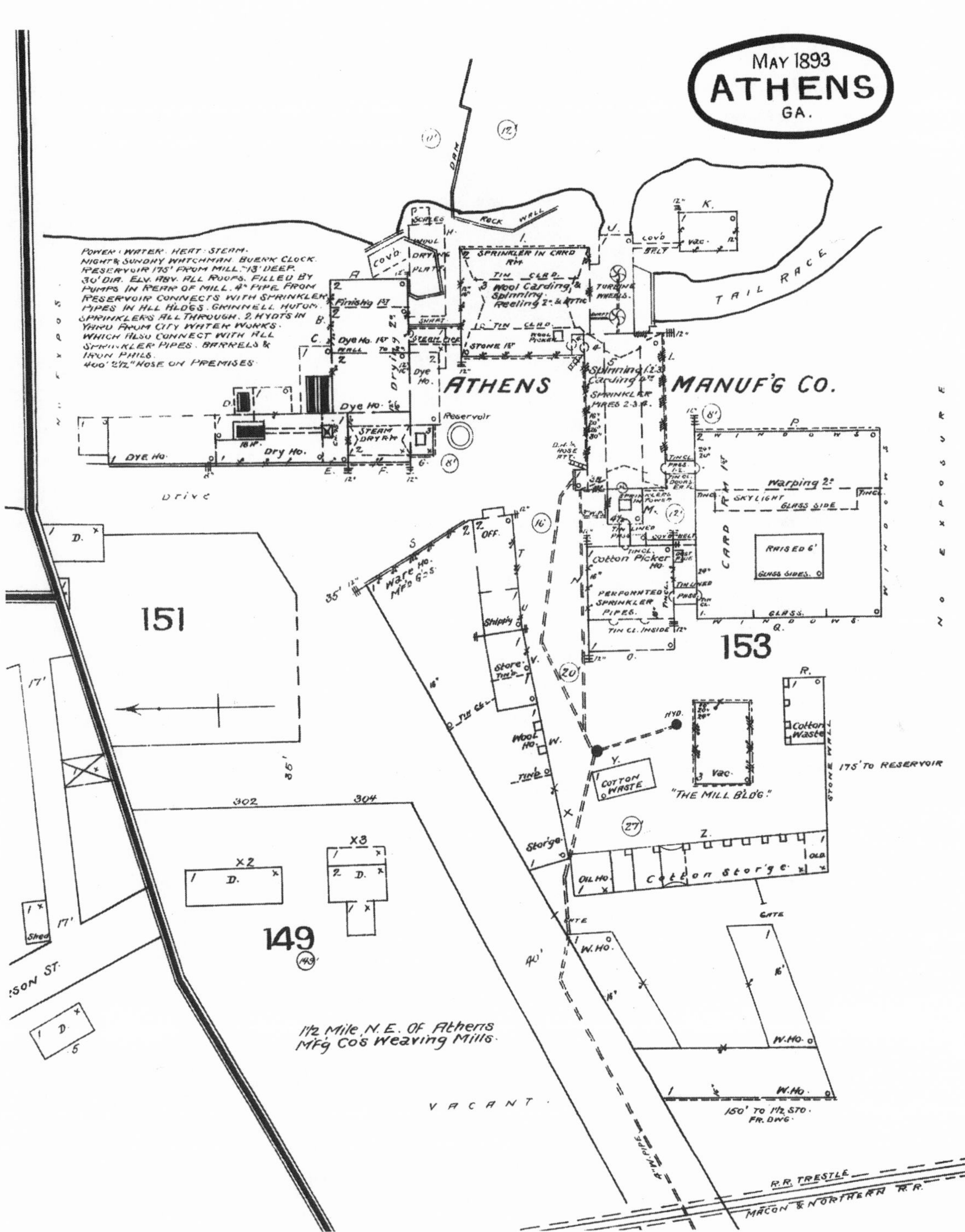
MAY 1893
ATHENS
GA.
ATHENS MANUF'G CO.
POWER: WATER. HEAT: STEAM.
NIGHT & SUNDAY WATCHMAN. BUERK CLOCK.
RESERVOIR 175' FROM MILL. 13' DEEP.
30' DIA. ELV. ABV. ALL ROOFS. FILLED BY
PUMPS IN REAR OF MILL. 4" PIPE FROM
RESERVOIR CONNECTS WITH SPRINKLER
PIPES IN ALL BLDGS. GRINNELL AUTOM.
SPRINKLERS ALL THROUGH. 2 HYDTS IN
YARD FROM CITY WATER WORKS.
WHICH ALSO CONNECT WITH ALL
SPRINKLER PIPES. BARRELS &
IRON PAILS.
400' 2½" HOSE ON PREMISES
DAM
ROCK WALL
TAIL RACE
TURBINE WHEELS
Wool Carding, Spinning, Reeling
Finishing
Dye Ho.
Dry Ho.
STEAM DRY RM.
Reservoir
Spinning 1.2.3. Carding 2
SPRINKLER PIPES 2.3.4.
Warping 2
SKYLIGHT
GLASS SIDE
CARD RM
RAISED 6'
Cotton Picker Ho.
PERFORATED SPRINKLER PIPES.
Ware Ho.
Store
Wool Ho.
COTTON WASTE
"THE MILL BLD'G."
Cotton Waste
175' TO RESERVOIR
STONE WALL
Cotton Stor'ge
Oil Ho.
GATE
W. Ho.
150' TO 1½ STO. FR. DWG.
NO EXPOSURE
drive
VACANT
1½ Mile N. E. OF Athens Mfg Co's Weaving Mills
R.R. TRESTLE
MACON & NORTHERN R.R.
4" W. PIPE
151
153
149
302
304
SON ST.

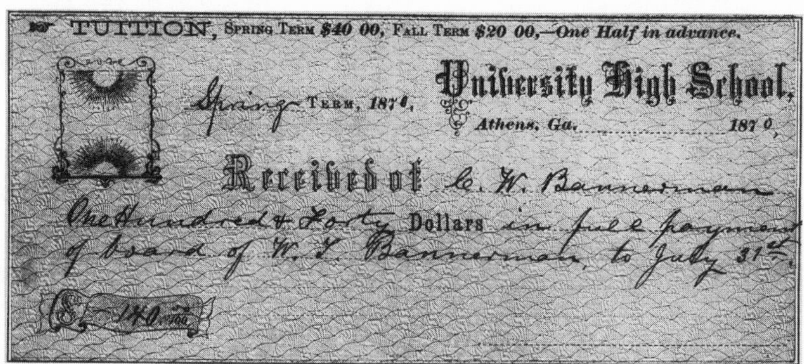

TUITION, Spring Term $40 00, Fall Term $20 00,—One Half in advance.

Spring Term, 1870, University High School,

Athens, Ga. 1870,

Received of C. W. Bannerman

One Hundred & Forty Dollars in full payment of board of W. T. Bannerman, to July 31st.

$ 140 00/100

University High School, sometimes called Rock College because the building was made of crushed rock and concrete, served as a school for Confederate veterans not yet prepared for college work. In 1870 $140 covered room and board for William T. Bannerman, class of 1873 at the University of Georgia.

The creation of the Beta Chapter of Sigma Alpha Epsilon in 1866 inaugurated the era of Greek fraternities at the University of Georgia. The addition of seven more fraternities by the 1880s spelled the decline of the Demosthenian and Phi Kappa literary societies, which had doubled as social and debating clubs before the Civil War. Pictured here are the brothers of SAE in 1883. Seated at the center is Chancellor Andrew Lipscomb, and among those standing are Patrick Hues Mell and Leon Henri Charbonnier, honorary members.

By the time of Muir's visit, the university was back in session, having reopened January 3, 1866, with seventy-eight students. Soon many veterans returned to school, recipients of legislative largess by which the state offered them tuition and other expenses. Most soldier students were ill prepared for college work and therefore attended "Rock College," the University High School, to prepare for college. In January 1867 thirty maimed Confederate veterans enrolled in the high school and received special attention from fellow students and townspeople as well. Clara Barrow wrote, "It is really touching to see them, sometimes as many as half a dozen together with only one arm." John Christy wrote in the *Watchman* that the sight of them occasioned "sad and bitter memories" but "proud remembrance of the Lost, but not Dishonored cause." By 1868 university enrollment had swelled to three hundred, the largest in the school's history. Not surprisingly, Chancellor Lipscomb found these students "much more manly . . . more obedient . . . more thoughtful and prudent" than students of old. Upon their graduation, enrollment dropped significantly. Not until the end of the century did the number of students reach three hundred again.

THE FREEDMAN'S BUREAU

The federal government in March 1865 created the Freedman's Bureau as a relief organization to lessen suffering and to get people back to work. The task ahead for black and white was to build a free-labor society through schools, churches, jobs, and reunited families.

U.S. Brigadier General Davis Tillson administered the Freedman's Bureau for the state of Georgia from September 1865 to January 1867. At the request of a committee of concerned white citizens, he traveled to Athens from Augusta in late autumn 1865 to address a large gathering of former slaves assembled in the Chapel on the university campus. Athens was overflowing with freedmen from Clarke and surrounding counties. Many were near starvation, and stealing had reached epic proportions when General Tillson arrived. In his address he advised the freedmen that there would be no land distribution—no "forty acres and a mule"—by Christmas as they had hoped, and warned them either to return to work (in most cases for former slaveholders) in order to make a living or face punishment for vagrancy and stealing.

The bureau acted as an employment agency, establishing minimum wages and supervising the drawing and signing of contracts. Those who returned to the farm had little trouble finding work, but those who remained in Athens had far more difficulty. Immediately after the war, there were few new jobs for urban blacks or whites, and returning veterans garnered many of the more desirable jobs formerly held by slaves. Impoverished families could ill afford to hire the number of servants they had owned before the war, so domestic jobs were at a premium as well.

Many blacks in Athens congregated in hastily built shanty settlements along the river bottomlands or on the outskirts of town. Whites dubbed the largest settlement on the Oconee's east bank "Blackfriars." When a smallpox epidemic broke out in the summer of 1865, the crowded black communities were hardest hit.

A former slave named Ike Derricotte related, "Them Yankees brought the smallpox here with them and give it to all the Athens folks, and that was something awful. Folks just died out with it so bad." In November 1865 the town council erected a makeshift hospital on the fairgrounds on the Watkinsville Road. One of Athens's leading citizens, Richard D. Moore, took charge. Dr. Moore, whom Sylvanus Morris called "the prince of doctors," had treated families of soldiers free of charge during the war, and now he did all he could to stamp out the epidemic, which peaked in December, claiming ten lives. During the first six weeks the hospital admitted

Prompted by Richard Moore, a local physician and university trustee, the citizens of Athens provided twenty-five thousand dollars to construct a new classroom building in 1874. Leon Henri Charbonnier, a Frenchman and a professor of science and engineering, designed Moore College, a Second Empire Revival building which is the only structure on campus to reflect French architecture. The large grassy area (center) served as drill grounds and athletic fields for the increasingly popular sports of baseball and football.

154 patients; but by mid-February the worst was over, and the hospital closed.

Freedman's Bureau funds built the Knox School in 1867, and two hundred former slaves enrolled. This first school ever open to blacks in Clarke County cost local citizens nothing to operate. The American Missionary Association (AMA) sponsored the teachers—northern whites, mostly women (initially two)—whom the hostile local press dubbed "pious young females, of the Puritan persuasion." AMA-sponsored black teachers, born and educated in the North, eventually replaced the white teachers, a situation local whites found more palatable. Named for Major John J. Knox, administrator of the Freedman's Bureau in Athens, the school was college preparatory but offered normal, grammar, primary, industrial, and music education as well. Tuition ranged from $.50 to $1.25 per month, and for $5.00 to $8.00 per month students could board in local homes.

There were no free black or white schools in the county until 1872, and none in the city until 1888. But schools to educate the freed slaves—the Knox Institute, the Methodist School (established 1876), and Jeruel Academy (later Union Baptist Institute), which opened in 1881 offering primary, intermediate, industrial, and nurses' training—established Athens as a center for black under-

The Knox School, located at the corner of Pope and Reese streets, was one of four private educational institutions for black students in Athens at the end of the nineteenth century. Renamed Knox Institute in the 1880s, it offered academic and industrial courses.

graduate education in Georgia for over fifty years after the Civil War.

Within a relatively short period, the Knox Institute encouraged remarkable progress among the emerging black community of educated free men and women. Blacks withdrew from white church affiliation and formed their own congregations. By March 1867 the new African Methodist Episcopal (AME) Church in Athens had 254 members, for example. Hill First Baptist Church organized in 1867 as well. In rural Clarke County there were many black churches that predated the war. Among these were Shady Grove, Chestnut Grove, and Billups Grove churches, built among trees to shade social and religious gatherings. Athens blacks formed social

Schools built for black children during the late nineteenth and early twentieth centuries were mostly modest facilities. Chestnut Grove School on Epps Bridge Road, built in 1896, is a rare surviving example of a typical one-room schoolhouse where one teacher instructed black pupils of all ages. It is listed on the National Register of Historic Places.

The construction of independent churches for black people increased throughout the southern states after the Civil War. The African Methodist Episcopal (AME) Church of Athens was organized in 1866 in a blacksmith shop on Foundry Street. Services were held in Union Hall until the completion of the church on north Hull Street in 1916. The handsome stained-glass windows and decorative beams showcased the emerging wealth of the black community in Athens.

Henry Woodfin Grady, chief spokesman for New South politics, was born in Athens in 1850. From 1879 to 1889, as editor of the Atlanta Constitution, *he regularly expressed his view that the South should develop its own industrial and commercial base. In editorials and speeches Grady pressed for harmony between the northern and southern states.*

and fraternal orders that became very important in establishing a sense of community and personal identity. In time black Athenians had their own press as well. But even as segregated society began, tension between the races flared when Reconstruction reached the local level.

THE POLITICS OF RECONSTRUCTION

During Reconstruction a strong Republican party developed in Clarke County. After rejecting President Andrew Johnson's reunification of the South and passing the Reconstruction Acts in March 1867, the Congress divided the southern states into military districts. Athens became headquarters for Georgia Military District 3 under the command of U.S. General John Pope, whose duty was to oversee the registration of those now eligible to vote for delegates to the new state constitutional convention—all of the freedmen and only certain classes of loyal white men. The dramatic and flamboyant Union League arrived in Athens in 1867 to consolidate black resolve. With "all the impressiveness of surrounding coffins, sculls and crossbones," wrote Augustus Longstreet Hull, "burnishing swords and pistols, the negroe was sworn to vote the ticket."

During the election for state and national offices, occupation troops kept watch as long lines of voters formed at Town Hall during four days of balloting (April 24–28, 1868). When the polls closed at 6 P.M., the Republicans had elected two former slaves, Alfred Richardson and Madison Davis, as the first two black men ever to represent Clarke County in the state legislature. Richardson was a carpenter and a tavern owner. Davis, a mulatto wheelwright, had been the slave of the Athens carriage maker Edward R. Hodgson. The two were expelled in a called session of the legislature July 4, 1868, but reinstated—one and a half years later—by congressional mandate. They won second terms in elections eleven months later.

According to Hull, white neighbors warned Richardson to prepare for twenty-five night riders, members of the Ku Klux Klan, "who raided his Watkinsville home for the second time in a month after his re-election." In the ensuing gunfire Richardson was shot in

A prewar graduate of the University of Georgia, Benjamin H. Hill returned to Athens from LaGrange in 1867, moving into what later became the President's House. After leaving for Atlanta in 1872, Hill became a major force in Reconstruction politics as United States congressman and senator. Like Henry Grady, Hill was a spokesman for the New South, arguing for better utilization of local resources and promoting education at all levels.

the side and arm; he fired back, fatally wounding a young Klansman. Richardson fled to Athens, where he found sympathy among both black and some white citizens. Later he and John Christy gave conflicting testimony before a congressional committee investigating Klan activities in Georgia. Meanwhile, in Watkinsville Richardson's home was burned to the ground. Governor Rufus B. Bullock offered a reward of five thousand dollars for the arrest and conviction of anyone connected to the attempt on Richardson's life. Richardson died of pneumonia in Athens on January 9, 1872.

If Hull found Richardson incendiary, "turbulent and dangerous," he deemed Davis a "leader of his race . . . always on the side of law and order." Davis withdrew in the race for a third term in the legislature. He served a stint as U.S. surveyor in Atlanta and then, at age thirty-three, returned to Athens as captain of Relief No. 2, Athens's first black volunteer fire company. In 1882 Davis became postmaster of Athens, an appointment that made him one of very few black postmasters in the state. His nomination was backed by Emory Speer, a local attorney elected on the Independent ticket as Clarke County's representative in the state legislature, but this support cost Speer his political career. Davis, termed "intelligencer and real estate agent" at the time of his appointment, served two terms as postmaster (1882–86 and 1890–93). Monroe B. "Pink" Morton, a local black real estate agent and politician, held the post from 1897 to 1902.

After 1872 blacks won no Clarke County representation, for Reconstruction was at an end. The freedmen never held local elected offices. The Democrats again emerged victorious in county elections; with Federal troops twice removed, it became obvious that there would be no real attempt to enforce the Civil Rights Act of 1875. Clarke County blacks, however, remained active in the Republican party, and several served as delegates to state and national conventions.

Black Athenians also developed a strong voice through the press. Few towns in Georgia had black newspapers in the late nineteenth century; Athens had three. Two nationally known black politicians, W. H. Heard (a preacher) and W. A. Pledger (a lawyer), edited and published the *Athens Blade* from 1879 to 1889. Under the motto

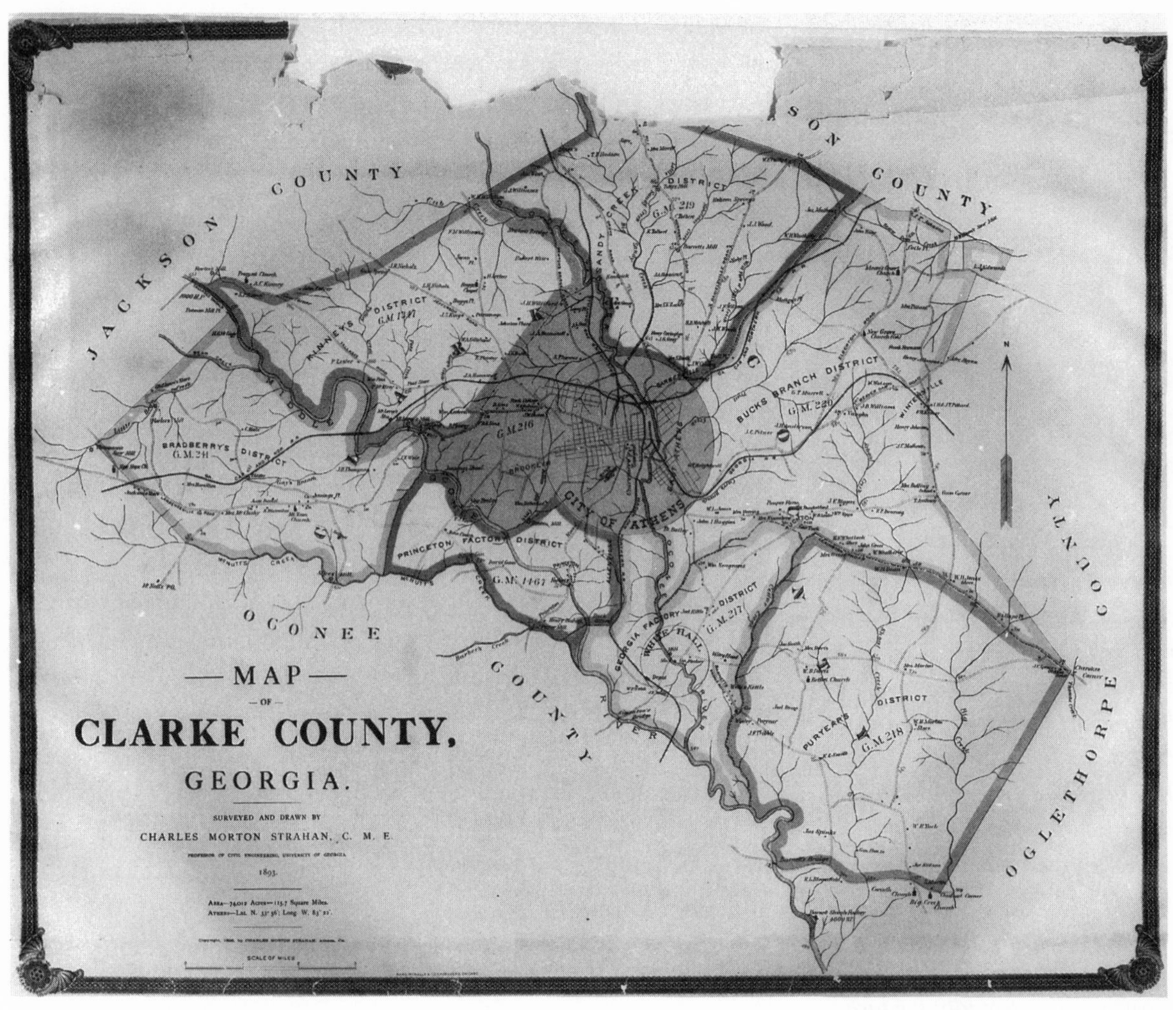

This map by Charles M. Strahan shows Clarke County in 1893, eighteen years after Oconee County was carved out of the southwest corner. Because of its size and central location, the city of Athens was by then the seat of government. Strahan, a professor of civil engineering, carefully mapped out churches, railroads, factory sites, and large parcels of privately held land.

"The Arm of Justice Cannot—Will Not Sleep," the *Blade* called for fair treatment for blacks. The *Athens Clipper* (1887–94) and the *Progressive Era* (begun in 1899) emphasized education.

After 1870 business and industry attracted new citizens, both black and white, to Athens. The population began to increase at about the same rate as in the antebellum decades. The population of Clarke County was 12,941 in 1870; 4,251 lived in Athens, and 8,690 lived in rural areas, with whites more numerous than blacks in Athens and blacks predominating in the county.

The growth of Athens toward the turn of the century continued at a steady pace without great boom or major recession. The Athens population in 1880 was 6,099; by 1890 it had reached 8,639. Skilled and unskilled jobs increased in number for both black and white workers.

THE FORMATION OF OCONEE COUNTY FROM CLARKE: WATKINSVILLE, ATHENS, AND THE GREAT DIVIDE

At the time the boundaries that divided Oconee from Clarke were defined by transient objects like mills and bridges, but basically all the acreage south and west of the Oconee River now belonged to the new county that bore the river's name. Watkinsville, divested of its status as seat of Clarke County in 1871 when the courthouse and jail moved to Athens, now became the seat of Oconee County.

A logical question is why Watkinsville became the county seat in the first place, and why, despite its "village" status, it remained Clarke's courthouse town for almost three quarters of a century. Initially, Watkinsville was selected because it was near the center of the county and therefore equally accessible (or inaccessible) to all other parts of the county. From the outset, politically influential professional men and wealthy landowners and cotton planters who held property south of the Oconee lobbied to make and keep Watkinsville the seat of Clarke County.

But while Athens and the region surrounding town and gown blossomed with a clever combination of industry and culture, Watkinsville, according to E. Merton Coulter, "remained a sleepy, country village without a railroad, known only as the county seat of

Clarke." While Athens experienced steady growth in population, Watkinsville seemed frozen in time. In 1841, when Athens became the terminus for the only railroad extending into northeast Georgia, the college town clearly became the center for commerce and trade, as well as the leader in manufacturing and education for all of Clarke and the surrounding counties.

Not only were the county's only two incorporated towns divergent, but there were vast distinctions in the rural landscapes surrounding each town as well. As an interface between mountains and the Piedmont plain, the county to the north and west featured small hill farms with a variety of crops and few slaves, while cotton plantations employing a large number of slaves dominated the south and east.

Despite these disparities, Watkinsville held tenaciously to her position as courthouse town, aided by a handful of politically powerful citizens from south of the river. Doubtless only the coming of war and the trauma of its aftermath postponed the inevitable. In February 1871 the county grand jury (with a majority of its members perforce from Athens and her environs) formally requested the state legislature to organize a new county with Athens as its seat, "for the reason that a large proportion of the litigation of our Courts, both civil and criminal, originates in and immediately around Athens, and a large majority of both parties and witnesses have no means of conveyances to and from the courts of Watkinsville, and for the additional reason that there is no accommodations [*sic*], whatever in Watkinsville for the colored people, who are required to attend court."

At the time, according to Coulter, four-fifths of the taxable property of the county lay in Athens and vicinity, with "a like percentage of the population," and Athens was the site of eleven-twelfths of the county's trade. Watkinsville leaders threatened reprisals—an embargo against trading with Athens and removal of their support for any Athenian candidate for county office—but in November undaunted Athenians signed a petition to move the courthouse and jail to the town hall. Athenians agreed to work for the passage of a bill to create a new county with Watkinsville as its seat, in exchange for support from Watkinsville of a change in the seat of Clarke County.

When the offices of the Clarke County government moved from Watkinsville to Athens, the town hall served as courthouse and jail. But in 1876 a splendid new structure opened off Prince Avenue in Cobbham. Designed by Leon Henri Charbonnier, the two-story courthouse served the county until 1913. Athens High School moved from Childs Street to the renovated courthouse building in 1914.

On November 24, 1871, the transfer became law. All county offices and all county business—the county courts and jail—moved to Athens.

More than three years passed before the state legislature created Oconee County and named Watkinsville its seat on February 12, 1875. The creation bill made its way through a labyrinth of Reconstruction and post-Reconstruction politics to give Oconee County one-third of Clarke's population and one-half of Clarke's land.

AGRICULTURE AND THE AGRARIAN WAY OF LIFE

The emancipation of the slaves in an area rooted in the plantation agrarian way of life coupled with the problem of depleted soil occasioned perhaps the greatest need for postwar economic adjustment. On the small farms and plantations slaves had worked side by side with their masters, developing a variety of skills. On the larger plantations they had worked at specific jobs supervised by an overseer; some seldom saw their masters. Therefore freedmen in search of work had varying degrees of skills or lack thereof.

Even while the local press urged agricultural diversification, cotton continued to cast its "strange spell." Clarke County farmers applied guano and phosphate manures in hopes of restoring the soil and increasing productivity. At the railroad depot village of Maxeys, David Crenshaw Barrow manufactured superphosphate for the merchant planters of Athens. New farm implements like John H. Newton's patented reaping machine to harvest wheat and Colonel M. C. Fulton's portable thresher aided production of diversified crops for market, and the Athens Wheat Club awarded prizes for the best crop.

According to Robert S. Gamble in his thesis "Athens: The Study of a Georgia Town During Reconstruction," cotton continued to be the cash crop. "Cotton bales barricaded both sides of Clayton and Broad Streets a week before Christmas (1869) and planters demanded not greenbacks but gold from cotton factors in Athens. . . . the effect on Athens trade was electric . . . cotton was the final arbiter of prosperity." With a ready supply of cotton, textile factories and related industries expanded rapidly after 1868, as new cotton warehouses emerged adjacent to town.

But cotton did not completely dominate the county, especially

During the late nineteenth century one of the largest farms in southeastern Clarke County belonged to the William W. Puryear family. This photograph, taken around 1915, shows Puryear's mill building and water wheel, cast in 1905 at the Athens Foundry to replace a smaller wooden one. Puryear milled corn in the fall and ginned cotton in the winter. When necessary he spent cold nights inside the small heated shed (right). Cut down in size, the water wheel became an attraction at Charlie Williams's Pinecrest Lodge.

after Oconee County split from Clarke. By 1880 only 8,202 of Clarke's 23,337 tilled acres produced cotton. According to the 1884 census, 7,393 acres were in corn; 3,178 in wheat, oats, and rye; and another 4,745 in miscellaneous truck crops. Gamble concludes, "In the 1890s national farm conditions were bad, but Clarke County's diversity plus a major market for almost all their products, including cotton, helped farmers."

Some county blacks managed to buy and keep land, but the vast majority of rural blacks, Peter Schinkel concludes in his thesis "The Negro in Athens and Clarke County, 1872–1900," "found their place as wage hands, croppers, or renters, and were unable to rise above it." Almost all freedmen outside of Athens were engaged in some sort of farm work. Very few found work in textile, paper, and fertilizer factories in the little settlements of mill villages that dotted the banks of the Oconee. These remained traditionally white. More blacks were attracted to Clarke by agricultural than urban opportunities, while the reverse was true for whites, who were attracted to Athens by a diversity of occupations.

The advent of sharecropping, with the landowner providing equipment, land, house, and food while the sharecropper received part of the crop at harvest in exchange for labor, changed settlement patterns in the county as well as the size and configuration of the farms. Sharecropping at least offered the former slave a fair amount of autonomy, although, according to Schinkel, "often the employee was caught in a credit bind that bound him again, even as a freedman." Interest rates for feed, seed, and fertilizer advanced to the "cropper" were 10 percent or higher, and the cost of a mule could be as high as two hundred dollars on a "time price"—an amount far in excess of the cash value.

The most progressive farmer in Athens was John Armstrong Meeker, a transplanted Yankee (a native of Newark, New Jersey) who lived with his widowed mother on Dearing Street in a house built by his wealthy father, Christopher Meeker, in 1859. After his father's death, John Meeker spent his considerable inheritance on adapting northern agricultural technology and machinery to southern soil. He bought two hundred acres of eroded land on both sides of the south end of Milledge Avenue and embarked upon an experiment, pioneering in Athens the use of clover to improve the land. He named his farm Cloverhurst and began to build haymows and barns and to raise oats and pigs and graze Jersey cows. According to Augustus Longstreet Hull, "hardly a day passed but some old ante-bellum Hayseed visited Meeker's farm to admire the progressive young farmer."

But few Clarke County farmers were progressive. Gamble concludes that the axiom "those who live close to the soil are painfully slow to change" held true, and "most Clarke County farmers clung to the artificial remedy of fertilizer."

NEW ENTERPRISES

Robert L. Bloomfield was a major contributor to the new spirit of enterprise that characterized postwar Athens. Bloomfield was one of many transplanted Yankees who prospered in Athens. He sent a son to fight for the Confederacy, and during the war took over the presidency of the Athens Factory. When fire destroyed a downtown block in 1867, the forty-four-year-old Bloomfield rebuilt the charred structures with his own money. In 1868 his cotton and woolen factory boasted 75 looms, 3,000 spindles, and 175 operators who produced 10,000 yards of cotton cloth and 7,500 pounds of cotton yarn. He transferred weaving operations to the newly purchased Cook and Brother Armory buildings and oversaw the production of the famous "daisy checks" gingham which won the gold medal at the New Orleans Exposition of 1876. Bloomfield also expanded the Athens Flour Mill.

The press hailed Bloomfield as the "spiritual as well as physical mentor of the Athens proletariat." He adopted a paternalistic attitude toward his mill hands, for whom he held family picnics on the sweeping lawn of his home. He plowed their gardens at his own expense, built their homes, and constructed for his workers a lovely little Neo-Gothic Episcopal chapel on Oconee Street (consecrated as Saint Mary's Chapel on Easter Day 1871) adjacent to the mill village. Years later (Bloomfield lived over fourscore years) oxen belonging to Bloomfield, a vestryman, hauled stone for the new Emmanuel Church when the parish moved from downtown to

Robert L. Bloomfield was one of Athens's most prominent citizens for more than forty years. Before the Civil War he helped organize the city's first fire department and the Athens Insurance Company. After the war, as president of the Athens Factory, Bloomfield greatly expanded the plant's operations. He was also a real estate developer, laying out the neighborhood that is now the Bloomfield Historic District near Milledge Avenue.

Prince Avenue in the 1890s. Parishoners dedicated their new bell tower to the Bloomfields, "since to him," according to the Reverend Troy Beatty, "is due very largely the fact that we have this beautiful and substantial church, built of granite, rather than of frame or brick as we first contemplated."

When a small group of Jewish people assembled in Athens after the war, it was Bloomfield who offered the first meeting place for the future founders of the Congregation Children of Israel in Athens. In summer 1872 Bloomfield, enthusiastic about the university's new College of Agriculture and School of Engineering, financed the refencing of the entire college campus.

Around 1867, J. J. Nevitt drew this picture of Dr. Matthew H. Henderson reading the service of morning prayer in the original Emmanuel Church at the corner of Clayton and Lumpkin streets. Nevitt, an architect from Savannah, designed the highly decorative stained-glass window at the east end as well as the altar rail for the present-day Emmanuel Church, which was completed in 1899.

The tireless Bloomfield also served as the prime promoter and first board president of the Northeastern Railroad. Groundbreaking ceremonies for the line from Athens to Clayton took place September 8, 1872, in the woodlands behind the Prince Avenue home of Marion Cobb under banners proclaiming, "The shrill note of the steam engine is but the strong voice of advancing civilization." Newly incorporated as a city on August 24, 1872, Athens issued stock in the Northeastern Railroad. Both black and white citizens were eager to buy shares in a frenzy of "railroad fever."

With the split of Oconee County from Clarke in 1875, Athens, now the seat of Clarke County, got a new charter and new source of income from city taxes. Now that Athens was firmly fixed as the seat of the restructured Clarke County, Mayor Henry Beusse (first to hold that title) and the city council (now composed of two councilmen from each of four wards) looked to the future with optimism. The face of Athens was changing, and builders enjoyed a heyday. The prestigious agricultural publication *Southern Cultivator* moved to spacious offices in a handsome new building at the corner of Lumpkin and Broad; Ferdinand Phinizy's commercial row of four stores wore fashionable new Victorian façades; and Dr. J. A. Hunnicutt built a new brick block in the business district on Thomas Street, demolishing the old Mitchell Hotel, once the site of a fête for President James Monroe.

Colonel Lewis J. Deupree, a wealthy citizen of Lexington, began construction of the most ambitious postwar structure to date, Deupree Hall, at the corner of Broad and Thomas streets. Here traveling shows and local productions took place until the construction of the New Athens Opera House in 1888.

A Confederate monument, the product of a three-year fundraising effort by the Ladies Memorial Association, was, in the words of the association president, Mildred Lewis Rutherford (an arch-

Ross Crane designed this early Italianate house for John Ferdinand Phinizy in 1857. Ownership changed hands several times before Dr. John Atkinson Hunnicutt and his wife, Mary Deupree Hunnicutt, purchased it in 1873. Hunnicutts lived here until 1967. Thereafter, fraternities, a private school, and various restaurants occupied the house until it was moved forward on its Milledge Avenue lot and eventually renovated for medical offices by 1990.

Broad Street in downtown Athens during the late 1880s was still an unpaved thoroughfare. This photograph shows Mr. Snodgrass's mule-drawn streetcar (center) and the cast-iron fence on the university campus (right).

Volunteer firemen posed for this picture on Broad Street just below Phi Kappa Hall on the university campus in the 1880s. The first volunteer force, Hope Fire Company, organized after fire destroyed the Athens Factory in 1849. A second company, Pioneer Hook and Ladder, formed soon thereafter. Although they received no compensation, the volunteer firemen earned great respect among citizens of the community.

Confederate who later became principal of the Lucy Cobb Institute), "reared on high" June 3, 1872, "so our children's children may from it learn how our own brave ones died."

In a preview of city-versus-county fiscal controversies to come, the Clarke County Grand Jury suggested in 1866 that the county and city buy the much-traveled lower toll bridge over the Oconee, then privately owned and poorly maintained. But three years passed before the city council voted to purchase and rebuild the bridge. With massive abutments shoring its sides, the bridge reopened in January 1870, just as Deupree Hall was completed.

Also in 1870 the Athens Street Railway Company, organized by William P. Dearing, surveyed a route between the city and the depot on Carr's Hill, and laid tracks across the new bridge to transport freight to town. Mules pulled heavy flatcars laden with shipments over the tracks, across the bridge, and to merchants' doors downtown. This venture was short lived, and not until the end of the century did the Georgia Railroad relocate its tracks and terminal from Carr's Hill to the Oconee's west side near Broad Street to extend the railway into the city.

City improvements came at a rapid rate. The Athens Board of Health was one of the earliest in the state. The city established a three-man police force in 1881. Bell Telephone installed lines for an initial thirty-five subscribers in 1882. In 1885 the city council au-

thorized the modest start of a street-paving program that would accelerate perforce toward the turn of the century. Replacing dirt streets and mudholes were streets of vitrified brick, granite blocks, and in some cases creosoted wood blocks.

But in the development of public schools Athens lagged behind other cities in the state. Even rural Clarke County offered a three-month school term paid for by the state for a dozen years before free education was available in Athens. Perhaps the plethora of private day schools—black and white—explains the fact that not until 1885 did Athens appoint a school board. The first regular sessions of Athens public schools began in the fall of 1886 with 1,085

In 1871 Athens replaced Watkinsville as the county seat. This 1893 Sanborn Fire Insurance Map of the downtown area lists the population as ten thousand. By this time the city had electric lights and streetcars, brick sidewalks, a paid fire department, and free postal delivery.

students, 20 teachers, and a budget of $10,146.13. Classes met in temporary quarters on Baxter, Foundry, Oconee, and Meigs streets. The Market Street School (later Washington Street School) for whites, located at the present site of the Georgian Hotel, and the Baxter Street School for blacks opened in 1887—two identical ten-room brick structures, the city's first public school buildings.

There were more than thirty private day schools of varying sizes in Athens by 1869. In 1862 the sophisticated Madame Sophie Sosnowski, daughter of the court physician to the grand duke of Baden and the widow of a Polish nobleman, arrived in Athens with her accomplished daughter, Caroline. They were refugees fleeing from the burning by Federal troops of Columbia, South Carolina, and the devastation of the girls' seminary where they had taught. For a time Madame Sosnowski held the position of principal of the Lucy Cobb Institute. Several years later she opened the Home School for young ladies, first in the Baxter house on Hill Street and then on Prince Avenue, in the former home of Joseph Henry Lumpkin, who had died in 1867. There boarding students (never more than twenty-five) lived with Madame Sosnowski and her daughters and granddaughters and studied with a moderate number of day students in the splendid parlors and on the broad piazzas of their Greek Revival "home" academy. Augustus Longstreet Hull praised Madame Sosnowski as "a princess in grace and courtesy of manner . . . highly educated, a brilliant musician and of very distinguished appearance. It was an education to a girl to be associated with Madame and Miss Callie." Until Madame Sosnowski's death in 1889, the Home School operated with great distinction, as did the Lucy Cobb Institute, led by the indomitable Mildred Rutherford. The Home School and Lucy Cobb Institute offered young ladies all the refinements of a proper Victorian curriculum.

"Miss Millie" Rutherford, according to the Athens historian James Reap, "was a strong believer in the Bible, the Lost Cause, and female virtue. She would not let the girls go out to the fence to talk with the boys. They were allowed only closely supervised visits in the parlors on the main floor and were forbidden to wave from the windows of their rooms on the second and third floor." But Miss Millie broadened their horizons as well. Each year Mildred Ruther-

Mildred Rutherford was teacher, principal, president, and director of Lucy Cobb Institute, serving the school for over forty years. Her tireless efforts in defense of the Confederate cause matched her devotion to education. She became historian general for the United Daughters of the Confederacy and president of the Confederate Southern Memorial Association. Her "Old South" lecture delivered in 1916 at a UDC convention was the first speech by a woman to be printed in the Congressional Record.

ford invited selected students to accompany her abroad, traveling via one of the great ocean liners. Wrote Bessie Mell Lane, "In all, 'Miss Millie' crossed the ocean eighteen times with small groups of students, teaching history, literature, and art as she went."

In order to fund a chapel for the institute, she encouraged her students to write to various philanthropists to solicit financing for construction. Young Nellie Stovall wrote to George I. Seney of New York, who agreed to underwrite a large portion of the cost. An Athenian, W. W. Thomas, designed the brick octagonal hall on the Milledge Avenue campus. Dedicated in 1885, Seney-Stovall Chapel was for many years the site of numerous concerts, performances, and ceremonies for the entire community.

Concerts and public exercises at the Lucy Cobb Institute were held in a bowling alley before George I. Seney agreed to provide ten thousand dollars for the construction of a chapel if the townspeople raised four thousand dollars.

Other private white city schools included the Grove School under the direction of Miss Mary Bacon and Miss Julia Moss; Athens Academy at Meigs and Harris Streets (later the public Meigs Street School); Mrs. E. A. Crawford's school; and schools headed by Mr. A. M. Scudder and Miss Emily Witherspoon.

Meanwhile, the University of Georgia in 1872 had become a land-grant school eligible for federal funds under the Morrill Act, passed by Congress during the war. The establishment of the State College of Agriculture and Mechanic Arts absorbed federal funds made available through that legislation and expanded the university's vision of service to the citizens of the state. Chancellor Andrew Adgate Lipscomb envisioned a university that would serve a broader spectrum of the needs of the state by offering courses in

This photograph, taken around 1892, shows a group of young girls on the front porch of the Lucy Cobb Institute. From its inception in 1859, the institute offered one of the finest liberal arts curriculums for young women in the southern states.

agricultural studies. At first there was some animosity between the agricultural students, who were offered free tuition and a three-year program, and students enrolled in the traditional liberal arts curriculum of Franklin College. But sons of poor farmers could now obtain a college education while gaining technical knowledge so necessary to the state's agricultural economy.

Some college students, however, were leaving their classes to join the volunteers when the United States declared war against Spain over Cuba, taking up the battle cry "Remember the Maine." Some of the Athens Guards drew assignment to the Second Regiment of the Georgia Volunteers. Among these were Captain J. H. Buesse, commander of the Guards; C. A. Vonderleith, first lieutenant; and Hershel Carithers, orderly sergeant. They trained in Tampa, but

In 1887 two permanent Athens public schools held their first regular session in four temporary locations. The following year two permanent buildings opened, one on Baxter Street, the other on Washington Street. This 1906 photograph captures the first tenth-grade class at Washington Street School.

Under the tutelage of Miss Julia P. Moss, students at the Grove School, in the side yard of the Moss house at the corner of Cobb and Franklin streets, recited before their families each spring. From this program it is evident that the school attracted youths from many of Athens's oldest families.

CLOSING EXERCISES

—OF THE—

BOYS AND GIRLS SCHOOL

TAUGHT BY

MISSES JULIA P. MOSS & SUSIE NEWTON.

Athens, Ga., June 17th, 1881.

Declamations and Recitations.

PROGRAMME.

James Barrow.......One of His Names.
Ernest Crimes.......The Little Soldier.
Wallace Mitchell.......Once More to be a School Boy.
Rutherford Lipscomb.......The Wish.
Munro Dearing.......Boys Versus Girls.
Pauline Harris.......Advice to Mama.
Willie Thomas.......The Wicked Nephew.
Frank Lipscomb.......The First Book.
Andrew Green.......The Miller of Dee.
Charlie Phinizy, (excused).......They Say.
Barrett Phinizy, (excused,).......Parting.
Lewis Russell.......The Twins.
Rosalie Wade.......A Dear Little Goose.
Albin Dearing.......Dollars and Dimes.
Tommie Gerdine.......The Kiss in School.
Edward Wade.......The Blue and the Gray.
Lamar Cobb, Jr.......Orator Puff.
Yancey Harris.......The Toast.
Sallie Hunter Moss.......Miss Annabelle McCarty.
Bolling Stovall.......(Excused.)
Hunter Golding.......Icarus.
Frank Thomas.......The Maniac.
Mid P. Barrow.......A. Fragment.
Guy Chandler.......Josh Billings on Gongs.
Eugene Wade.......Parhassius.
Edward Russell.......Horatius and the Bridge.
Gerald Green.......The Flying Machine.
Newton Lowrance.......Bernardo del Carpio.
John Moss.......Fitz James and Rhoderick Dhu.
Birdie Moss.......The Dove.
Sallie Harris.......Kentucky Belle.

ADDRESS BY

M. P. BARROW, ATHENS, GA.

During the Spanish-American War this training camp for volunteer soldiers was set up west of Athens. Officers' tents appear in the foreground. Log structures (privies and cookhouses) separate the officers from the enlisted men, whose tents stretch far into the distance toward the Athens skyline. This high ground (located near the present intersection of Broad and Hawthorne streets) came to be called Brooklyn, named after the soldiers from the New York borough who encamped here with the Fifth New York Regiment.

saw no active service. They were mustered out in February 1899.

While these Athenians were in Florida, the Yankees returned to Athens. Local boosters were successful in securing the location of a regimental camp near Athens, and an influx of northerners ensued. Three regiments—the Fifth New York, the Fifteenth Pennsylvania, and the Twelfth New Jersey—soon encamped on the high ground west of town beyond Phinizy's branch under the command of General W. C. Oates, a former Confederate who had lost an arm in battle at Missionary Ridge.

Augustus Longsteet Hull observed, "The soldiering was play. The young officers were hospitably entertained by the citizens and the young ladies showed none of that aversion to the Federal soldier which had led to the arrest of their mothers a third of a century before. Several of these ungrateful men came back afterwards and actually carried off some of our loveliest girls before the very eyes of their fathers; and some of the New Jersey soldiers came back and entered college to take a course in football."

Hull recalled various entertainments including a "free show," which he described as a "sham battle between the Jerseymen and the Quakers" in which "lots of Uncle Sam's powder was burned," much to the delight of the assembled crowd. But he pondered the various reactions of the locals to the presence of the federal soldiers in Athens. When the entire brigade marched down College Avenue in a public review, Hull stood near an old veteran who had lost an arm at Spottsylvania. When Hull asked him what he thought of the parading troops, the former Confederate replied, "I think if I had a gun I would like to shoot into them."

But the soldiers were notorious for spending all their pay as soon as they got it, and that made local merchants happy. When the Fifth New York was ordered to Cuba and the other two regiments were sent home in February 1899, the camp stood deserted. Nonetheless, reported Hull, "The retail merchant jingled the harvest in his pocket."

Despite the departure of the troops, local businesses encountered

Officers and a dog at an encampment of Spanish-American War volunteers just outside Athens in 1898.

Athens families entertained Spanish-American War trainees encamped in and around Athens. These Cobbham belles pose in a side yard at the corner of Hill and Franklin streets with souvenirs of war: a Company D tent and regimental caps and sword. Not all Athenians were as hospitable to the soldiers as these young ladies, for the volunteers were the first federal troops some of the older generation had encountered since the Civil War.

no dirth of other new customers. Indeed, by 1899 railroad facilities were bringing new citizens to Athens and Clarke County to spend their money and start new enterprises. Although the first automobile appeared on the streets of Athens that year, it was rail transportation that shaped the county with a proliferation of depot communities soon dotting the map. Meanwhile the invention of the streetcar and the advent of a street railway in Athens in 1888 opened the way for greater mobility and, subsequently, the possibility of new neighborhoods; the phenomenon of the "streetcar suburb" was on the horizon. Town and county at the turn of the century were on the move.

5

Rails and Roads: The Changing Face of Clarke County

Railroads and roadways enabled the county to prosper and the city of Athens to grow. Dotting early twentieth-century maps as rail lines and roads spread across the county were depot towns; farms; country schools, stores, and churches; and mills and villages at shoals and dams along the county's abundant waterways. Communities at Allentown, Barbersville, McNutt's Creek, and Tuckston were among the county's hamlets at the turn of the century; and Winterville was destined for incorporation as Clarke County's second significant railroad town. Athens grew as the central marketplace fed by the county and serviced increasingly by rail and (with the advent of the automobile) road.

Charles Morton Strahan—teacher, civil engineer, and for fifty years a member of the faculty of the University of Georgia—played an important role in the development of Clarke County in the early century. From 1890 to 1908 he served as surveyor for the county; from 1908 to 1919 he was the county engineer. As engineer he mapped the county and extended its system of public roads. With the advent of the automobile, he pioneered innovative road-building techniques soon used throughout the nation. His low-cost method (shared through the Good Roads School he conducted at the university in 1909 and the Roads Extension Department, begun in 1911) combined sand and clay as a topsoil for paving roads. His refined method for surface paving treatments became known as the Clarke County method. He helped draft the legislation that created the Georgia Highway Department in 1918 and became the department's first head.

The Georgia, Carolina, and Northern Railroad reached Athens in 1891, connecting the city directly to Atlanta. This meant quicker and less expensive service to the entire eastern seaboard. A passenger station for what became known as the Seaboard Air Line was located on north College Avenue. This 1975 drawing depicts the depot shortly after discontinuation of passenger service.

In Athens he drew plans for many buildings, including the connecting colonnade combining the Ivy Building and Old Library on the campus into the Academic Building, the Holman Building, and the new (1912) Clarke County Courthouse. He laid out a 1927 subdivision from the large McWhorter estate, and developed the grounds and designed a rectory and parish hall for Emmanuel Church. In the 1930s he served as chairman of the county commissioners.

Five rail lines—the Seaboard Air Line, Southern, Georgia, Central of Georgia, and Gainesville Midland—serviced Athens and environs. Augustus Longstreet Hull observed in his *Annals of Athens*, "Nothing brings about such changes in a town as a railroad. Not only the character and volume of business, but the physical features of a railroad town undergo a complete change." He reflected, "The building of the North Eastern road converted a beautiful grove alive with birds and squirrels, where a limpid brook hurried along by mossy banks to the quiet river, into a bustling scene of activity, noisy with the clatter of wagons, the whir of machinery and the passing of trains. The Macon and Covington then invaded the sanctity of the City of the dead, raised an unsightly trestle over beautiful monuments, cut an enormous gash through the hills and came into the very bosom of the city. The Georgia Railroad must needs cut down trees, remove old land marks, blast away a hillside and run its trains across the public street. The Georgia Carolina & Northern then with a whiff comes in and goes out touching lightly on the edge of town, crossing the river on a high bridge and leaving behind a deep rock cut and a smell of powder."

Winterville, a farming community east of Athens, is Clarke County's only other incorporated municipality. When the Georgia Railroad established "Six-Mile Station" as a wood-and-water stop, the community soon called Winterville began to grow. Pictured here is the century-old one-story wood depot that served passengers and farmers who shipped their grain along the rails from Winterville.

By the turn of the century, Hull lamented that the new citizens attracted by railroad facilities brought with them the demand for new houses and lots. He wrote: "Then history repeated itself and the handsome old lots were cut up and sold off or built up with cottages. Old homes have passed from the hands of the family. New neighbors with bay windows and little hoods and towers and ginger-bread work are crowding them; fine old trees have been cut down; the familiar mud is gone; the gentle cow no longer lies across the pedestrians way."

THE DEPOT TOWN OF WINTERVILLE

One of the best examples of a depot town that thrived with the growth of the railroad in Clarke County was Winterville. The town straddled the county line between Oglethorpe and Clarke at the headwaters of Beaverdam Creek. When the state legislature in 1906 allowed local citizens to decide into which of the two counties the divided town should fall, Wintervillians voted themselves into Clarke County and elected W. R. Coile mayor and John Pittard clerk. Winterville, incorporated in 1904, remains today the only incorporated town in the county other than Athens.

The area had an exotic history as part of a land grant from the state of Georgia to a Revolutionary War hero, Count d'Estaing. The count, a French citizen, deeded the land to Madame Gouvain in exchange for her valuable plantation in the West Indies. She was an intimate of the Empress Josephine and the widow of Ange de la Perriere (a French general) and Michael Gouvain (once private secretary to President James Monroe). For many years Madame Gouvain lived in Athens; around 1810 she moved into a frame French chateau her second husband built for her. (The house was later demolished to make room for the Georgia Railroad depot.)

Members of a sturdy German family named Winter settled in this area in the early 1850s. Diedrich Heinrich Winter of Bremerhaven came first, followed by his cousin John Winter from province Hanover and Heinrich's brother Christopher. The settlement became known as Winters. When the Georgia Railway extended its line toward Athens from Union Point, Heinrich Winter was the first section foreman, and "Winter's Station" was a water-and-wood stop for a train drawn by a little locomotive called the *Fairywestward*. When the line extended to Athens, the village was sometimes called Six-Mile Station. In 1866 John Winter, a shopkeeper, became the community's postmaster, and the village officially became Winterville. Heinrich (now Henry) was put in charge of the railroad's new water-pumping equipment. He gave forty years of service to the railroad before retiring as one of the "oldest and most valuable employees" on the line.

Fertile country and large farms surrounded Winterville and made it a lively marketplace and shipping center. Gothic Revival cottages and two-story homes soon adorned Main Street, which ran parallel to the tracks. Nearby in Oglethorpe and Madison counties was the thirty-square-mile "Smithonia," the plantation of the millionaire farmer James Monroe Smith, known locally as Colonel Jim because of his Confederate service. Wrote Georgia historian Numan V. Bartley, "In addition to as many as ten thousand acres in cotton and other crops, a thousand head of cattle, and three hundred swine, the plantation contained a cotton gin, a dairy, a fertilizer factory, a cottonseed oil mill, a brickmaking factory, sawmills, a planing mill, separate grist mills for grinding corn and wheat, a blacksmith shop, a woodworking shop, and two stores selling $75,000 to $100,000 in products annually. . . . He incorporated his own town, Smithonia, with post office, hotel, and other buildings. Vendors, drummers, and the like stayed at his hotel, although the town's other residents were mainly foremen and other employees on the plantation. The twelve hundred or more blacks lived in settlements scattered around the plantation, where several churches and six schools for black children provided services."

From Smithonia (population one thousand) Smith ruled an empire of farming and allied interests, shipping goods through the depot at Winterville and often carting country hams and other produce by four-horse wagon to Athens. In 1888 Smith's freight bill for February alone at the Winterville depot was a then-staggering eleven hundred dollars for goods he had shipped to his plantation. Smith realized that transportation—getting goods to market to buy and sell—was basic to building his agricultural fortune, and in 1889 he completed construction of a rail line from a point near Winterville to Smithonia.

Smith's wealth had a great impact on the economy of Winterville and Athens. He invested in lots and buildings (including warehouses) in Winterville and bought buildings and one triangular block in downtown Athens, for which he paid $61,800 in 1912. Athenians hoped one of his new buildings would be their third skyscraper, but according to E. K. Lumpkin, "He is only going to have it two or three stories high. Most everybody is indignant with him for not putting up a large, handsome building there instead." Smith was a stockholder in twenty-five banks in the area; for a time he held controlling interest in an Athens newspaper and served as president of an Athens oil and fertilizer company while owning a cotton mill.

In every respect, the controversial Smith himself seemed to his contemporaries larger than life. He served terms in the state house and senate and in 1906 ran unsuccessfully for governor. In the course of building his empire, Smith used convict labor. E. Merton Coulter wrote, "In 1892, Colonel Jim paid Clarke County $466.68 for some of its misdemeanor prisoners. In 1899 he was the highest bidder for those convicted at the first term of Superior Court. There were fifteen of them, and Colonel Smith paid $50 apiece for them." It was at the time common practice in the state of Georgia for

On June 23, 1891, the first electric streetcar moved down the roads of Athens. Power plants at Mitchell Bridge and Tallassee Shoals provided the electricity. The cars ran along Prince and Milledge avenues, Barber and Lumpkin streets, and the Boulevard.

counties to gain revenue by hiring out at auction persons convicted of misdemeanor crimes within each county's jurisdiction. The state hired out convicted felons, and Smith took advantage of those laborers as well.

Smith died at his plantation in 1915. Today Smithonia plantation is "Beaverdam Farm," the home of the singer Kenny Rogers and his wife, Marianne, a native Athenian.

By 1920 Winterville had 510 citizens, five general stores, one drugstore, a bank, two garages, two cotton gins, two grist mills, good country doctors, and an annual Winterville Community Fair. Children from small surrounding rural areas (like Dunlap, Hutchins Grade, and Murelle's) commuted by train to attend Winterville schools, getting off at the quaint clapboard railway station and joining town students. Winterville continued to prosper with the railroad in an agricultural economy.

THE STREETCAR SUBURBS

As transportation grew, so also did the population. In 1900 Clarke County had a population of 17,708. By 1940, 28,393 people lived in the county. During this forty-year period the population of Athens doubled, from 10,245 in 1900 to 20,650 in 1940.

A promoter from Texas named Snodgrass introduced the first passenger street railway cars in Athens in 1888, and the town was never the same again. He obtained a charter for the Classic City Street Railway Company and shipped in mules to power his cars. Mayor H. J. Rowe recalled "the breaking in of the little Texas mules that were shipped untamed from the wilds of the former independent Republic on the Rio Grande" and the "daily exhibitions of cowboy skill and resourcefulness and opposing mulish stubbornness." He wrote, "The little rails were laid on Broad, College, Clayton, Lumpkin, Hancock, Pulaski, Prince and Milledge, the little cars were unloaded and placed upon the rails, and the little mules were hitched to the cars and Athens had made a step forward." The company motto was "twenty-seven car miles per bale of hay." The cars were named Lucy Cobb, Pocahontas, and No. 2.

In time Snodgrass became homesick, sold his enterprise, and went back to Texas. Local promoters were eager to replace the mules and electrify the streetcars. E. G. Harris soon bought the streetcar line

The introduction of electric streetcars in Athens led to the growth of a new residential area along the Boulevard. It also stimulated the construction of new houses near already-established avenues like Prince and Milledge.

William Winstead Thomas was a trained civil engineer. A successful businessman as well, Thomas is best remembered for his architectural work from the 1880s and 1890s. Thomas is credited with the design of the Seney-Stovall Chapel, the William P. Welch and Joseph H. Fleming homes, probably White Hall, and his own mansion.

(which had gone into receivership) and went into business with the Athens Park and Improvement Company. They extended the line for electrified streetcars down Boulevard through the company's new three-hundred-acre residential development north of Prince Avenue and west of Barber Street. They subdivided the land for sale, setting aside twenty-one acres for a park at the edge of the city limits. Large new Queen Anne and Gothic Revival houses were soon under construction in Athens's first "streetcar subdivision."

With the advent of the automobile, the suburbs moved further out, and an extension of Boulevard west of the park (called Buena Vista) developed. When the Southern Manufacturing Company bought land along the railroad tracks for a factory, a mill village of factory workers' homes grew up there among more substantial houses on streets with Indian names like Nantahala and Hiawasee. In 1922 the Georgia General Assembly passed an act incorporating a large area of this western extremity into the city limits. Mayor and council created the city's Fifth Ward, and Wallace Bell, a real estate agent and a resident of Nacoochee Avenue, was the first councilman elected to represent the new ward.

Another new area (now Midtown), partially laid out in the 1880s by Robert L. Bloomfield in meadowlands east of Milledge Avenue, developed incrementally as one of Athens's modest neighborhoods created to house the town's expanding middle class. Proximity to the Milledge Avenue streetcar and the appeal of its parklike setting adjacent to the great houses of Milledge quickly made "Bloomfield" one of the town's most popular suburbs.

W. W. Thomas, an engineer and architect (and later Southern Mutual Insurance Company president), completed his own lavish Beaux Arts Milledge Avenue residence in 1896 and then designed flamboyant turreted houses along the popular and stylish street. One of his new houses was the stunning setting for a party honoring President-elect William Howard Taft when he visited Athens in 1908. The wealthy cotton factor Billups Phinizy, a long-time president of Southern Mutual with a myriad of business interests in Athens and beyond, built a Queen Anne house on Milledge before the turn of the century, as did many other prominent Athenians of this era.

The highly decorative entryway of W. W. Thomas's house on Milledge Avenue is pictured here around 1900, soon after its completion. In designing the house Thomas paid careful attention to details in the public rooms, adding such touches as paneled wainscoting, decorative cornices, and friezes with plaster swags.

Present-day Cloverhurst Avenue was a private driveway to an elaborate Victorian Romanesque 1890s villa of towering turrets and mansard roofs crowning a hill west of Milledge, formerly part of John Meeker's experimental farm. Judge Hamilton McWhorter (then general counsel for the Southern Railroad in Georgia, Alabama, Florida, and Mississippi) bought "Cloverhurst" in 1901 and moved his family from Lexington, Georgia, to Athens. After his death the house was demolished. The land was sold and subdivided in the 1920s.

In the 1920s and 1930s some of Athens's most prominent citizens were playing a nine-hole golf course and enjoying the Cloverhurst Country Club, where Springdale and Bobbin Mill now converge. The club held dances and parties, expanded the golf course to eighteen holes, and added a swimming pool. When the club dis-

This 1890 Queen Anne house belonged to Billups Phinizy, one of Athens's most influential citizens. Among his many business interests were the Southern Mutual Insurance Company, the Georgia Railroad and Banking Company, and the Athens Railway and Electric Company. His home, now demolished, featured extensive boxwood gardens facing Milledge Avenue.

"Cloverhurst," the imposing home of Judge Hamilton McWhorter, stood just west of Milledge Avenue adjacent to the avenue that bears his name. This large Queen Anne mansion, as well as those belonging to neighbors William Pinckney Welch, J. H. Fleming, and Billups Phinizy, illustrates the new development on and just off Milledge Avenue during the 1890s.

banded in the depression years of the late 1930s, this land too was subdivided for residential lots. For a time high school football teams practiced on a field that was part of this property. Two other small clubs were the Westlake Country Club and the Jewish Country Club on Pinecrest Road.

A. G. "Lon" Dudley, newly elected mayor of Athens, was responsible for the success of the new Athens Country Club on the Jefferson Road. Largely through his efforts, the club remained in operation throughout the depression. Dudley was a self-made man who prospered as a mill owner, buying into the Climax Hosiery Mill, where he had begun work as a young boy, and eventually becoming president of the Athens Manufacturing Company when Climax obtained the controlling shares of that venerable Athens institution. Dudley recruited the famous golf-course designer Donald Ross to lay out a fine new course in 1926 for the Athens Country Club. When hard times came along, Dudley had no intention of letting his prized course fail; when some members could not afford to pay dues, Dudley paid for them. He served as mayor of Athens from 1926 to 1936 and again from 1938 to 1940. When he began his tenure as mayor, the city's budget was $220,000. By 1936 it had risen to $421,000. Dudley, according to Morgan Redwine, who wrote of him in the *Athens Observer* in 1990, relied heavily on "Captain Jack" Beacham, his city engineer and unofficial chief administrator throughout these years of rapid change.

As the central business district expanded into residential streets downtown, Cobbham evolved from a pastoral setting for a few houses into a true in-town neighborhood. Phinizy Spalding, Georgia historian and a noted preservationist, wrote, "For the generation from roughly 1880–1914, Cobbham was *the* place to live. It was during this period when the full block lots, some running larger than four acres, were broken up and Athens's finest Victorian architecture began to replace gardens, barns, pastures, or side yards."

One of the houses that occupied a full block in Cobbham was the early residence of Moss Side, built originally circa 1839 by Hiram Hayes and bought in 1863 by John Dortch Moss and his son Rufus Lafayette Moss, who had served on the staff of his Cobbham neighbor, Confederate General Howell Cobb. Rufus Moss also managed

Cobbham was the only place to live for many Athenians. Seen here is the artist Lucy M. Stanton, who lived and worked at 552 Cobb Street from 1908 until her death. Best known as a painter of miniatures, Stanton worked in oil, watercolor, pastel, and clay. Examples of her art are found in the permanent collections of the Metropolitan Museum of Art, the National Portrait Gallery, the Philadelphia Museum of Art, and Emory University.

the Pioneer Paper Mill and Princeton Factory. A city councilman and bank director, he was prominent throughout his life in civic affairs. Moss became a director and promoter of the Northeast Railroad, which connected Athens to north Georgia, where coincidentally he owned considerable property in the popular Tallulah Falls resort area.

His youngest son, William Lorenzo Moss, was born at Moss Side on August 23, 1876. After graduation from the University of Georgia in 1897, Lorenzo Moss earned a medical degree at Johns Hopkins, where years later as a member of the research staff there he perfected a method of blood typing that by 1921 was used in about 90 percent of the hospitals in America. Moss gained worldwide recognition for classification of blood types and his other pioneering work in immunology.

Lucy M. Stanton was a Cobbham neighbor and contemporary of Lorenzo Moss. An important twentieth-century painter of miniatures, this Atlanta native lived, painted local portraits, and infused culture and a collective conscience in the community from the Cobb

Street studio and house she designed and built. An early feminist, she held the first women's suffrage meeting in Athens in her home and remained active locally in the movement. She founded the Georgia Peace Society in her home when the United States failed to join the League of Nations after World War I. A founding member (with other women artists, including Jennie Smith, Mary Franklin, Millie Dearing, Laura Blackshear, Jean Flanigen, and Sally Goodwin) of the Athens Art Association (1919), she brought the first traveling art exhibit to Athens at her own expense in 1907 and lobbied for a permanent art gallery at the university. She died in Cobbham in 1931 at the age of fifty-five.

Jennie Smith was another artist of considerable reputation who lived in Cobbham, in a cottage that doubled as her studio on the Lucy Cobb campus. Born in Athens in 1862, this Lucy Cobb alumna studied art in Baltimore, New York, and Paris before returning to her alma mater as head of the art department, a position she held for more than fifty years. Although she instilled in many young women an appreciation for art and doubtless trained many budding

Harriet Powers (1837–1911), a black woman living just outside Athens, completed this appliquéd Bible quilt around 1886 and exhibited it that year at the local cotton fair. Jennie Smith, an artist and teacher at Lucy Cobb Institute, purchased the quilt four years later; it now belongs to the Smithsonian Institution. Powers's Bible quilt is an excellent example of African-American material culture. Although it is distinctly American in its narrative subject matter, the appliqué technique, where cutout shapes are sewn onto a larger fabric, has its roots in West African culture.

In 1891 twelve Athens women organized the Cobbham Garden Club. At the first meeting Ann Olivia Newton Cobb was elected president of the organization, which was the forerunner of the first Garden Club of America.

America's first garden club convened in the Cobbham home of Mrs. E. K. Lumpkin in 1891. From the beginning members met every other week to exchange plant cuttings and conduct botanical experiments. The membership soon opened to any interested Athenian. All were invited to participate in the club's pioneering flower and vegetable shows.

female artists, perhaps her greatest contribution was as patroness of another woman later recognized as a profoundly important folk artist, an African-American named Harriet Powers. Born into slavery in 1837, Harriet Powers lived in Clarke County in the Bucks Branch and Sandy Creek districts. She lived on the edge of poverty during her years of freedom. Poverty and providence brought the two women together when Jennie Smith began efforts to purchase an intricate and intriguing narrative Bible quilt designed by Harriet Powers and exhibited by her at a local cotton fair in 1886. Powers was reluctant to sell her beloved creation but finally arrived by oxcart at Jennie Smith's front door with, according to Smith, "the precious burden in her lap encased in a clean flour sack, which was still enveloped in a crocus sack." Probably because Smith exhibited the Powers quilt in the "Negro Building" in the 1895 Cotton States and International Exposition in Atlanta, Harriet Powers received a commission from the faculty ladies of Atlanta University to sew a second biblical quilt as a gift for Charles Cuthbert Hall, chairman of the university trustees and president of Union Theological Seminary. Both quilts are historically significant examples of the appliqué techniques traceable to West African culture. Both are mirrors of a narrative folk tradition ripe with religious symbolism, accounts of actual historical and natural events, and traditional motifs steeped in mythology. Gladys-Marie Fry, Powers's biographer, concludes, "In Harriet Powers' quilt lies an almost intriguing classic tale of the South: the skilled work of the slave craftsman imbedded in the creator's African heritage and preserved by the patron." Harriet Powers died in Clarke County in 1911, Jennie Smith in 1946. The Smithsonian Institute now owns the quilt Miss Smith bought; it hangs in the National Museum of American Art in Washington, D.C. The commissioned quilt is now in the permanent collection of the Museum of Fine Arts in Boston.

IMPROVEMENT AND EXPANSION

Cobbham residents and others nearby must have gained a measure of security when the city expanded fire protection with the 1901 construction of Fire Hall No. 2 at the intersection of Prince Avenue

NEW YORK
Herald Tribune
Annual International Flower Show Section

SECTION XI | SUNDAY, MARCH 18, 1934 | TWENTY PAGES

Painted for the Herald Tribune *by* Calvert Smith

Founding of America's *First Garden Club*—Athens, Ga., 1891

and Hill Street, directly across from the new Gothic Revival stone sanctuary of Emmanuel Church (completed in 1899). Brick Victorian structures in a triangle behind the firehouse housed stables, ice cream parlors, butcher shops, and more.

New streetcar tracks extended past Cobbham out Prince Avenue, where yet another "subdivision" was developing at Normaltown around the campus of the State Normal School. Established by the state legislature for the training of teachers for rural schools, the Normal School opened in 1891 in "Rock College," the 1862 rock building that originally housed University High School. Federal troops had occupied this site at the close of the Civil War, and from 1872 to 1891 the university operated an experimental farm here. The Athens City Council in 1892 appropriated five hundred dollars for wire cots, tables, chairs, buckets and other necessities of life to help launch the Normal School at its meager beginnings. Rock College became Gilmer Hall in honor of Governor George R. Gilmer. Over the years the campus improved and expanded through generous private support coupled with increased state funding as the need for teacher training became acute.

The United Daughters of the Confederacy donated twenty-five thousand dollars for the construction of Winnie Davis Memorial Hall (built in 1902), and the Elijah Clarke Chapter of the Daughters of the American Revolution contributed to the construction of an infirmary. Mrs. Jefferson Davis herself endorsed the idea of the memorial to her daughter. She wrote to Mildred Rutherford in Athens, "My dear child often said: 'If I only was well enough off to give to Confederate orphans, to endow a college, or even a chair in one, I should be extremely happy. Do you think, dear, I could ever afford it?' It is a matter of great pride and rejoicing to me to know my and her dear friends will do this, and I am sure she knows it and rejoices in Heaven over the tender offering. May God speed you in your effort."

The great philanthropist George Foster Peabody took a special interest in early-twentieth-century Athens and gave twenty-five thousand dollars for the construction of a library (completed in 1910 and now the Navy Supply Corps Museum). Born in Columbus, Georgia, in 1852, Peabody had little formal education,

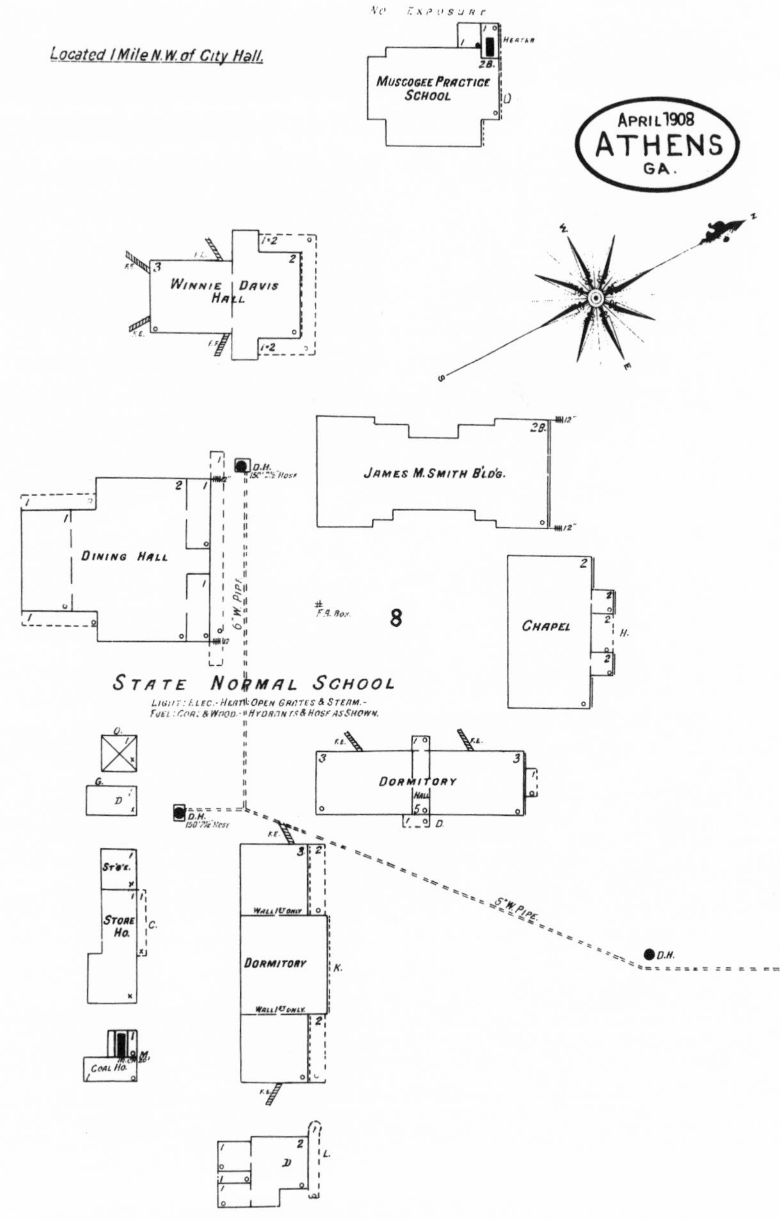

A 1908 plan of the State Normal School campus.

This 1920s photograph shows the Barnett Shoals dam and electric plant. Built in 1912–13 by Athens Railway and Electric Company employees, it produced electricity for a large section of Athens and nearby Watkinsville. Georgia Power purchased the plant in 1927 and maintains it today. The building at the top center is the former Star Thread Mill, founded in 1898.

attending preparatory school in Danbury, Connecticut, for a few months only. Nonetheless, he made a fortune as a banker and a developer of the Edison Electric Illuminating Company (later General Electric). In 1906 Peabody retired at the age of fifty-four to pursue philanthropy full time. Among his rather eclectic interests were the University of Georgia and the Normal School.

In 1928, when legal requirements for teacher certification changed, the name of the Normal School changed to Georgia State Teachers College. Under the direction of President Jere M. Pound, the school educated as many as one thousand women a year. The college operated independently until 1932, when it passed by law under the control of the University of Georgia, which turned the buildings on "Coordinate Campus" into dormitories for university women. Throughout all these stages, the neighborhood around the campus continued to grow as a community of shops and residences.

Normaltown in its infancy, like other new areas of town, benefited from a significant event of far-reaching consequences in 1896. The development of a new hydroelectric station at Mitchell's Bridge generated enough current from the "white coal" of the Middle Oconee River to light Brumby's Drugstore downtown on December 12 and thereby introduced electric lighting to Athens. New stations at Tallassee Shoals and Barnett Shoals generated power to run streetcars, light city streets and homes, and—at first—power at least two cotton factories.

The Eight Beautiful Woodlawn Lots

SHOWN ON PLAT BELOW WILL BE SOLD THIS AFTERNOON

A T

Auction to the Highest Bidder

On terms of One-fifth Cash, balance in 4 years at 8%. This street is already established---Fine elegant houses already erected and occupied by OWNERS. Two additional homes to be erected in the near future and both will be built for owner's use.

$2.50 Gold Pieces Given Away Free

at the Sale and a Brass Band will furnish the Music.

The above Prices on Lots have no connection with the Auction Sale. Buy them for what you can.

Come out at 5:30 this Thursday afternoon and buy one or more of these beautiful lots.

Be there to vote for the contestants for the diamond Ring and the diamond LaValliere. Each grown person attending entitled to 750 votes. You don't have to buy to vote.

ERWIN & COMPANY

The Woodlawn Avenue neighborhood adjacent to Milledge Avenue dates from 1913. Many families bought their lots at auction and built houses in the Craftsman style, which featured the natural use of fieldstone, shingles, and stucco.

In 1910 all property belonging to the Athens Electric Railway Company and its owners (W. S. Holman, J. Y. Carithers, A. P. Dearing, J. A. Hunnicutt, and C. D. Flanigan) transferred to the Athens Railway and Electric Company, headed by W. T. Bryan and a board that included Holman, the Hodgson brothers, Billups Phinizy, and John R. White. In 1927 this company became part of the Georgia Power Company.

The extension of streetcar tracks out Milledge and Lumpkin and the increasing popularity of automobile ownership hastened development of Five Points and environs. Much of the land was originally the 161-acre antebellum farm of Alonzo Church, who had built "Homewood" (now the oldest *in situ* residence in Athens) as a presidential retreat and retirement home a brisk buggy ride away from the noise of the early campus. By the early 1900s the land was known as the Scott Homeplace and included a country club and lake. Below Hampton Street (later Hampton Court) the Lily Land Company offered home lots for sale. In 1913 the Georgia Development Company formed to develop other sections near Homeplace. They named the land west of Five Points Milledge Park and began a planned community along curvilinear streets with Milledge Circle the major thoroughfare. The suburb developed in the 1920s and 1930s and included the town's first apartments—named Milledge Park, Milledge Circle, and Henrietta—and a small shopping district at Five Points.

Barrow Elementary School, named for Chancellor David Crenshaw Barrow, opened on Lumpkin Street in Five Points in 1923. Patty Hilsman was the first principal of the Spanish mission–style brick school. John Stegeman, an Athens physician who was a student at Barrow in its first years, recalled an event that took place in 1927. "Charles Lindbergh, back from France after his historic New York-to-Paris flight, flew over our school." The famous aviator was scheduled to "buzz" all the schools in Athens. At the school's semicentennial celebration Stegeman recalled, "Right on schedule we saw our great hero approach from the west. He flew low over the school, banking in a big circle, leaning far out of his cabin and waving. . . . We were all maniacs in a mob scene. As 'The Spirit of St. Louis' leveled off and flew toward the city, we all rushed headlong down Pinecrest, onto Lumpkin Street, and dashed wildly toward town. Eventually we realized we were being badly outdistanced, and now had to walk sheepishly back to school to face our teachers' ire."

By the next year, 1928, news events around the world were brought home via Athens's first radio station, WTFI. In Five Points and other neighborhoods, residents soon acquired radio sets. When the station moved to Atlanta in 1937, a new, privately owned radio station, WGAU, began.

BLACK NEIGHBORHOODS

Some blacks—domestics and professionals—lived in predominantly white neighborhoods early in the century, but black neighborhoods increasingly became distinct and segregated from white neighborhoods. Probably this separation occurred as free blacks formed a sense of community through black churches and black educational institutions. Sara Glickman in a study of African-American neighborhoods in the Georgia Piedmont wrote of changing times for black Athenians: "In Athens, the occupations which showed the greatest increase relative to their numbers were black professionals and businessmen [and women]—preachers, teachers, lawyers, doctors, store owners, real estate agents, newspaper reporters, editors, and postal workers—whose primary clientele were blacks." Indeed, the achievements of Athens blacks in the decades following the Civil War were remarkable, especially since by the end of the war only a handful of free blacks in Athens were literate.

One exceptional black Athenian was Lucius Henry Halsey, a young slave who belonged to a university professor. As a teenager Lucius sold rags to earn money to buy books. With the help of some young white children and an old black man, he taught himself to read. After emancipation Halsey became a licensed preacher in the African Methodist Episcopal (AME) church and later became bishop and the founder of Paine College.

The wealthiest black citizen in Athens was Monroe B. "Pink" Morton. A former hotel porter with little formal education, Morton rose to become a successful contractor. His projects included a new

Monroe B. "Pink" Morton, one of Athens's most prominent black citizens.

courthouse for Washington, Georgia, and a government building in Anniston, Alabama, as well as a number of commercial buildings in downtown Athens.

As an active member of the Republican party and a delegate to the 1896 national convention, Morton was an elected member of the committee that notified William McKinley of his nomination as the GOP presidential candidate. In 1897 Morton received an appointment as Athens's second black postmaster, a position he held from 1897 until 1902. Morton became an entrepreneur and editor of a black newspaper. In the city he owned from twenty-five to thirty parcels of property, valued at more than eighty-five hundred dollars, which included the Samaritan Building, the Morton Theater, and a handsome marble building on Clayton Street.

Morton built an imposing two-story house for his family on Prince Avenue near the quintessentially fashionable intersection of Prince and Milledge avenues. "A few other Athens black citizens, including Madison Davis and Henry Derricotte, a prominent carpenter, also owned two-story homes in white neighborhoods," according to Sara Glickman.

While some servants' quarters (usually one-story frame structures with shingled roofs) sat on the lots of older homes and housed black "help," most Athens blacks lived in black neighborhoods. By 1900 there were 5,190 blacks living in Athens; Sanborn Insurance maps show that by 1913 servants' quarters behind town houses had all but disappeared, and all-black neighborhoods had proliferated. T. J. Woofter, Jr., in a 1913 survey of black settlement patterns in Athens, explained, "They live in several different localities, and yet there are very few blocks in which both white and colored people live. . . . While the color line can be drawn on the map of Athens, this segregation is due to economic and social, not to municipal, laws." Unlike many other southern cities, Athens never enacted a residential segregation ordinance.

By the turn of the century, most blacks in Athens were building or renting small houses on narrow lots in several expanding, self-contained settlements. Among these were the West Hancock district, platted as Lynwood Park in 1906, and the Reese Street neighborhood. Lynwood Park lay between Milledge Avenue and the city limits, and became a little town within itself. In 1918, 1,136 of the city's 6,300 blacks lived in the area. Many owned their own homes and worked nearby. Professional black people—doctors, lawyers, and educators—occupied the larger homes on higher sites, while tradesmen and unskilled workers lived in the district in more modest housing on lower lots. T. J. Elder, an educator, lived in a substantial home in Lynwood Park, as did Andrew Jones, a physician. The community built its own grocery stores, churches (including Ebenezer Baptist Church on the corner of Chase and Reese streets), and hospitals, all within walking distance of one another. Most residen-

Inspired by the motto "Your school is always the best in everything," the Knox Institute's football team went undefeated during the 1920 and 1921 seasons. The team played home games at Chase Street Park against other schools for black students, including Clarke Institute and Morehouse College.

tial structures were modest vernacular house types such as L-shaped cottages and square houses with pyramidal roofs.

A broad cross-section of black Athenians lived in the Reese Street section, just west of downtown, where a residential hierarchy also developed. Here lived, for example, the minister and physician Charles Haynes, who founded the nursing department at Athens High and Industrial School in 1918, and Ida Mae and Lace Hiram, a husband-and-wife dental team. Practicing dental medicine in Athens for fifty-five years, Ida Mae Hiram was the first woman to pass the Georgia Dental Board examination.

White developers of adjacent Milledge and Prince avenues overlooked the Reese Street area because the hilly terrain made building difficult. Nonetheless, a significant black neighborhood developed. House styles included mostly simple wood-framed one-story structures built close to the street, with pyramidal roofs and front porches offering relief from summer's heat. Shotgun-style houses, Craftsman bungalows, and two-story gabled houses appeared here as well.

Knox Institute operated for sixty years on Reese Street, until the school closed in 1928. J. Thomas Heard established another (though much smaller) private high school for blacks in 1912. Athens High and Industrial School, built in 1913, became Georgia's only black public high school in 1916. In 1922 AHIS was one of the first black schools accredited by the state.

In 1910 the E. D. Harris Drug Store opened in the Morton Building in downtown Athens. Not long after this the business moved into new quarters in the Samaritan Building on Washington Street. Local black citizens, including the physicians W. H. Harris and Blanche Thompson, owned and operated the drugstore.

MORTON THEATRE
Monday, November 2nd

The Black Patti Musical Comedy Company

Presenting a new Musical Play, entitled

Lucky Sam
From Alabam

Headed by Sissieretta Jones, Harrison Stewart

40—PEOPLE—40

Join the Army of Laughter

Seats on sale at Harris' Drug Store

The Morton Theater, built in 1911, was a showplace for black entertainers. As a centerpiece for the Athens black community, the Morton also became a stage for local events.

Hill's First Baptist Church on the corner of Pope and Reese streets, designed with Gothic Revival detailing in a modified cross plan, called members to worship by the ringing of the bell in its two-and-one-half-story steepled tower. Both figuratively and literally, the church stood at the heart of community life.

Though not a residential neighborhood, "Hot Corner" downtown was a home away from home for many black citizens. Here "Pink" Morton's building dominated one corner of the intersection of Washington and Lumpkin Street, which was the center of black commercial, financial, professional, and social life. At Hot Corner were numerous offices (many in the Samaritan Building and Union Hall) for black doctors, lawyers, dentists, and others, as well as black-owned restaurants, two poolrooms, lodge halls, barbershops, insurance companies, two undertaking establishments, and the Morton Building, a center for the black middle class. In the Morton Building, above professional offices, a magnificent two-story opera house with horseshoe wrap-around balcony, flawless acoustics, and pagoda-style boxes formed an elegant setting for all sorts of cultural events, statewide professional meetings, black community events, and traveling vaudeville shows. Playing to local audiences (with seating for white people in a special section in the balcony) were a bevy of black stars of the era, including Louis Armstrong and Duke Ellington; Cab Calloway, Jimmy Lunceford, and Bessie Smith; as well as Butterbeans and Susie and the Black Patti Musical Company. Each May black schools performed operettas at the Morton, and each New Year's Day the entire black community gathered here to celebrate the Emancipation Proclamation. Morton's son Charlie managed a movie house in the opera house in the 1930s after the 1920s heyday of vaudeville.

The passage of Jim Crow laws and the financial reverses of the early 1920s dealt harsh blows to the black middle class community in Athens as elsewhere throughout the South. After the boll weevil destroyed the cotton crop and the depression hit the nation, many black Athenians moved north in search of better opportunities. Eventually, the large lodge halls adjacent to the Morton Building were demolished, but the Morton Building and a few other commercial structures endured, adapting to change on Hot Corner.

DOWNTOWN DEVELOPMENTS

Hilltop residents could watch the quickly changing skyline of downtown Athens from their verandas. The building boom of the 1880s and 1890s continued unabated into the early twentieth century, as much of downtown assumed a character and appearance little changed today.

By 1904 Athens had a new city hall. Crowned by a cupola topped by an eagle weathervane, the imposing granite Beaux Arts structure rose ninety-nine feet above the town's highest point and included city offices and council chambers, an armory for the local militia, and soon adjacent office space for the very aggressive Athens Cham-

Built at a cost of fifty thousand dollars, City Hall sits on College Avenue at Washington and Hancock streets. The water tower, erected in 1893, remained standing until 1951.

This bird's-eye view of Clayton Street dates from around 1920. At the left foreground is the Shackelford Building, which housed several small businesses, including Orr Drugs. The Athens Railway and Electric Company had, by this time, relocated its main offices to the former Southern Mutual Insurance Building, which had been moved up College Avenue when the company directors decided to erect a new seven-story skyscraper on the original lot.

ber of Commerce, founded in 1903 and primed for expansion and progress.

James Knox Taylor, architect of the U.S. Treasury Building in Washington, D.C., designed the handsome Renaissance Revival Federal Building in 1905. The three-story brick and stone structure across College Avenue from City Hall housed the post office and the federal courthouse.

Not for long did City Hall dominate the townscape. When the Southern Mutual Insurance Company completed a $250,000 seven-story building on College Avenue in 1908, it was state-of-the-art: Athens's first skyscraper, the largest ferro concrete office building in the South, the first example of Commercial-style architecture in northeast Georgia, and a model of fireproof construction.

The president of Southern Mutual, Billups Phinizy, organized the financing for another landmark, a new hotel on the former site of the Washington Street School. The elegant Georgian Hotel, de-

When the Georgian Hotel opened, it drew praise as one of the state's finest hostelries. The architect introduced modern conveniences including private baths and running water. The refurbished main dining room remains one of Athens's most elegant restaurants.

Deliverymen in horse-drawn wagons carried Athens's very own cherry-flavored drink, Bludwine (now called Budwine), to local merchants at the turn of the century. The drink was formulated and merchandized by a Watkinsville native named Henry C. Anderson, but by the 1920s the company was run by Joseph Costa, owner of a popular Athens ice cream parlor. Budwine is still in business today, owned and operated by two local entrepreneurs.

signed by the Atlanta Architect A. Ten Eyck Brown and completed in 1909, was Athens's first fine hotel. Mayor H. J. Rowe felt that opening this first-class hotel "did more to help build Athens than any other movement ever started in Athens." The dining room, Palm Garden, ballroom, coffee shop, marble-lined lobby, and distinctive stained glass windows and skylights drew rave reviews. The 125-room fireproof hotel featured steam heat, running water, and private rooms (75 with baths) for $1.50 to $3.50 per day. Not only would guests to Athens find fashionable accommodations, but the townspeople had a new center for social life. Some guests even stayed on as permanent hotel residents.

A few automobiles were on the streets in 1909, but buggies, wagons, surreys, runabouts (one-seated open carriages and roadsters), stanhopes (open horse-drawn carriages with with two or four wheels and one seat), horses, trolleys, and bicycles were all popular means of transportation. Just around the block in his small electrical shop on Washington Street, a young Athenian named Ben Epps tinkered with early motorcycles and automobiles and experimented with monoplane and biplane designs. Only four years after the Wright brothers' historic 1903 flight in a biplane at Kitty Hawk, Epps designed, built, and flew briefly (before it crashed) the first

airplane in the state of Georgia. He designed and flew other new planes in 1909, 1911, 1916, 1924, and 1930. Young Epps established a reputation as one of the true pioneers of early aviation. In 1919, when he and a partner opened the Rolfe-Epps Flying Service (offering flight instruction, passenger flights, and aerial photography), Athens truly went airborne. Epps died when his plane crashed on takeoff in 1937.

W. S. Holman built Athens's tallest building for $175,000 in 1913. The modern, 168-room, nine-story "skyscraper" stood on the corner of Clayton and Lumpkin streets, on the original site of Emmanuel Church. For many years the Holman Hotel competed for customers with the Georgian. The Citizens and Southern Bank redesigned the interior and exterior of the Holman building for its Athens headquarters in the early 1960s.

The new Clarke County Courthouse, designed by A. Ten Eyck Brown and executed by Charles Morton Strahan, opened in 1918 on the corner adjacent to the Georgian where C. A. Tucker's blacksmith shop once stood. A hybrid of Neoclassical and Beaux Arts architecture, the two-hundred-thousand-dollar building housed offices for elected county officials: the ordinary (the chief executive), the county treasurer, the clerk of the superior court, the tax receiver and tax collector, the county surveyor, and the coroner. The courtrooms of Judge Charles H. Brand (who later represented Clarke County in the United States Congress) and Judge Henry S. West were on the second floor. On the fourth floor Sheriff Walter E. Jackson lived with his prisoners in jail facilities that included cells (two padded for the insane), a hospital room, kitchen, laundry

Ben Epps poses in front of his garage on Washington Street with his pioneering airplane built in 1907. For the next twenty-three years Epps spent much of his time designing, building, and testing his own planes. In 1919 Epps, along with Monte Rolfe, opened a flying service on rented land that is now the site of the Athens Municipal Airport–Ben Epps Field.

room, and an open rooftop court where prisoners exercised. With the completion of the county courthouse, the city, county, and federal governments all conducted their affairs within two blocks of one another in a business district bound to the north by the Lickskillet residential area.

Fire Hall No. 1 moved to Thomas at Washington Street in 1912, and the first motorized fire truck moved into the proud new building. Another motorized truck replaced the horse-drawn wagon at Fire Hall No. 2 in 1913 in an effort to modernize the municipal fire department established in 1891. City-employed fire fighters now replaced the colorful and valiant volunteer fire companies. City fire-fighting equipment, however, was still grossly inadequate. In 1921 a devastating fire swept through numerous western-edge properties downtown along Clayton Street from Jackson to Thomas and down to lower Broad Street's "Deupree Block." Many of the city's handsomest brick, late-nineteenth-century structures were destroyed in this fire, which started in the Max Joseph Building, a four-story structure on Clayton Street that housed the Denny Motor Company, a restaurant, meeting rooms for fraternal orders, and the Athens Typographical Union. The fire, fed by an explosion of gas tanks stored in the basement, leapt across streets and did extensive damage before the fire department, aided at the last by reinforcements arriving by train from Atlanta, could bring it under control. The city of Athens soon made more serious financial commitments to the purchase of up-to-date fire-fighting equipment.

Michael Brothers, the city's first and finest department store, was a total loss in the fire. The brothers, Simon and Moses, commissioned the famed Atlanta architect Neel Reid to design their new store, a Renaissance Revival building completed in 1923. The new store was an even greater success than the old. The distinguished building is still considered Neel Reid's finest commercial structure.

The Michaels were highly respected for their generosity and philanthropy as well as for their business acumen. Moses Michael, the product of Athens private schools, graduated from the University of Georgia in 1878 at the age of sixteen. He and his brother built one of the largest wholesale and retail dry-goods firms in the state. Moses was active in many fields, serving as president of the Athens

Chamber of Commerce, vice-president of the Athens Savings Bank (which he founded with clothier Myer Stern in 1892), and treasurer of the Athens Board of Education. H. J. Rowe called him "one of the great civic leaders of this city and section, possessing executive ability of remarkable nature." He was a director of the Hebrew Orphans Home in Atlanta and raised funds for the National Jewish Hospital for Consumptives in Denver.

The Michael brothers in 1902 built two startlingly identical and monumental Neoclassical mansions side by side on Prince Avenue between the Taylor-Grady House and the Grant-Hill House (now the President's House) on Prince Avenue. Moses Michael lived in his house until his death at the age of eighty-two in 1944.

Moses Michael served as president of the Congregation Children of Israel, whose synagogue, built in 1884, stood on Hancock Street across from the courthouse, growing and prospering along with other downtown houses of worship. First Presbyterian and First Methodist churches remained at their original locations downtown, while Emmanuel Church moved out to Prince Avenue at Pope Street in 1899. In 1915 First Christian built a new sanctuary on the corner of Pulaski and Dougherty streets across from their former church building (built in 1884). In 1916 a prosperous black urban congregation built their handsome, architect-designed AME Church on Hull Street. The congregation organized originally in 1866 in a blacksmith shop on Foundry Street. In 1917 Roman Catholics built Saint Joseph's Church on the site of T. R. R. Cobb's small law office, where the congregation initially had held services. The T. R. R. Cobb House next door served Saint Joseph's as rectory and parish hall for many years. In 1921 the congregation of First Baptist Church worshiped for the first time at their present church on Pulaski Street; for thirty-eight years (from 1860 to 1898) First Baptist had occupied the corner of College and Washington streets. Places of worship anchored downtown physically and spiritually and lent charm and dignity to the townscape.

From 1888 to 1932 the center of the town's eclectic cultural life was the Colonial Theater (called the New Opera House until the Michael brothers bought, renamed, and remodeled it in 1906). Located on Clayton Street across from the Georgian Hotel, the

Moses and Simon Michael founded the wholesale and retail dry-goods firm Michael Brothers in 1882. Their twin Neoclassical houses and the Taylor-Grady and Grant-Hill-White houses made Prince Avenue one of the most palatial streets in all of Georgia.

theater could seat 1,006 in its luxurious balcony, gallery, and orchestra sections. Literally thousands of actors and actresses, from professional companies to local and amateur talent, trod the boards of the Colonial. The theater employed two orchestras and in 1915 installed a great Wurlitzer pipe organ—reputedly the first of its kind in the South—to accompany silent films. The aging Sarah Bernhardt performed here in her farewell tour of America in 1916; Geraldine Farrar played Carmen at the Colonial in 1925; and here Will Rogers wowed Athens audiences with his one-man show in 1927. Will Rogers, Jr., later wrote to Athenian Jack Martin, "While Will Rogers had his biggest success in the theatrical centers of New York and Los Angeles, I think he was proudest of the fact that he was one of the few 'big names' who could go into any little town anywhere in the country and feel perfectly at home."

Even a few sporting events played the Colonial. The majority presented details of Bulldog football games "live" via Western Union Telegraph. An announcer shouted play-by-play results through a megaphone to the audience, while the fans cheered their team. In 1919 a standing-room-only crowd followed the Willard-Dempsey

championship boxing match from Toledo, Ohio, "live" in the same manner.

In 1916 Confederate veterans were guests of honor at the Colonial for a major event in the life of all of northeast Georgia: the exclusive regional premiere of the widely acclaimed D. W. Griffith film *Birth of a Nation*. The *Banner-Herald* proclaimed, "These brave fighters of the sixties will attend in a body to see many stirring scenes that will carry them back to the days when they were in the trenches before Richmond, Vicksburg, or Appomattox."

The press reported, "There was not a performance given which did not at times find the house in tears, some sobbing, and once or

This turn-of-the-century photograph pictures a group of fashionable young Athenians. Isabel Thomas, daughter of W. W. Thomas, is standing at the top with a large feathered hat, and her sister, Gertrude, is seated at the front, second from the left.

twice women became a little hysterical—so moved were they by the powerful picture and its effective presentation."

Ironically, the great success of this early film foretold the eventual demise of the Colonial, for the silver screen (especially with the advent of "talkies") soon forced legitimate theater out of business. In the 1920s three new movie theaters opened in downtown Athens: the Palace, the Strand, and the Elite (later the Georgian). When the plaster ceiling of the Colonial caved in in 1932, the city engineer, Captain Jack Beacham, condemned the building as a menace to public safety. Soon the crumbling landmark was demolished.

A series of grand opera seasons featuring Italian opera stars and local choruses at Woodruff Hall on the university campus included ambitious productions like *Rigoletto, Orpheus,* and *Lucia di Lammermoor* in the late 1920s. But Athens had turned to movies and sporting events as entertainment for the masses. The Morton became a movie theater, and even professional productions on campus became more of a rarity.

Banking played a key role in downtown development, and Bankers Row on Broad Street for many years housed much of the financial community. In the early twentieth century the Athens Savings Bank stood on Broad, flanked by the National Bank of Athens at "Bank Corner" (at Broad and Jackson Street) and the American State Bank. Other banking establishments by the 1920s included the Commercial Bank of Athens, People's Bank, Clarke County Bank, and Georgia National (founded by John J. Wilkins, the president of University Savings Bank, in 1903).

New warehouses and freight depots grew up along Foundry Street as Athens became a major center for transportation and trade. According to the *Banner,* Athens was one of the largest cotton markets in the world in 1910, handling more wagonloads of cotton than any other town in Georgia. In bumper years more than 150,000 bales passed through the Athens warehouse district. Dean William Tate remembered a 1920 scene: "Cotton weathers well, and hundreds of bales were on the sidewalk—one on the edge of the street, one on the sidewalk, a third atop these two. . . . It was all down one side of Broad, one side of Lumpkin, in fact, on every street corner where space permitted."

When cotton was king the intersection of Broad and Oconee streets was a bustling corner. This picture from the early twentieth century shows bales of cotton lined up outside a warehouse, now Farmer's Hardware.

In 1923 E. W. Carroll, secretary of the Chamber of Commerce, reported that Athens was the second largest cotton manufacturer in the state. Related industries included twelve cotton-manufacturing plants and a cotton-oil refinery, two oil mills, a sulfuric acid plant, and three fertilizer plants. A veritable army of salesmen (two hundred) made Athens their headquarters. Serviced by five rail lines, the city was a hub for wholesale grocers. Athens had 105 miles of streets, and improved highways spread throughout Clarke County.

The municipal water plant pumped one million gallons of water a day. The city YMCA had a new one-hundred-thousand-dollar recreational and meeting facility. Numerous doctors now hung their shingles in town and treated patients at three new hospitals that opened between 1918 and 1920: Athens General Hospital on Prince Avenue, Saint Mary's Hospital on Milledge, and the Clarke County Tuberculosis Sanitarium (now part of Memorial Park). The Chamber of Commerce boasted of the healthful condition of the town: "Athens enjoys the lowest death rate in the South, the second in the U.S."

During the first two decades of the twentieth century, cotton culture remained unmechanized in most of Georgia. Most farmers were tenants and lived as before—in unpainted houses with no electricity, telephone, or running water. After World War I, as prices plummeted and the boll weevil took its toll, cotton production dropped throughout the state, never to regain its prewar high.

World War I had caused cotton prices to soar and then plummet. The demand for cloth and uniforms proved a boon to Athens textile industries as cotton prices rose to unprecedented highs. Cotton was still the principal crop in the county, and the worn land increasingly required larger amounts of fertilizer to produce a crop. According to James Reap, "While many of the small farmers did not prosper under this one-crop agricultural system, the cotton factors, fertilizer manufactures and farm implement suppliers in Athens reaped a substantial profit."

The depression that hit rural Georgia began in 1920 and lasted until World War II. Diversification and a balanced economy helped Athens and Clarke County weather the storms of the 1920s—the devastation wrought on crops by the Mexican boll weevil and the Great Depression—that ushered the decade in and out. While some businesses, banks, farms, and fortunes failed, the area fared far better than most, aided in part by the presence of the university and a building program there fostered by the New Deal. Even during the depression university enrollment increased.

David C. Barrow, a graduate of the University of Georgia, joined the faculty in 1879. After serving as dean of Franklin College, he succeeded to the chancellorship, a position he held from 1906 to 1925. Under Barrow's administration the modernization of the university moved forward rapidly. Barrow added schools and colleges and invited women to join the faculty.

THE EXPANDING CAMPUS

When Walter B. Hill, class of 1870, was elected chancellor in 1899, he became the first nonminister in almost a century and the first alumnus ever to head the university. After Hill's death six years later, David Crenshaw Barrow, a grandson of the Revolutionary War hero James Barrow, held the post of chancellor for nearly twenty years, from 1906 to 1925. These two progressive alumni coaxed the university into the twentieth century. Under "Uncle Dave" Barrow (a sobriquet of affection bestowed on him by his students) enrollment grew from four hundred to more than sixteen hundred students. Larger enrollments and the creation of a number of individual schools and colleges (among them Pharmacy, Forestry, Education, Commerce, and Journalism) led to a vastly expanded campus and transformed a small college into a true university.

New buildings constructed during the century's first decades intermingled Victorian Romanesque, Beaux Arts, and Neoclassical design with the earlier architectural styles of historic North Campus. In 1903 Charles Morton Strahan's elaborate Corinthian colonnade joined the Academic Building and the Library just inside the Arch, making the two classic structures appear as one. George Foster Peabody endowed a new university library (now the Georgia Museum of Art), and Neel Reid designed a strikingly beautiful classical building (later named Brooks Hall) to house the Departments of Commerce and Journalism.

The Conner Act of 1903 created the new, all but autonomous State College of Agriculture and Mechanical Arts. For twenty-five years Andrew M. Soule, a Canadian who proved a tireless agronomer and aggressive administrator, directed a rapidly expanding agricultural academic fiefdom from his "command post" in Agricultural Hall (later renamed Conner Hall) south of the university. Soule was an expert in spending new federal funding now available to agricultural colleges. F. N. Boney, university historian, wrote: "Determined to reach the state as the university had never done before, and hailing his operation as 'the college with the state for its campus,' . . . Soule [in 1908] chartered a special train to tour the state. Flatcars carried livestock, produce, and modern machinery, and Soule and his aides went along to spread the good word about scientific agriculture."

In 1907 the trustees of the University of Georgia turned over 830 acres—the new "enlarged" campus—to the State A & M College. According to Soule, the land was secured "by subscriptions made by the alumni and the good people of Athens." He wrote of the land, "The location is naturally picturesque though the farm was in a decadent condition." He reclaimed the land "from an unsightly condition into a series of beautiful fields and woodland areas" and made it, he said, "one of the most attractively situated educational institutions in the South."

Agricultural Hall was completed in 1909 at a cost of one hundred thousand dollars. The impressive Renaissance Revival structure was the first campus building to have central heat. Soule wrote of Ag Hall, "It stands in a commanding position on the top of Lumpkin Hill, overlooking the classic city of Athens." Indeed, it all but dwarfed Rock House, the beloved home of the antebellum governor Wilson Lumpkin, which became a diminutive neighbor.

Soule built facilities for farm mechanics, agricultural engineering, and veterinary medicine as well as greenhouses, barns, sheds, and cottages for the college's livestock farm. The John J. Wilkins family of Athens turned over their farm to the college for Camp Wilkins, a center for conferences and summer sessions. By 1932 Soule was directing a staff of 129 on campus and 220 county-extension and home-demonstration agents all over the state.

Campus beautification became the order of the day. According to F. N. Boney, "Professor McHatton, beginning the first landscaping program on either campus, introduced bermuda grass as an attractive alternative to the clay and weeds on north campus. Following a common practice of the times, he used twenty-five to fifty convict laborers, who were housed at a stockade nearby on the Oconee River."

In 1918 the university admitted women to its regular undergraduate program for the first time. As the women's suffrage movement reached fruition and women gained the right to vote with the passage of the Nineteenth Amendment to the Constitution on August 26, 1920, Mary Lyndon and Ann Wallis Brumby, the univer-

Since its completion, Memorial Hall has functioned principally as a student activity center. Sanford Stadium, built in a valley just below Memorial Hall, opened in 1929, providing a much-needed facility for university football games. Named in honor of Steadman V. Sanford, a former president of the university and chancellor of the system, the stadium grew to seat more than eighty-seven thousand people by 1991.

sity's first women deans, oversaw the steady integration of women students into campus life, with university enrollment swelling to one thousand for the first time. In 1933 Mary Creswell, one of the first women to graduate from the university, became the first dean of the new School of Home Economics.

Harry Hodgson, an Athens businessman and a 1893 graduate of the university, mounted a massive campaign among alumni and others to raise a fund for the completion of a hall on campus to honor the forty-seven University of Georgia men who died in World War I. More than a thousand university men served in the war. Many were infantry officers active in the last great battles on the western front. Local men and young university students were among that number. During the seventeen-month U.S. involvement in the war, Athens citizens and college students (many enrolled in the Student Army Training Corps) had fought food shortages, a severe and in some cases fatal flu epidemic, and a harsh winter.

Donations for the memorial exceeded one million dollars, including Rockefeller Foundation money and sixty thousand dollars from the university's wealthy friend and benefactor George Foster Peabody. As Memorial Hall neared completion in 1925, Chancellor Barrow (then in his final year of office) composed the words that rim the hall's rotunda: "In loyal love we set apart this house, a memorial to those lovers of peace who took arms, left home and dear ones and gave life that all men might be free."

Next door to Memorial Hall another impressive project soon was under way, for in the wooded valley that separated the north and south campuses, preparation for the construction of Sanford Stadium had begun. To prepare the site, convict labor diverted Tanyard Branch (which ran through the ravine), sealed it in a concrete tunnel, and forever changed the landscape of the campus.

The complexion of athletics changed as well. For Georgia football's first two decades (1892–1911) teams played on the old Herty Field behind the Chapel; from 1911 to 1929 Sanford Field (today the site of Stegeman Hall) was the intercollegiate and intramural playing field. A low-key program that allowed the legendary dean of men Herman J. Stegeman to coach baseball, basketball, track, and football as late as 1920 soon changed as football mania increased and alumni and others made more mobile by the advent of the automobile rolled back into town to see the Bulldogs take the field. As spectators swelled the small college town on autumn weekends and demanded professional athletic staffs to coach the team, the need for a new stadium became acute. On October 12, 1929, the Georgia Bulldogs played their first game in their brand new thirty-three-thousand-seat Sanford Stadium, defeating the Yale Bulldogs 17–0.

The superstructure of the university's administration soon changed as well. In 1932 a reorganization of state higher education under Georgia Governor Richard B. Russell—a University of Georgia alumnus (class of 1918) and for many years chairman of the Senate Armed Services Committee—created a unified system under a board of regents and brought the College of Agriculture (and the State Normal School) under the administration of the University of Georgia. When the regents named Chancellor Charles Snelling chairman of the board in 1932, Dean Sheldon B. Sanford succeeded Snelling and became the first to hold the title of president of the University of Georgia since 1860. Three years later Sanford was named chairman of the Board of Regents. The handsome and highly respected dean of the School of Law, Harmon W. Caldwell, then became president of the university. By 1935 enrollment had mushroomed to over twenty-five hundred students; by 1937 enrollment exceeded three thousand for the first time.

President Caldwell oversaw a construction boom that transformed the campus before the outbreak of World War II. Funding from the Public Works Administration (an arm of President Franklin D. Roosevelt's New Deal designed to rebuild the nation's depressed economy) helped construct seventeen new buildings—dormitories, classrooms, cafeterias, labs, and the Fine Arts Building—and renovated many older campus structures as well.

The Joseph Henry Lumpkin School of Law located on campus for the first time in 1932. Law alumni raised eighty thousand dollars to construct Hirsch Hall on North Campus, and faculty and students moved from cramped quarters downtown in a building on the north side of Broad Street into the new facility.

In 1935 and 1936 the Georgia Rehabilitation Corporation, a government-sponsored agency designed to retire worn-out farm land, acquired the mansion home White Hall and 1,875 adjacent acres from descendants of Clarke County's greatest antebellum industrialist, John Richards White. The agency deeded the land and mansion to the University of Georgia. South of the Whitehall–Watkinsville Road 750 acres of Clarke County land became the Whitehall Experimental Forest, and the White Hall mansion came under the auspices of the School of Forestry.

CHANGING TIMES

For a week in January 1932 all the banks closed during a federally mandated moratorium. Athenian Paul Hodgson recalled, "I had just entered the University and my daddy had given the registrar my forty dollars and told him if the price of cotton went down one-half

Franklin Roosevelt received an honorary doctor of laws degree from the University of Georgia in August 1938. Congratulating the president is Steadman V. Sanford. After brief remarks Roosevelt journeyed to Barnesville, Georgia, to deliver a scathing political speech against Senator Walter F. George, who was running for re-election. In spite of Roosevelt's personal popularity, the senator was re-elected.

cent (from five-and-a-half cents), he would have to withdraw me."

The price of cotton did not go down, and after the Great Depression some small businesses in Athens were able to get loans from the reopened local banks. But many retailers lost out, and the larger manufacturing companies had to get financial assistance from the federal government through funds made available through the National Recovery Act (NRA), part of President Franklin D. Roosevelt's New Deal.

In the mid-1930s the Hodgson enterprises included a cottonseed-oil mill, a cottonseed-oil refinery, and the Empire State Chemical Company on the Winterville Road. "In the fall after the cotton was picked and ginned," recalled Paul Hodgson, "the seed would come in and be put in warehouses. The lint off the cottonseed was bought for gunpowder by Hercules Powder. The hulls went basically for cow feed. We would crack the hulls to get the seed. When the seed got real hot in the presses, it would be squeezed out for oil." The oil was sent to a separate building at the Hodgsons' refinery and made into shortening, which sold around the Southeast for southern cooking. The star customer was the Southern Cotton Oil Company (Crisco) which operated out of New Orleans.

Hodgson remembered, "We sold shortening in 2-, 5-, or 10-pound tin buckets or in commercial vats of 150 pounds. As you drove around the surrounding countryside, nearly every farmhouse had a tin of Hodgson's Crystal Flake Shortening sitting out on the porch." All the cottonseed grown within a forty-mile radius came in in the fall, but tank cars imported cotton oil from farther south year round.

Many companies diversified after the depression. Moss Manufacturing Company became the Athens Lumber Company. Armstrong and Dobbs, which had been a coal and cottonseed company, began to sell oil for heating and then got into the building-supply business.

Athens had the Seaboard Airline Railroad but lost out to Gainesville and Atlanta in attracting a depot for the more aggressive Southern Railroad. Atlanta was surpassing Athens by leaps and bounds as the crossroads for the entire New South. Athens's economy remained a cotton economy through the first half of the twentieth century. Atlanta was sawmill and timber country; all around Athens timber was cut down for acre upon acre of cotton fields. Behind General Hospital in the 1930s, for example, was a two-hundred-acre cotton patch. Other cotton fields lined the Lexington Highway and the Winterville Road all the way to Whitehall.

Few students could afford to buy cars to travel those roads. All through the 1930s students hitchhiked, lining up at major intersections to be picked up by obliging townspeople who were going the students' way. Kappa Alpha fraternity, for example, had in those days one car, which the students drove in shifts. There were few joy rides. Even the city of Athens had only one police car and two motorcycle policemen.

Hard times hit the housing market as well. Many old Athens families were finding it difficult to keep up the great mansion houses in which they had lived gracious lives. One by one some of the old landmarks came on the market, but in depressed times potential buyers for big houses were few and far between. Historic real estate in Athens underwent a decided change as Greek organizations on

In 1896 W. W. Thomas completed a house for his family on Milledge Avenue. Thomas's design reflects the Beaux Arts style made popular during the Columbian Exposition in Chicago. After Thomas's death the house passed into the hands of other owners. In 1913 James Y. Carithers, organizer of the Athens Electric Railway, bought the house, now owned by Alpha Gamma Delta sorority.

campus began to purchase and save some of the finest homes in Athens (principally Milledge and Prince Avenue residences).

One of the first great mansions to change from residential use was the great Greek Revival house that Athens's premier antebellum architect, Ross Crane, had built for himself in 1842. In 1924 the house sold out of private ownership to the Athens Lodge, Order of Elks, for a lodge hall. In 1929 Sigma Alpha Epsilon (SAE) fraternity bought the landmark for $12,500. It has remained a fraternity house ever since.

Kappa Alpha Theta sorority acquired the magnificent Greek Revival A. P. Dearing House (built in 1858) in 1938. The following year Alpha Delta Pi sorority moved into the Italianate Hamilton-Hodgson House, and Alpha Gamma Delta bought W. W. Thomas's Beaux Arts residence from the Carithers family.

Other historic structures, many of more modest size and many in varying states of deterioration, were demolished in an early wave of urban renewal to make way for federal housing in 1938. An increased number of low income families had migrated to the city from the farms, increasing the demand for low rent housing. The city's first urban renewal projects were Parkview Homes (to house 154 white families) and Broadacres (for 126 black families). To provide low rent housing, Athens employed a formula of in-town neighborhood demolition that then recycled the land and offered it to private enterprise for urban redevelopment. Rehabilitation or renovation of existing, though sometimes deteriorating, structures seldom found favor until the historic preservation movement gained momentum in the 1970s. Athens was destined to lose many of the landmarks and neighborhoods that had defined and distinguished its past.

Even the Lucy Cobb Institute bowed to changing times and troubled finances, closing its doors and turning its buildings over to the university in 1931. Clearly the closing of the Lucy Cobb Institute, a school so closely identified with the history of affluence in Athens, signaled a changing of the guard and marked the passing of an era for the self-styled Classic City.

Even though the university neglected the Lucy Cobb Institute for decades after acquiring it, building and acquisitions at the university helped sustain Athens and Clarke County during the Great Depression. During these years the demographics of the county shifted. By 1940 (after the migration of many blacks away from the county during the depression years), nearly two-thirds of the county was white. Only 27.3 percent of the county population was rural.

Manufacturing establishments—principally textiles—employed one-fifth of the county's workforce of twelve thousand people in the early 1940s. Farm-related jobs employed only 9.4 percent of the total number of workers in the county. In addition, 17.2 percent worked as domestics; 13.9 were sales or clerical employees; and 7.4 were professionals (doctors, lawyers, and teachers). Most working women in the county were employed in traditionally accepted fields for women. They worked as domestics, teachers, home-extension agents, and nurses.

The advent of World War II would bring many changes for women and for men in Clarke County. As storm clouds gathered in western Europe, students and townspeople gathered at newsstands downtown each afternoon to await the Atlanta papers so that they could read what the Germans were doing in Poland and Czechoslovakia. Town and county would soon march to a different drummer. Athens would soon turn from a college town to a military town.

6

The Urbanization of Clarke County

Athens's new Neoclassical U.S. Post Office building, a WPA project, opened on Hancock Avenue in 1941 not a moment too soon, for city and county were on a course of rapid expansion that would see the population of the city double over the next four decades and the combined city and county census reach 74,498 by 1980. Seemingly overnight, suburbs, highways, shopping centers, and commercial and industrial development swept through the county, all but consuming the last remaining vestiges of rural landscape. While Athens remained the second largest cotton market in the state from 1930 to 1950, the local postwar economy soon diversified the county's industrial base; a new era had begun.

THE WAR YEARS

Matters domestic—depression, cotton, and altercations political and athletic—preoccupied many Athenians as Hitler marched across Europe. Athens was still "small town." In 1940 most businesses and banks were home-owned, and salaries were marginal as draft registration began and newly mobilized National Guard units camped on the university's polo field. Some 3,631 students survived on hope, good will, and very little spending money under the tutelage of an underpaid faculty.

In the early 1940s football mania knew few bounds. Coach Wallace Butts succeeded Harry Mehre in 1939 and began a twenty-year gridiron reign with players like Frank Sinkwich (1942 Heisman trophy winner) and Charlie Trippi, who led the Bulldogs to a national championship by defeating UCLA in the Rose Bowl on New Year's Day 1943.

This photograph appeared in newspapers on December 24, 1942, under the heading "How Hollywood Helps Georgia Footballers." At right is a wooden model of Ann Sheridan, a movie star who is cheering on members of the football team before the Rose Bowl game. Led by Charlie Trippi and Frank Sinkwich, Georgia defeated UCLA 9–0 on New Year's Day.

A former Georgia football star was elected mayor of Athens in 1940. Robert "Bob" McWhorter was Georgia's first All-American, a running back on the football team from 1910 to 1913, captain of the baseball team, and a member of Phi Beta Kappa. He held a law degree from the University of Virginia and served on the law faculty at the University of Georgia. McWhorter was mayor throughout the war years until 1947. That year Jack R. Wells, a state legislator during World War II who had moved to Athens from Atlanta, won election. Although often controversial, Wells remained mayor for twelve years, his tenure interrupted but briefly by his defeat by Ralph Snow, a popular Athens businessman who served as mayor from 1958 to 1961.

Students postponed confronting the inevitable reality of war as long as possible. LaGrange Trussell Dupree, a former university student from Athens, remembered her 1941 commencement in a class of eight hundred: "I recall a keen sense of excitement and anticipation, despite mounting tensions abroad that would send so many in our class from graduation into military training and then off to war. But we were young and optimistic then. 'Little Commencement' dances traditionally held earlier in the spring initiated the commencement season with big bands like Glen Miller and Artie Shaw. It seemed to me in those years our hearts were always in our throats."

The university's political and academic fortunes, by contrast, enjoyed few victories or celebrations, thanks to gross interference by an alumnus, Governor Eugene Talmadge. Talmadge persuaded the Board of Regents to dismiss the dean of the College of Education, Walter D. Cocking, because of his alleged support for racial integration. Cocking was an Iowan and Jewish, and many accused the governor and his supporters of anti-Yankee sentiment and anti-Semitism. In the summer of '42 members of the Student Political League (financed by another alumnus, Georgia's attorney general, Ellis G. Arnall) toured the state denouncing Talmadge. By September 1942 the university had lost its accreditation from the Southern Association of Colleges and Secondary Schools. Arnall defeated Talmadge in the gubernatorial election later that year. Through legislative restructuring of regents' appointments, Governor Arnall accomplished reaccreditation, but restoration of the university's good reputation was far more difficult to achieve.

University enrollment dropped dramatically as young male students entered the armed services and went to fight a war from which about two hundred sons of the university would never return. With the exodus of college men came an influx of military trainees from all over the country who swelled the population and strained town and campus facilities. In 1940 a new Civilian Pilot Training Service instructed about 250 trainees in leased classroom space downtown in the yellow brick Costa Building on Washington Street. A diminished ROTC program and an enlarged Army Signal Corps and Army Specialized Training Program operated on campus throughout the war. But the navy's preflight school had the greatest impact on Athens.

Georgia's powerful United States senator, Richard B. Russell, and Congressman Carl Vinson, alumni of the university, used their considerable political influence to have the University of Georgia

During World War II thousands of students trained at the naval preflight school in Athens. The navy expropriated numerous campus buildings and erected several others. Here the cadets are running an obstacle course where Boyd Graduate Studies Center now stands.

named as one of five naval preflight schools in the nation. More than six thousand men enrolled in twelve-month classes in Athens when the navy took over much of the campus and renovated the interiors of Old College and Candler Hall (renamed for the duration of the war Ranger Barracks and Yorktown Barracks respectively). The navy headquartered in Baldwin Hall and built several new buildings and recreational facilities, including a gym and swimming pool (later called Stegeman Hall), a new track, four football fields, and a field house (later Alumni Hall). Thus the navy helped bolster the local wartime economy, leaving at war's end a legacy of expanded and renovated campus facilities for which the military had borne more than half the cost. Also thanks to the military, the Athens airport got its first paved runways.

Athens became, for a time, a military town, as soldiers and sailors filled streets, shops, and sleeping quarters. The city council finally allowed movie theaters to open on Sundays to entertain the servicemen. When the Signal Corps students became unduly rowdy in public, however, the council passed an ordinance stopping the sale of beer after midnight. A few Athens women went off to join the WAVES, WACS, or WASPS; but the majority stayed at home or in school. Some took Red Cross courses in home nursing at the Michael brothers' twin houses on Prince Avenue or worked at a cannery on Boulevard. Ration cards, Civil Defense blackout curtains, "victory gardens," the absence of many local men and fear for their safety abroad became facts of life.

POSTWAR ECONOMY

After the war many of the soldiers and sailors who had trained in Athens returned to live and work or finish college. The GI Bill funding college tuition for veterans swelled postwar enrollment and initiated a vast expansion of university and town. Some locals felt this was the second invasion of the Yankees. Even Coach Butts began to recruit northern white boys for his team. The military prefabs (temporary housing) left over on Ag Hill were soon full of young families, typically consisting of a veteran turned family man–student and a working wife.

Outsider-owned businesses multiplied, and mill villages became a thing of the past as locally held corporations that owned the mills sold their properties and offered mill workers an opportunity to buy the homes in which they were living. In some cases, as at Princeton Mill, houses were moved away from the mill site.

Thomas Textiles bought the factory at the old mill site at Whitehall and for many years operated the last remaining water-powered textile plant in Clarke County. The company manufactured clothing rather than the cloth originally produced there. Chicopee Mills, a division of Johnson and Johnson, in 1947 moved into the old Confederate armory, which they bought from the Check Factory, the weaving division of Athens Manufacturing Company. Chicopee, the last to make cloth at one of the county's earliest manufacturing sites, removed the battlements and enlarged the building. In the 1980s the company sold the factory building to the university for conversion to administrative offices and quarters for the Small Business Development Center. The old mill is a study in microcosm of restoration and adaptive use in Athens's historic Warehouse

Lamar Dodd painted Winter Valley *in 1944. During this period Athens and its environs captured Dodd's imagination: "I was fascinated by the monumental quality of the city," the artist recollects. The houses in the foreground were located between North Avenue and the Seaboard Railway. Pictured in the background are the Methodist church, the City Hall dome, and a water tower, then adjacent to City Hall.*

District. It recalls the early manufacturing center's important role in Athens and Clarke County and meets modern needs. The renovated structure is one of the very few architectural artifacts from early Georgia water-powered technology remaining in the state.

By 1949 J. H. Hubert's private bank, founded in 1927, received a state charter as the Hubert State Bank. This bank changed owners and its name, to First American Bank and Trust, in 1962. By 1950 the homegrown Southern Mutual Insurance Company had assets totaling almost $2.5 million; the home-owned National Bank of Athens listed resources in excess of $10 million; and the Athens branch of the Citizens and Southern system—one of twenty-six offices in Georgia and South Carolina—was thriving. Athens was becoming an increasingly attractive place in which to do business.

Two World War II memorials made their mark on the area—the Simon Michael II Memorial Clinic and Memorial Park. In 1944 Max Michael outlined his family's plan to construct a memorial to his son Simon, who had been killed in the war. The Michaels constructed a building facing Hancock Street on City Hall Square to house all the health clinics of the Athens Junior Assembly (later the Athens Junior League), a social and service group founded in 1935 by twenty-five young Athens matrons to channel volunteer efforts to meet the welfare needs of the town. Within ten years the Junior Assembly had become Clarke County's chief source of charity maternity and baby care. The Simon Michael Clinic, dedicated in March 1946, logged 22,238 patient visits by 1948.

Memorial Park, the first city-owned park, developed around the old tuberculosis sanatorium, which was soon converted into a recreation hall. The park and later the zoo were joint efforts of the city and county. Soon the city had plans for another park, a memorial to Mayor A. G. Dudley, the last president of the Athens Manufacturing Company, who had died in 1947.

CULTURAL AMENITIES

In 1939 the Garden Club of Georgia began a fund to create, with the university's landscape architecture department, a series of gardens as a memorial to the twelve founders of the Ladies Garden Club of

In 1941 John Held, Jr., drew this view of the original Founders Memorial Garden planted around an old smokehouse. After World War II, Hubert B. Owens designed an adjoining two-and-one-half-acre arboretum as a memorial to those who had served in the war.

Athens, America's first garden club. Their plans came to fruition in 1946 with the dedication of Founders Memorial Garden, two and one-half university campus acres of formal boxwood gardens, two courtyards, terraces, and a perennial garden arboretum—a natural laboratory for botany, forestry, and landscape design along Lumpkin Street surrounding a handsome residence built in 1857 to house university professors. Hubert B. Owens, sometimes called the "father of landscape design," fashioned a garden that drew copious praise. In April 1955 the *Atlanta Constitution* hailed the garden as "a spot of beauty, charm and tranquillity . . . one of the floral showplaces of the nation." In 1964 the Garden Club of Georgia restored and furnished the university-owned house as a museum and Garden Club headquarters. Professor Owens became the founding dean of the School of Environmental Design in 1969. More than five hundred students earned degrees with the internationally renowned dean, who served terms as president of the American Society of Landscape Architects and as president of the International Foundation of Landscape Architects.

Owens designed numerous residential gardens in Athens and advised many avid local gardeners. When the Greek Revival Grant-Hill mansion on Prince Avenue was acquired from the descendants of industrialist-banker James White to serve as the President's House for the university, Dean Owens redesigned the gardens to accommodate receptions and other social events. Dr. and Mrs. J. C.

In 1949, after sixty-six years of ownership by descendants of James Richards White, the Grant-Hill-White-Bradshaw House was sold to become the home of presidents of the University of Georgia. Generous gifts from the Bradley Foundation of Columbus, in cooperation with the University of Georgia Foundation, enabled the sale of the house to the Board of Regents. Dr. Charles B. Knapp is the fifth university president to reside with his family in the restored landmark.

In 1945 Alfred H. Holbrook moved to Athens, and later that year he presented his art collection to the university. While director of the museum he acquired more than twenty-five hundred objects for the museum from other sources.

Rogers were the first presidential couple to occupy the newly refurbished landmark, followed by Dr. and Mrs. Omer Clyde Aderhold and their daughter, who lived in the house throughout his seventeen-year tenure (1950–67) as president of the University of Georgia.

After the war a seventy-year-old retired New York lawyer and art collector, Alfred Heber Holbrook, came to Athens to study art at the university and to find a home for his impressive art collection. He quickly formed a mentor-patron relationship with Lamar Dodd, an energetic and highly acclaimed artist who in 1938 at the age of

During the 1950s the face of the university campus changed rapidly. Structures like the Greek Revival Lucas House were demolished to make way for classrooms, dormitories, and a new library. The Lucas House, which originally stood at Jackson and Baldwin streets, was moved near the site of Memorial Hall around 1912. The university demolished it in the early 1950s.

twenty-nine had become head of the university's fledgling art department. Through their combined efforts the university opened the Georgia Museum on November 8, 1948, in the basement of the Peabody Library. The original permanent collection—just over one hundred works of art—was Alfred Holbrook's gift in memory of his wife, Eva Underhill Holbrook. Holbrook served as the museum's director and chief benefactor for twenty-five years, personally presenting more than nine hundred works of art to the collection. Wrote the art historian Mary Levin Koch, "An admirer of American art, he made purchases remarkably rich in both diversity and quality . . . as a firm believer in continuing education, Holbrook instituted an outreach program that provided hundreds of people with the opportunity to view museum quality art." At the time there were only two other art museums in the state: the High Museum in Atlanta and the Telfair Museum in Savannah.

Both library and museum quickly outgrew their allotted spaces. The library moved to spacious new quarters in the Ilah Dunlap Little Memorial Library, completed in 1953 at a cost of $1,948,932.

Lamar Dodd, a native Georgian, joined the faculty of the University of Georgia Department of Art in 1937. A year later he became department head. In On the Campus, *painted in 1939, Dodd successfully captured the familiar surroundings of North Campus as well as the mood of quietude and seriousness associated with this period in American history.*

Architect Wilmer Heery renovated the entire old library into a museum, which opened to the public in 1958. Holbrook died in Athens in 1974, just five months shy of his one hundredth birthday.

In 1954 the University of Georgia once again transacted a property deal with the navy. The U.S. Navy Supply Corps School moved from the New York Naval Yard to the Piedmont city of Athens, far removed from coastal waters. The university wanted to sell its Coordinate Campus at Oglethorpe and Prince avenues, formerly the State Normal School (and at the time home to UGA freshmen and sophmores). Georgia Congressman Carl Vinson and Senator Richard Russell convinced the navy to relocate on the university's land. The navy agreed to buy the campus for $450,000. At the thirty-fifth anniversary celebration of the navy's move to Athens, Captain Leonard Sapera, the school's commanding officer, said of the purchase, "It was the fourth greatest land deal made in U.S. history after the Louisiana Purchase, the purchase of Alaska and the Island of Manhattan." Here the navy trains its business managers. More than four hundred officers graduate from a basic six-month course each year; another eighteen hundred, including many foreign officers, attend some of the other eighteen graduate courses.

In 1955, a year after the "naval invasion" of Athens, a Kellogg Foundation grant of $2.5 million built the Georgia Center for Continuing Education on Lumpkin Street on campus land once part of Governor Wilson Lumpkin's farm. The concept of a conference center was a new one nationally. The Georgia Center, state-of-the-art by its completion, became an instant local attraction—a real drawing card for Athens and Clarke County as well as for the university. The design of its 444-seat auditorium drew on plans for the United Nations General Assembly Chamber. Thomas Church, a California landscape architect, designed the graceful grounds around the building, which included conference rooms and guest quarters, indoor and outdoor dining areas, offices, and soon broadcast facilities for educational television station WGTV on Channel 8. The contemporary center brought thousands of people to Athens for course work and conferences.

The Georgia Center proved a boon to the Chamber of Commerce in recruiting business executives and industries to Clarke County.

Hugh Hodgson, chairman of the university's music department from 1928 to 1960, was a leading figure on the Athens cultural scene. He served as organist for several local churches as well as for Saint Luke's Church in Atlanta, where he was also choirmaster. His regular concerts, given on the university campus, introduced many students to classical music. Hodgson composed choral and piano pieces, a ballet, and a concerto for piano and orchestra.

Local boosters had a nucleus on which to build in the early 1950s. In 1951 Clarke County landed its first major "outsider-owned" industry when Dairy Pak, a company based in Cleveland, Ohio, opened a new branch in Athens for the production of milk and juice cartons. The following year Gold Kist began a poultry-processing operation in Clarke County. General Time opened a $2.5 million plant on Newton Bridge Road, where the first Athens-made Westcloxes and Seth Thomases came off the production line in 1954. And in 1957 Westinghouse moved some of its corporate executives to Athens from Sharon, Pennsylvania, to run a new plant.

Roads were not even paved in the new subdivision of Beechwood when local real estate agents began selling large lots for houses to incoming executives. Named for its beech trees, the residential area of modern ranch-style houses soon consumed the Beacham farm on undulating acres that sloped from a newly extended road, West Lake Drive, to the Oconee River. As in other towns across America, the ranch-style house came in vogue in Athens thanks to an increasing dependence on the automobile. Just as the Boulevard and Bloomfield sections were Athens streetcar suburbs of the late nineteenth and early twentieth centuries, now Beechwood became one of the city's first modern suburbs made possible by the mobility afforded by the automobile. Buyers could move out and spread out on wide lots in low-pitched, rambling brick houses that featured such amenities as built-in garages and private outdoor living areas to the rear (rather than the verandas or front porches of earlier and more compact houses on smaller lots "in town"). Tree-shaded Beechwood lots boasted frontages of 100 to 120 feet, a princely property for executives transferred to Athens, Georgia, from urban northern centers.

The advent of home air-conditioning made Athens and its suburbs more attractive to natives and newcomers alike. When air conditioning expanded beyond movie theaters to stores, schools, churches, and workplaces, Athens, like other cities and towns in the deep South, became comfortable during periods of fierce heat. Architects lowered ceilings and eliminated front porches as they designed longer and lower air-conditioned houses.

RACIAL DESEGREGATION

In January 1961 two young black Georgians ended 160 years of segregation when they enrolled in the nation's oldest chartered publicly supported university. Charlayne Hunter and Hamilton Holmes, both former valedictorians of Atlanta high schools, gained admission by order of the U.S. Federal District Court after numerous administratively thwarted attempts to gain acceptance at the University of Georgia. Their matriculation was the beginning of officially integrated public education in the state of Georgia.

The eyes of the nation focused on Athens as the two honor transfer students arrived for registration. Hamilton Holmes lived off campus in the residence of a black Athens family. Charlayne Hunter lived alone in a small suite in Myers Hall. Had she not lived in a dormitory, according to Thomas G. Dyer, "the institution would have violated its own rules, which required all females under the age of twenty-three to reside on campus."

Initially most of the white students, according to Dyer, "greeted their classmates with little more than curiosity. . . . By and large the vast majority of the student body regarded the new students coolly and dispassionately." But before the two students had even entered a classroom, amid rumors that Governor Ernest Vandiver would order President Aderhold to close the integrated university, approximately four hundred students gathered, a crowd that reportedly grew to a thousand as they marched in protest through the streets of Athens. Only the adept skills of the legendary and highly respected dean of men, William Tate, quieted the crowd and averted violence.

Dean Tate's style was to remain in the middle of a potentially unruly crowd and keep talking because, he said, "If you're out front [of the crowd], you might get hurt." Calvin Trillin reported in the *New Yorker* that when the crowd became threatening, Dean Tate began confiscating student identification cards through "an astonishing operation that combined an iron grip, to prevent the prisoner from escaping; a swift movement toward the wallet, to help the boy find the card; and a kindly hold, to keep the terrified boy from falling."

Douglas Kiker described Tate the following day in the *Atlanta Journal:* "He's big. He's aggressive. He looks mean, and he can act mean. But he's really a sentimental fellow, with a heart of gold and an abiding consuming love for the University of Georgia and the students who attend it. And they know it."

Escorted by Dean Tate, plainclothes detectives from the Athens Police Department, and a throng of news reporters, the two black students attended classes the next day without serious incident. Tate biographers John W. English and Rob Williams wrote, "Of all the words written about the desegregation of the University of Georgia, none captured the personal struggle of leadership of Bill Tate better than the wire service photograph, reproduced around the world in newspapers and magazines, of a glaring Tate taking the identification card of a student who had uttered a racial slur as Tate walked Charlayne Hunter to class. The caption read: 'God's Angry Man.' "

But that evening, Wednesday, January 11, following a Georgia Tech victory over Georgia in a basketball game in drafty and leaky old Woodruff Hall gym, violence broke out. Leaving the arena, a

Few Georgians loved their university more than William Tate. As a student, teacher, and dean his affiliation with the school spanned fifty years. Many remember Tate best as the voice of reason during the first tense days of racial desegregation on the university campus in 1961.

large groups of students headed up Lumpkin toward Myers Hall. Growing into an angry mob of several hundred, the crowd threw bricks at Hunter's dormitory, started fires and shouted obscenities while waving a banner that read "Nigger Go Home." University officials and Athens police worked to restore order, but their requests for reinforcements from the Georgia State Patrol drew an unduly slow response (a "procedural misunderstanding," officials claimed). Police finally resorted to tear gas and hoses to disperse the mob. Hunter remained inside (taking refuge in a basement room),

One hundred and sixty years of racial segregation in Georgia public education ended when Hamilton Holmes and Charlayne Hunter entered the University of Georgia. While a student disturbance on their first day of classes resulted in the removal of the two black students by state troopers, public condemnation of the violence led to their reinstatement. They are pictured here in 1985 with university president Fred C. Davison at the inaugural Holmes-Hunter lecture given annually in their honor.

while rocks, bottles, and bricks sailed through the night, smashing sixty window panes in her dormitory, ten in her room.

"As soon as the crowd had retreated into the mist of tear gas," wrote English and Williams, "Dean [of Students Joe] Williams ordered the removal of Charlayne Hunter and Hamilton Holmes from the University for 'their own protection and the well-being of 7,000 other students.'" An injured and bleeding Dean Tate rode with the two students and guards in a state patrol car which sped them through the night to their homes in Atlanta.

On Thursday Dean Williams announced, "They will be withdrawn until such time as the members of my staff and I determine that it is safe and practical for them to return to school." The faculty met in the University Chapel to decry violence and demand the black students' reinstatement. Governor Vandiver, according to Dyer, "publicly condemned the violence and backed away from the massive resistance slogan 'No, Not One.'"

Dave Garroway on the NBC "Today" show was strongly critical of the University of Georgia and its students. Said Garroway of the demonstrators, "They were a mob and they won. If you were living in any part of the world, including this country, what would you think? You have the answer from University of Georgia officials." Then he read the University's suspension statement.

Hunter and Holmes, again by court order, returned to campus January 16 and attended classes. Legal challenges and physical violence had ended. Dean Tate wrote in his annual report for 1960–61: "Four boys were suspended, two others withdrew while suspension was pending, about seventeen were placed on probation for their part, and a total of 94 interviewed in one way or another."

Four months after the desegregation of the University of Georgia, U.S. Attorney General Robert Kennedy came to campus to deliver the tenth annual Law Day lecture at the School of Law—his first formal address since assuming office in the administration of his brother, President John F. Kennedy. "When your moment of truth came," he told his audience, "the voices crying 'force' were overridden by the voices pleading for reason. . . . You are the wave of the future—not those who cry panic. For the country's future you will and must prevail." Kennedy received a standing ovation.

Hamilton Holmes received a bachelor of science degree cum laude in 1963. Among his academic honors was admission to Phi Beta Kappa. He graduated in 1967 from Emory University School of Medicine and practiced orthopedic medicine before heading the medical staff at Grady Hospital in Atlanta. In 1983 he became a trustee of the University of Georgia Foundation. His son is a graduate of the University of Georgia.

Charlayne Hunter (now Hunter-Gault) received a bachelor's degree in journalism in 1963 and went on to a distinguished career as a writer for the *New Yorker* and the *New York Times* and as a news reporter and analyst for the "MacNeil/Lehrer News Hour" on public television. She served on the advisory board of the university's Henry W. Grady School of Journalism and Mass Communication and in 1988 gave the commencement address at graduation ceremonies in Sanford Stadium at the University of Georgia.

During its bicentennial year the university established the Holmes-Hunter Lecture Series to honor its first black graduates. Annually a distinguished scholar or public figure lectures on race relations, aspects of higher education with implications for race relations, or black history.

Despite the fact that events at the University of Georgia struck the first blows for integration in education in Georgia, desegregation of other schools in Athens (as well as throughout the state) was slow in coming. The new all-white Athens High School was only two years old when the 1954 U.S. Supreme Court decision in *Brown* v. *The Board of Education* declared racially "separate but equal" education unconstitutional. In 1955 the court ordered desegregation "with all deliberate speed." In 1956 the city and county public school systems merged, and the all-black Athens High and Industrial School (one of the first accredited black public schools in the state) moved from Reese Street to Dearing Extension, to a new building (named Burney-Harris High School in 1964 in honor of Mrs. A. H. Burney and Samuel F. Harris, former principals and prominent educators). In 1963, under the "freedom of choice" plan adopted by the school board, four young black girls—Wilucia Green, Margie Green, Agnes Green, and Bonnie Hampton—integrated the public school system in Clarke County.

The Susan Building on the corner of West Hancock and Chase streets was the first maternity hospital in Clarke County for black women. Money to erect the medical center came from the local black community and from former Athens residents. The center's founder, Dr. Andrew Jones, ran the medical operations there from 1946 until 1953, when he sold it to Dr. Donarell R. Green. Green, a cofounder of the Northeast Georgia Medical Association (an organization of black physicians), practiced privately in the Susan Building through the mid-1970s. The property was renovated in the early 1980s to house the law offices of Thurmond and Thurmond. This photograph shows visiting physicians during a medical conference held at the center.

Michael Thurmond represents the Sixty-seventh District in the Georgia House. As a legislator Thurmond first focused on rewriting the tax codes and the problems caused by teen drug abuse and teen pregnancy.

Not until 1970 did local school officials prepare to merge totally the separate black and white school systems. Combining two high schools that had not only racially separate but also intensely independent and loyal student bodies, each with its own set of athletic rivals, proved difficult. Despite the efforts of biracial planning committees to seek solutions in advance of a merger, unrest broke out on April 16, 1970, with student violence and vandalism at both Burney-Harris and Athens High School. Superior Court Judge James Barrow issued an injunction restraining thirteen named students and John Does (one through one hundred) "from any acts which might interrupt normal school operations." There followed about a week of racial turmoil and widespread absenteeism. Meetings and negotiations continued throughout that spring and the following summer. Michael Thurmond, then a student at Burney-Harris High School, later reflected, "The April disturbances had proven that a great deal of work remained to be done before the September merger deadline."

In the fall Burney-Harris opened as an integrated junior high school, and Athens High School became Clarke Central High School. The Burney-Harris blue and gold Yellow Jackets and the red and white Athens High School Trojans athletic teams merged as the Clarke Central Gladiators; team colors were red and gold. Blacks and whites shared student leadership roles and formed a coalition for as peaceful a transition as possible.

One of those student leaders was Michael Thurmond, the youngest of nine children in a close and supportive family. He had attended all-black public schools in Athens for eleven years before his senior year, when he was elected copresident of the student council at the newly consolidated Clarke Central. That year he was a football player, coholder of the hundred-yard-dash track record, and a graduation speaker. He subsequently earned a B.A. degree cum laude from Paine College, where he was president of the student government and editor of the school paper. He earned a law degree from the South Carolina Law Center and returned home to practice law and edit for a time a black newspaper. In 1984 Michael Thurmond became the first black elected to the Georgia General Assembly from Athens since Reconstruction and the only black representing a majority white district (in this case 62 percent white).

The first black elected to the Athens City Council was Charles Mack, who served from 1974 to 1975. Ed Turner, a black educator elected in 1980, served eight years on the council.

ADVANCING ATHENS

The Chamber of Commerce reorganized in 1961 as the Athens Area Chamber of Commerce, forged ahead, and changed its slogan from "Tradition with Progress" to "Advancing Athens." The meaning of the change was less than subtle in a period of rapid and sometimes unbridled growth. Between 1960 and 1970 the combined population of city and county increased over 40 percent, topping the state's 16.4 percent increase and the nation's 13.2 percent population growth. Urban dwellers made up 68 percent of the county population by 1977. The vast majority of these citizens were white (79.6 percent in 1970), and the Clarke County School District ranked sixteenth in size among the state's 188 school systems.

During the 1960s and early '70s the university tripled in size and expanded to South Campus into state-of-the-art science facilities. Meanwhile, industrial development and massive infusions of federal money sent Athens and Clarke County into a developmental frenzy.

A number of new schools—both private and public—opened in Clarke County in the 1960s and 1970s. New public schools on the growing east side of Athens included Patti Hilsman Middle School (1965), Barnett Shoals Elementary School (1968–69), and Cedar Shoals High School (1971). A private college preparatory school, Athens Academy, opened in 1967 on residential property at the then-hilly corner of Prince and Hawthorne Avenues in a red barn and a handsome Colonial Revival house (formerly the home of Dr. Harvey W. Cabaniss, Sr., and his family). The academy grew and moved to property donated by Marion Ivey, an Athens realtor, on rolling acres just into Oconee County south of town. The house itself was moved straight out West Lake Drive. Sawed in half and then reassembled, it underwent another metamorphosis on yet another hill as an impressive residence facing Greenbrier Court.

In 1961 local citizens elected Robert G. Stephens, Jr., to Congress. During his sixteen years in the U.S. House of Representatives, Stephens concentrated on issues involving housing and banking. He is photographed here with his son, Lawton, a representative to the Georgia House for the Sixty-eighth District from 1987 until his appointment in April 1991 as judge of the Superior Courts for the Western Judicial Circuit.

Athens Federal Savings Bank rearranged the configuration of the home's former site and built a branch bank of marble there.

Meanwhile other private schools opened in town as well. Athens Christian School went up in temporary buildings just north of town in 1970, offering classes in all grades. In 1978 Athens Montessori School was incorporated. And Saint Joseph's Catholic School, opened in 1949, enrolled students through the eighth grade in expanded classroom space.

An impressive YMCA complex on Hawthorne Avenue opened in 1967. The old YMCA building, constructed on the corner of Clayton and Lumpkin streets in 1889, was demolished in the early 1970s. The land became a parking lot for the Holiday Inn. The Young Women's Christian Organization occupied the Stevens Thomas House on Pulaski Street, a site they had acquired in 1911. On the corner of that lot they had erected in 1913 a then-modern gymnasium and swimming pool. (Later, in 1981, the women's organization moved out to new facilities on Research Road and the house became law offices).

The hospitals too expanded to serve the growing populace. The Hospital Authority of Clarke County, with a seven-member board, assumed ownership of Athens General in 1960. Additions and renovations followed in rapid succession throughout the sixties and seventies. In 1968 the hospital grew from 196 beds to 274. In the

The history of Athens Regional Medical Center dates to 1919, when a twelve-bed medical facility opened in a private home. Two years later Athens General Hospital, as it was then called, opened at its present site on Prince Avenue. Since that time the hospital has undergone six major expansions, enlarging its physical plant and patient-care facilities, and introducing the most technologically advanced equipment available. Modern additions include new operating rooms, a birthing center, a substance-abuse treatment center, and a separate out-patient surgery facility. Today the Athens Regional Medical Center staff handles major trauma cases for all of northeast Georgia.

eighties Athens General literally gobbled up the properties surrounding it (including residences large and small, a church, and a shopping center) as it mushroomed with new buildings and services and (by 1989) a new name as Athens Regional Medical Center.

Athens's first hospital, founded in 1906, grew as well. Under the administration of the Order of the Missionary Sisters of the Sacred Heart of Jesus, who took over the physician-owned hospital in 1938, Saint Mary's Hospital grew out of its expanded buildings on Milledge Avenue, selling that property (demolished in the early 1970s) and constructing a large new hospital on Baxter Street in the mid-1960s. Saint Mary's continued to operate as a nonprofit facility without any tax or financial support from the city or county and without any subsidy or grant from the Roman Catholic church. Like Athens Regional Hospital, Saint Mary's continued to expand in the 1980s as Athens became the medical center for thousands of patients across northeast Georgia.

Three movements swept rapidly through the town and county—urban sprawl, urban renewal, and demolition of many of the earliest houses and in-town neighborhoods. With annexation on January 13, 1963, the city limits incorporated thirteen square miles.

Clarke County's first hospital opened in 1906 under the direction of Drs. Henry M. Fullilove and J. Peeble Proctor. In 1938, a year after this facility closed, the Missionary Sisters of the Sacred Heart of Jesus reopened the institution as Saint Mary's Hospital. The present Baxter Street building opened in 1965. Saint Mary's offers state-of-the-art equipment with diagnostic procedures such as ultrasounds, CAT scans, and nuclear medicine. Saint Mary's places special emphasis on community health-education programs, and the hospital was one of the first in Georgia to offer a home healthcare program with a full range of services.

Clarke, the smallest county in the state in area, ranked fourteenth in population. The Athens Industrial Development Corporation had helped attract one hundred plants employing six thousand workers. And by 1963 Athens had its first shopping center, Beechwood. The shopping-center syndrome soon expanded across suburbia. Across from Beechwood construction began on the Alps Road Shopping Center on the former site of a drive-in movie theater built on a cow pasture and cotton field. Other shopping centers opened on the east and north sides of town.

As franchised businesses gained popularity across the United States in the 1950s and 1960s, Athens began to feel the visual impact of "signature architecture" (Howard Johnson's orange roof, for example) and "portable identifiers" (such as Kentucky Fried Chicken's giant bucket sporting the bearded Colonel's enlarged visage; McDonald's golden arches; and eventually the emblazoned Taco Bell). Through the ensuing years city council wrestled with sign ordinances as the contemporary urban boulevards of Athens (Baxter, Broad, Alps Road, and more) filled with a carnival of neon signs, plastic architecture, and billboards that created a "pop art" townscape along increasingly numerous urban thoroughfares.

URBAN RENEWAL

In 1964 the city and the Department of Urban Renewal launched the largest and most ambitious program in the history of Athens, a two-part undertaking designated Project 50 and Project 51. Julius Bishop, president of Athens Federal Savings and Loan Association, was mayor (1963–75); Paul Hodgson, great-grandson of the founder of the city's first stagecoach line, directed urban renewal. Bishop and Hodgson carried out a plan inaugurated by a former mayor, Jack Wells. Hodgson replaced the city's first urban renewal director, R. W. Bowstum, the retired captain of the Navy Supply Corps School.

Project 50 affected an area south and north of Baxter Street between Finley and Hull Streets extending to Cloverhurst Avenue. By March 1967 this project was complete, with the purchase of forty acres of land for more than $1 million, the relocation of eighty

Hands-on rehabilitation characterized the renaissance of historic Cobbham. John English is seen here replacing the Gothic Revival trim on the porch of his Prince Avenue home.

families, the rebuilding of streets, and the sale of all of the land to the University of Georgia for more than $200,000. Explained Mayor Bishop in a review of his twelve-year administration, "Due to a system of credits through the urban renewal program, the city was able to do this for a cash outlay of just over $10,000 and still have over $400,000 in credits remaining. The University in turn placed more than $12 million worth of improvements [including the high-rise dormitories Russell, Brumby, and Creswell] on this land which was formerly a slum in the heart of the City of Athens."

Project 51 involved the condemnation, purchase, and subsequent demolition of slightly more than 3 percent of the city's land—128 acres or an area equivalent to 160 football fields—on both sides of College Avenue in the northern part of downtown. Affected as well was the area bounded by the Seaboard Railroad to the north and the Oconee River to the west, acreage that included several parcels along Washington and Pulaski streets. The $5.5 million Project 51, involving 310 parcels of land and 350 structures, demolished slums and historic landmarks alike (including Athens's only synagogue and the old Southern Mutual Building) and relocated (or sometimes

In 1971 the imposing 1905 brick and stone structure on downtown College Avenue that originally housed the main post office and federal courts was threatened with demolition. The First American Bank and Trust Company stepped in and saved the building. After careful restoration and renovation the structure became the bank's home office. This action marked the earliest significant adaptive re-use of a commercial building in downtown Athens.

The Ware-Lyndon House, a two-story Italianate building, overlooks downtown Athens at the north end of Jackson Street. It is the only surviving structure from the once-fashionable Lickskillet neighborhood. Built by Edward R. Ware, a prominent physician, the house was sold to Edward S. Lyndon in 1880. Lyndon was a druggist and owner of Lyndon Mill, forerunner of the Athens Lumber Company. Purchased by the city of Athens in 1939, the landmark underwent major restoration in 1960. Since 1973 the Ware-Lyndon House has served as a community arts center and is an excellent example of preservation and utilization of a historic structure. This photograph, circa 1850, shows Andrew Jackson Lyndon, Jr., nephew of Edward Lyndon, seated on the front steps.

dislocated) "no income" families in a massive effort to clear out substandard housing and stimulate development. The three R's of the project were revitalization, redevelopment, and rehabilitation. Project 51 rerouted streets, created a four-lane bypass north of Athens (on land the city would sell to the state), and with the aid of the Athens Public Housing Authority, built new housing for the elderly and indigent.

Demolished was the early Athens neighborhood Lickskillet, which included some of the oldest houses in town. At one point, there was even talk of tearing down City Hall. Original revitalization plans called for the demolition of the old Federal Building for a parking lot. Instead, in 1971 First American Bank bought the government building and adapted the interior for their headquarters.

"If progress can be measured in what is torn down," proclaimed the *Athens Daily News* on February 26, 1967, "then Athens's ambitious urban renewal program is well on its way to complete success."

"A climb to the top of the courthouse and [a] peek due north will give the viewer a panoramic look at intentional devastation," the paper reported. With the "antiquated" and "dilapidated" gone, the paper proclaimed, "the year 1967 is going to be remembered as the year buildings started going up in the project instead of coming down." What went up over the next several years was a federal housing project (Bethel Homes), a ten-story high-rise apartment complex for the elderly (Denney Towers), a new federal building (named for Robert G. Stephens, the retired Tenth District congressman), a motel and shopping and dining complex (History Village), offices and business establishments, a public library, and parking lots. The city cut short Thomas Street and Strong Street in order to curve and widen Dougherty and destroyed many of Athens's prized old trees in the process. History Village investors moved the Federal-period Hoyt House (once the home of a Presbyterian minister, Nathan Hoyt), from State and Hoyt streets to their newly acquired acres and converted the old brick buildings of the Athens Boiler and Machine Shop for shops and offices.

Among the houses on Hancock Avenue slated for demolition was the city's oldest surviving residence, the Church-Waddel-Brumby House, built in 1820 for Alonzo Church, later president of the

University of Georgia, and sold to university president Moses Waddel soon thereafter. In the 1960s the house belonged to the Brumby family, whose ancestors had purchased the property from the Waddels in 1834.

Local citizens, alarmed at the prospect of the loss of yet another historic landmark, banded together to form the Athens-Clarke Heritage Foundation (ACHF) to preserve this two-rooms-up, two-rooms-down historic residence. In October 1967 ACHF arranged for the removal of the house from its original lot on the north side of Hancock between Jackson and Thomas streets to a site several hundred feet away on a corner newly created by rerouting Dougherty Street. There the house sat forlornly for four years, boarded up on a weed-choked lot, while its supporters sought restoration funding and its detractors ridiculed the effort to save the house. But in 1972, thanks to funding from the city and local citizens and a grant from the U.S. Department of Housing and Urban Development (HUD), ACHF restored the house to its original appearance and deeded it, furnished with period antiques (most provided by Albert Sams, a local philanthropist and retired businessman), to the city of Athens.

The 1820 Church-Waddel-Brumby House is one of the few surviving structures from the city's earliest decades. The house was built for the Alonzo Church family but never occupied by them; its first resident was most likely the Reverend Moses Waddel. Owned thereafter by Sarah H. Harris and then Colonel Benjamin F. Hardeman, the house finally passed to the Brumby family.

Operated as a house museum and Athens Welcome Center, the Brumby House, landscaped and loved, became a popular tourist attraction.

ACHF also managed another preservation coup during this period. When owners of the historic Franklin House (the old Athens Hardware building) planned to demolish the historic structure for new commercial development, the foundation hurriedly raised seventy-five thousand dollars through individual contributions, guaranteed loans, and an emergency grant from Governor Jimmy Carter in order to buy the property and the demolition contract. Through the Georgia Department of Natural Resources, the foundation secured yet another grant—this one for thirty thousand dollars—to stabilize the structure. Hugh Fowler, an Athens businessman, bought the building in late 1971, removed rear additions, began restoration, and in the early 1980s sold it to new owners who completed an award-winning and thorough renovation for offices.

Federal dollars continued to pour into Clarke County, affecting almost all aspects of community development. The U.S. Environmental Protection Agency (EPA) built a research laboratory in 1966, and the U.S. Department of Agriculture (USDA) constructed

The parlor of the Church-Waddel-Brumby House is restored to its original elegance. The handsome Adamesque mantel features two engaged reed columns, each crowned by a sunburst. The wood paneling and molding are original to the house. The mirror, more than a century old, and round mahogany tilt-top table—also original to the house—are on loan from the Brumby family.

the towering Richard B. Russell Agricultural Research Center in 1970, changing the landscape on College Station Road as the city grew eastward past the university's dairy barns and pasture lands to Barnett Shoals Road and beyond.

Athens became one of the most successful participants in the nation under the federally funded Model Cities Program. As a Model City from 1970 to 1975, Athens received $9,479,000 in federal grants from HUD as well as matching grants (state and federal) of more than $6,150,000. And so the city got a new transit system, child-development and senior-citizens programs, preschool and adult education, recreation and parks improvements, youth counseling and police-community relations programs, water and sewer improvements, bridges, streets, sidewalks, and more. The projects created jobs and expanded the area's economic base.

After Model Cities funding, Community Development funds infused $9.7 million in federal money into the city for further public improvements over the next three years. All of these programs helped attract new industries and new people—the employed and the unemployed—to Clarke County.

VANISHING ATHENS

Several natural disasters hit the city amid this prosperity. In the summer of 1964 a devastating flood occurred when eleven inches of rain fell on portions of the city in about three hours. Two tornadoes in 1973, two months apart, caused extensive property damage. The first, on March 31, killed one person, destroyed more than one hundred trailers, and damaged or obliterated houses in Forest Heights subdivision and along Prince Avenue and the Boulevard area. On May 28 the second tornado followed much the same path from Holiday Estates and Forest Heights to the Navy School, Boulevard, and Pulaski and Tibbits streets before exiting via the edge of East Athens. Damage was extensive. The storm ripped through the rear of the YMCA building on Hawthorne Avenue (crowded at the time with young boys assembled for activities). Fortunately, it was

In 1974, when developers threatened to demolish the historic Franklin House, local preservationists banded together and in two weeks managed to raise the necessary funds to save the building. A nineteenth-century structure, the Franklin House was originally a hotel and later the Athens Hardware Store. Today it houses several businesses.

According to a legend dating from the late nineteenth century, Professor William Jackson, in order to preserve a favorite white oak tree, deeded the tree into its own possession. Over the decades the tree became diseased. Acorns were gathered from it, and in 1946, four years after the great tree fell, one of the seedlings was replanted at the spot where the original tree had stood at the intersection of Dearing and Findley streets. Pictured here planting the new tree are Patsy Dudley, Elizabeth Magill, Mayor Robert L. "Bob" McWhorter, LaGrange Trussell, and Katherine Michael. The Junior Ladies Garden Club still maintains the tree and its small plot.

after school hours when the raging storm completely destroyed the Oglethorpe Elementary School nearby. The fire department responded to sixteen calls and two major fires as trees fell on houses and blocked many city streets. Although local hospitals treated numerous cases of minor injuries, miraculously no lives were lost. But much of the historic landscape, including hundreds of Athens's prized old trees, was gone.

Demolition, both natural and man-made, seemed the order of the day as Athens began to lose more and more of its historic structures. Among the landmarks vanished forever from the townscape were the twin Neoclassical Michael mansions, demolished in the early 1960s for two unremarkable office structures dwarfed both figuratively and literally by their monumental neighbors (the Taylor-Grady House and the President's House). Similarly, other stately structures along Prince, once one of the nation's finest boulevards, fell to the wrecking ball, replaced by commercial and professional buildings, parking lots, and eventually fast-food establishments. A few great mansions remain scattered along Prince Avenue, recycled reminders of an earlier and more graceful time and place.

One graceful reminder is the 1847 Franklin-Upson House on

Prince Avenue, a monument to historic preservation and adaptive use. In 1974 the city's oldest bank (then the oldest bank in the South operating under its original charter), First National (later Trust Company Bank), bought the Greek Revival mansion from descendants of the Upson family, who stipulated that the house could not be destroyed. The bank undertook a sterling restoration of the house, adapting the main structure for offices and adding a modern though thoroughly compatible rear wing for a vault and drive-through windows. The giant magnolia-flanked mansion with its Doric columns, silver-plated doorknobs, parquet floors, nine-foot windows, and fourteen-foot ceilings, was listed on the National Register of Historic Places in 1973. The bank received numerous awards for the restoration. The Athens-Clarke Heritage Foundation hailed the end result as "a model for the whole country of both the aesthetic and the practical possibilities in the adaptive use of a beautiful structure."

But the destruction of a treasury of other historic sites was not peculiar at the time to Prince Avenue, for Milledge Avenue and Dearing Street suffered bitter losses as well. Gone, for example, were the Queen Anne Phinizy-Hodgson House (replaced by the Varsity, set anachronistically among a grove of enormous old magnolia trees) at Broad and Milledge; the William Dearing House at Milledge and Dearing (for the Medical Arts Center Building); the Italianate, cupola-adorned Thomas-Swift-Cofer House on Dearing (for the Dearing Garden Apartments); and the graceful Mell residence (built in 1848) for a new Milledge Avenue sorority house, Zeta Tau Alpha. Many other Greek Revival, Italianate, Queen Anne, Gothic Revival, and vernacular style houses disappeared.

Athens Federal Savings and Loan Association (later Athens Savings Bank) on Hancock Street replaced the sadly deteriorated Gerdine House (circa 1834); a university parking lot at Hull and Florida avenues gives no clue that it was once the site of the Greek Revival home of Dr. Crawford W. Long, discoverer of the anesthetic effect of ether; and Magic Years of Learning Day Care Center on Harris Street replaces the stately antebellum home of John B. Cobb. A complete list would form a litany of irrevocable loss in terms of architectural heritage in a city proclaiming itself the Classic City.

Under the leadership of its president, Thomas H. Milner, the First National Bank of Athens (later the Trust Company Bank of Northeast Georgia) renovated the historic Franklin-Upson House as a branch bank in 1974. This adaptive use of this landmark set high standards for historic preservation in Athens and received local and state awards and national recognition.

One of Athens's earliest examples of preservation, however, occurred in 1966 when the city of Athens purchased the deteriorating Taylor-Grady House and in 1968 leased it to the Athens Junior Assembly. The Junior Assembly in turn raised the funds to restore the house, furnished it through generous donations of period pieces (many from Albert Sams), and generated revenue to maintain the building and grounds through rental fees. Listed on the National Register of Historic Places in 1976, the house became a National Historic Landmark in 1988—the only site in Athens to receive this significant designation. This popular tourist attraction, a house that the New South spokesman and famed journalist Henry Grady recalled as his "old Southern home with its lofty pillars, and its white pigeons fluttering down through the golden air," became the setting for many weddings, receptions, and other social affairs.

DOWNTOWN REVITALIZATION

In January 1965, in a study commissioned by the Athens Area Chamber of Commerce, the architectural planning firm of Heery and Heery submitted a report entitled "The Classic City?" They noted that the town still could boast "a number of exceptional examples of Classical and Greek Revival architecture" and "several handsome, almost European-like, tree-lined boulevards." They acknowledged the dominant influence of the university on the state and region and the town's traditional place as the business and shopping center of northeast Georgia. "Athens," they said, "is certainly among the more important cities of the state with a somewhat special role and a strong economy. But there are dark clouds on the horizon." Downtown was in trouble. "The fact that the town center has been failing has resulted in an economic deterioration of property values as well as a loss of visual quality," said the report. "This materially and spiritually affects the future of Athens."

Heery followed with a proposal that included a plan to turn Clayton Street from College to Thomas streets into a pedestrian mall. While this imaginative scheme failed to gain approval, the chamber and the city did begin to focus upon historic downtown as the heart and soul of the city, a spiritual as well as a visual forum or meeting place for the community. They began to take important steps to insure the continued viability of downtown as the social, retail, and financial center of Athens and Clarke County.

Downtown merchants formed the Athens Downtown Council in 1973 to work together toward economic revitalization. The Federal Tax Reform Act of 1976 stimulated rehabilitation of historic structures by providing tax credits to investors. Citizens approved a constitutional amendment to create a special downtown tax-assessment district in 1976. Through the efforts of the Athens-Clarke Heritage Foundation, the Downtown Historic District was placed on the National Register of Historic Places in 1978. This designation enabled downtown property owners to become eligible for federal tax credits in renovating their properties. That year the city formed the Athens Downtown Development Authority (ADDA), a public corporation designed to stimulate investment through economic incentives. Through ADDA local banks and sav-

City Hall, one of the most imposing structures in downtown Athens, occupies the highest point in the central business district. L. F. Goodrich, an Augusta architect, designed the building, which was completed in 1904. A transportation mall built in the mid-1980s on College Avenue and Washington Street complements the extensive landscaping of City Hall grounds.

ings and loan associations created a loan pool at 5 percent interest. Upshaw Bentley, an Athens attorney who served the city as mayor from 1976 to 1979, hailed this arrangement as "a significant partnership between Mayor and Council and the private sector . . . a positive impact on the revitalization of downtown."

The Athens Transit System began service in the city November 1, 1976, providing bus transportation in and out of downtown. A series of successful restorations at Clayton and College in 1979 signaled the "corner comeback" and generated enthusiasm for other projects. ADDA director Joe Burnett said of the period, "We focused considerable attention on 'paint-up, fix-up' projects . . . a new paint job or exterior cleaning, a new sign or an awning. In some cases aluminum siding or stucco panels, the '50s fad, hid lovely architectural detail on original façades on turn-of-the-century buildings rich in architectural detail."

Downtown beautification became a priority under the Bentley administration. The city's Department of Recreation and Parks planted numerous trees and shrubs, and landscaped streets, parking lots, and the grounds of City Hall (including a new plaza for the double-barreled cannon). An underground system of wiring enabled the city to remove downtown utility poles and unsightly overhead wires; a new sign ordinance went into effect; and City Hall got a face-lift inside and out.

Around the perimeter of downtown the construction of a southeast bypass progressed. Athena and Paradise Valley industrial parks developed along the northeast bypass. Athens continued to attract new industries. Among these were Kendall and Reliance Electric (in 1968), Del Mar (1970), DuPont (1972), and Certain-Teed (1975). Older homegrown industries thrived as well. They included the McGregor Company and Tanner Lumber Company, founded in Athens in 1888 and 1897 respectively, and several companies founded in the early twentieth century, including L. M. Leathers, Athens Coca-Cola Bottling Company, Benson's Bakery, and Wilkins Industries.

A feisty new weekly newspaper started up in town as well, when two young Georgians began publishing the *Athens Observer* in an artist's loft downtown. In 1974 a Greensboro native named Pete McCommons and a young man from Thompson, Chuck Searcy, found themselves temporarily out of work. McCommons (a graduate and a former member of the faculty of the University of Georgia) had worked for a labor union, and Searcy, a Vietnam veteran, had been working for George McGovern's campaign for the presidency. Almost on a whim, the two small-town boys began on a shoestring—with the help of any number of students and local citizens—what would become a highly popular and successful publication. Publisher McCommons would reflect: "*The Observer* came along at a time when there was a burgeoning group of people here with a '60s mentality. The '60s seemed to arrive in Athens in the '70s. Activist students and professors on campus seemed ready for a new voice, and mainstream Athenians seemed titillated by our more liberal yet folksy editorial approach. We lucked into the right time and place to start a weekly."

With no staff and no writers, the paper, desperate for copy, stumbled into the tradition of encouraging talented local people to contribute columns. Don Nelson, later the editor, joined the staff as a photographer, teaching himself as he went along and developing his photos in an old bathroom he converted to a darkroom. The first run of ten thousand copies free to the public simply whetted the appetite of Athenians for more. For a time volunteers delivered the paper door to door. Eventually the paper turned to paid subscriptions and went from free classified ads to regularized billing for advertising in order to insure its stability as a new institution in Athens.

THE UNIVERSITY

During the administration of President O. C. Aderhold, enrollment in the university doubled. His vigorous building program increased the value of the physical plant to $100 million, including a $15 million science center and a $4 million sports coliseum (opened in 1964) and enlarged football stadium.

A young Alabaman, Vince Dooley, began his legendary twenty-five-year career as head football coach at the University of Georgia in 1964. Although the university had been integrated since 1961, a decade passed before black athletes played intercollegiate sports for the Bulldogs. Ronnie Hogue, a basketball star, was the first black to

Few individuals have had greater impact on sports at the University of Georgia than Vince Dooley. As head football coach, Dooley amassed a 201-77-10 record, including a national championship in 1980. Under Dooley's leadership as athletic director, Georgia teams in men's and women's programs led the Southeastern Conference in combined all-sports points throughout the 1980s.

As a teacher and faculty advisor at the University of Georgia, Dean Rusk, a native Georgian, made himself readily available to students and became a popular figure campuswide. Traveling tirelessly across the state, he served as a goodwill ambassador on behalf of the university.

play a major sport at Georgia (1971–73); Horace King was the school's first black football player (1972–74). There was little emphasis on women's sports until the mid-1970s.

Veterinarian Fred C. Davison, the thirty-seven-year-old vice-chancellor of the University System, began a twenty-year tenure as president of the university in 1967. He inherited the presidency at a volatile time characterized by student unrest, an assertive and diverse faculty, and institutional growing pains. Record legislative appropriations to the University System in 1967 provided a windfall of over $34 million for the University of Georgia, a 70 percent increase over the previous year's allocation. With this sudden largess the university immediately hired 450 new faculty members. Enrollment soared, and the influx of new faculty families to Athens proved a boon to local realtors and lending establishments.

Thomas G. Dyer wrote, "By 1967 signs appeared of a shift in student attitudes and a drift toward student activism." Even on this traditionally conservative campus, where in 1966 five thousand students and some faculty signed petitions "affirming" U.S. involvement in Vietnam, a number of Georgia students joined the national mainstream opposing the war in Vietnam. "At the same time," according to Dyer, "a variety of other causes and movements such as feminism and civil rights activism gained footholds on campuses and attracted adherents." Several hundred students marched and staged a "sit-in" in the Academic Building in 1968 for "coed equality" and fewer regulations for all students. Dyer judged the spring protests of 1968 "rather feeble compared to the strident and violent protests occurring elsewhere." He adds, however, that by 1970 "virtually all distinctions in conduct regulations based upon gender had disappeared."

In spring 1970, however, the killing of student demonstrators on the campus of Kent State University quickly intensified the antiwar movement on the Athens campus. Demonstrations began in earnest, growing at one point from one thousand marchers on the president's home to four thousand dissenters parading down Milledge Avenue to the Academic Building to demand cancellation of classes in protest of the events at Kent State. Once again Dean William Tate was a calming presence, donning love beads and

sitting among student activists. Three students were arrested and released before another march began. Dyer concludes, "The close involvement of faculty members in the protest helped to prevent violent confrontations."

Ironically, 1970 was also the year in which former U.S. Secretary of State Dean Rusk joined the faculty as Samuel Sibley Professor of International and Comparative Law. Rusk had orchestrated foreign policy throughout the administrations of Presidents John F. Kennedy and Lyndon B. Johnson. In 1977 Philosophical Hall (later Waddel Hall) became the Dean Rusk Center for International and Comparative Law.

By the mid-1970s student activism at the University of Georgia gave way to a new conservatism and a wave of student pranksterism, including nude "streaking" on campus and on city streets. Once again Athens made the national news.

On a more pastoral note, the early years of the Davison administration saw the establishment of the University of Georgia Botanical Garden. In 1968, 293 Clarke County acres and five miles of nature trails along the Oconee River became a "living plant library." Dr. Francis E. Johnstone, a university horticulturist, was the garden's first director. In 1973 the Callaway Foundation of LaGrange, Georgia, provided a grant for a botanical headquarters facility as the focal point of all garden activities.

A $6 million journalism-psychology complex opened in 1968.

Since 1858 the wrought-iron arch on Broad Street at College Avenue has been the main entryway to the University of Georgia campus from downtown Athens. Francis Chapin captured the venerable symbol in this 1952 lithograph. To the left is the ornately columned Academic Building; and beyond the arch Chapin depicts the old Colonial Hotel and the City Hall cupola.

The university established the School of Environmental Design in 1969 and soon expanded the Institute of Ecology under the direction of Eugene Odum, internationally renowned as "the father of ecology." The library got a new annex. Governor Jimmy Carter participated in 1974 ceremonies naming the large library addition in memory of Senator Richard B. Russell.

The School of Forest Resources received an award from the Georgia Trust for Historic Preservation in 1978 for restoring White Hall to its original 1892 splendor. This showplace, built by the Athens industrialist John Richards White, went on the National Register in 1979. Funds derived from the sale of insect-killed timber at Whitehall and other university-owned forests made the restoration of the vacant property possible.

University enrollment doubled in twenty years (1960–80) to twenty-five thousand students as the building boom continued. Campus architecture became increasingly indistinguishable from that of other major state universities across the nation, but the historic North Campus, listed on the National Register of Historic Places in 1970, continued to serve as a reminder of the timeless classical origins of the college and a town.

Thus local citizens fifty years of age and over had seen town and county transformed over the previous four decades. In 1940 they may have been residents fanning themselves on front porches as they listened to radio news reports of Hitler's latest perfidy. In 1980 those same residents might watch a black running back carry the ball for the Bulldogs on color television sets in air-conditioned suburban family rooms. Town life became more comfortable and yet more complex.

7

Into the Eighties and Beyond

The changes wrought in the 1960s and 1970s and the federal dollars that infused the local economy threw Athens and Clarke County into the national mainstream. The decade of the 1980s became a time for maturing, for coming to terms with those changes, and for rediscovering that which was unique and valuable in defining this place. It was a time of self-awareness and re-evaluation.

The key issues in the 1980s for both county and city were quality-of-life issues: maintaining a sense of place in an ever-changing environment; protecting natural and historic resources and their accessibility while encouraging quality development and economic diversity; insuring equality; and improving education, housing, health, and human services for all citizens.

One of the thorniest issues of the 1980s was zoning—land-use regulation. Planning became ever more a priority and a necessity. The Athens–Clarke County Planning Commission, the Northeast Georgia Area (later Regional) Planning and Development Commission, Chamber of Commerce subcommittees, mayor and council, and the county commission dealt daily with matters of land and property usage as the county's population increased. Most of the county's growth in the 1980s took place in the unincorporated areas. Inside the city limits of Athens the population grew very little, despite a couple of annexations during the decade.

Clarke County easily led northeast Georgia (an area generally considered to include fifteen counties) in growth throughout the decade. Clarke held its own around fourteenth in ranking among the state's most populous counties. According to census figures Clarke County's population increased by roughly 17.6 percent (from 74,498 in 1980 to 87,594 in 1990). The population of Athens grew by 7.5 percent (from 42,549 to 45,734) as the city retained its position as the seventh largest in the state and for the first time surpassed Augusta, now ranked eighth. Like the "bedroom" counties surrounding ever-burgeoning Atlanta, the counties around Athens felt a real spillover in terms of population growth as well. Oconee County, for example, grew more than 40 percent over the decade, while Madison increased by 18.6 percent, Jackson by 18.4 percent, and Oglethorpe by 9.3 percent.

Pete McCommons summed up the 1980s in an article for *Athens Magazine* (December 1989) entitled "What a Difference a Decade Makes." He wrote, "Everything's bigger: the university, the hospitals, the banks, the churches, the housing projects, the luxury homes, the streets, the courthouse, the football stadium, the music industry." Some of the changes reflected national trends; others were unique to this place.

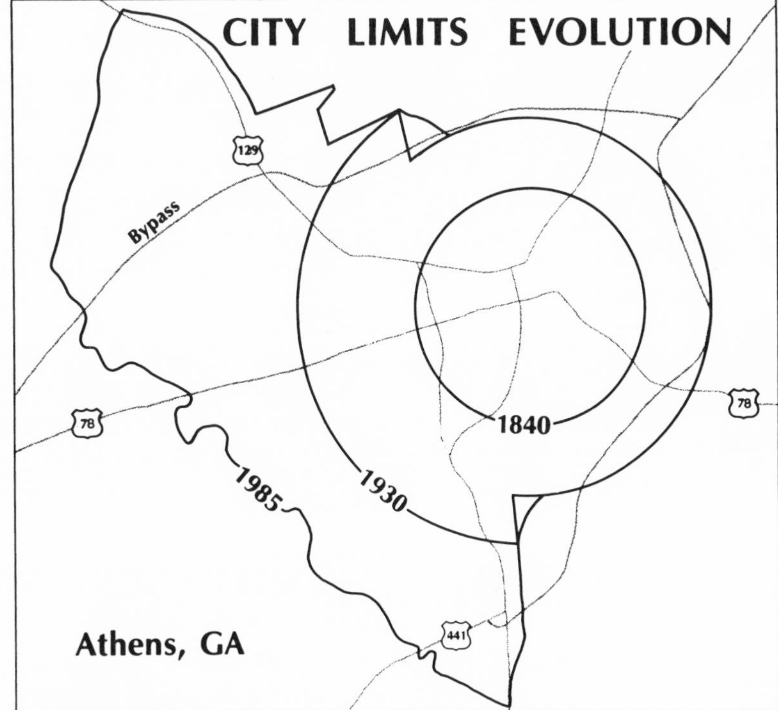

In 1840 the University Chapel was the fixed center of Athens city limits. Corporate expansion in the early twentieth century continued to radiate from this center in a more or less circular fashion. According to geographers, small southeastern towns, particularly in the Georgia Piedmont, often grew in this fashion. However, in the 1980s Athens, like other growing urban centers, finally broke this circular pattern. Thereafter additional land to the west was surveyed and attached to the circle.

By 1983 Athens was the seventh largest municipality in population size and Clarke still the smallest county in geographical size in the state. As the county became increasingly urban, demands for public services beyond the city limits accelerated. Suburbanites expected all the amenities (some for which city dwellers felt they picked up the tax tab), and county government grew in order to meet many of those demands.

CITY AND COUNTY GOVERNMENTS

The Georgia legislature had passed an act creating the new Board of Commissioners of Clarke County on March 29, 1973. The act had increased the number of county commissioners from three to five and provided for the creation of the office of county administrator. All commissioners, including the chairman, were elected "at large" for four-year terms. Elections were staggered to fill three posts in one year and the other two posts two years later. A veteran commissioner, James Holland, won election as chairman of the new board. He was re-elected chairman throughout the 1980s. Clerk of the Court Ben Lumpkin assisted the commission, but not until 1983 did the Board of Commissioners change their structure to a council-manager form, hiring a full-time professional administrator to carry out commission policy.

Commissioner Jewel John, elected in 1975, reflected at the end of the 1980s on the rapidity and necessity of change within the structure of county government. "When I first came into office, I remember the county treasurer sitting at his rolltop desk in the basement of the courthouse with his huge ledger book before him writing all county checks out by hand," she said. "The county no longer has the office of treasurer, and we are into our third generation of computerization."

The predecessor of the county commissioner was the commissioner of roads and revenue, a title prescribed by the legislature in the 1870s. The county commissioners administered policies and operations of the state within the county's boundaries and provided for the needs of the people living within those boundaries. As an arm of the state, the county operated welfare and health programs,

From 1872 to 1990 the Athens city government consisted of an elected mayor and council. The four men who served as mayor over the last twenty-five years are pictured together at "Night in Old Athens" on North Campus in 1989. They are (left to right) Julius Bishop (1964–75), a businessman and banker; Upshaw Bentley (1976–79), an attorney; Lauren Coile (1980–87), a businessman; and Dwain Chambers (1988–91), also a businessman.

built and maintained roads, and conducted the courts of law that were part of the state justice system.

By the 1980s the days of massive federal financial infusions were waning. But local governments had gained a potential windfall when the state passed legislation in 1976 enabling cities and counties to levy and split revenues from a local option one-cent sales tax. In addition, after July 1, 1985, counties could impose a special-purpose local option sales tax, adding another one-cent tax on every dollar.

In the 1980s, as the county population increased, problems involving solid and hazardous waste disposal, deteriorating roads and bridges, and overtaxed sewer and water facilities demanded attention. The county contracted with the city for water and sewage facilities, while the city contracted with the county for landfill. The county provided the same services as the city, with the exception of garbage collection and bus transportation. Citizens living in the unincorporated areas of Clarke County expected the county to maintain roads and sidewalks and provide public utilities and fire and police protection as well. Planning and building inspection were joint city-county services. Despite the creation of its own parks and recreation department, the county contracted with the city for many recreational programs. Lines of responsibility could sometimes be confusing in this city-county maze. At work, for example, were three separate police forces—city, county, and university—and in matters of law enforcement questions of jurisdiction often arose.

Given the rapid growth of the county, many citizens felt that a merger of the two governments would mean more efficient and more economical government. Special referendum elections brought "consolidation" of city and county government before the voters three times in twenty years. Voters thrice defeated consolidation at the polls (March 12, 1969; May 24, 1972; and February 18, 1982). In each referendum consolidation failed by small margins; city totals narrowly favored and county totals narrowly defeated creation of a single countywide government. For example, in 1982, 10,002 voters (out of 25,465 registered voters) cast ballots in the referendum. In the city the vote was 2,611 to 2,120 in favor of consolidation; in the county the vote was 2,388 to 2,883 opposed. Perhaps one of the reasons county voters did not favor consolidation was that city residents subsidized many county services. County residents, fearing increased taxes, perceived little incentive to support consolidation.

Nonetheless, by the end of the 1980s a group of local activists calling themselves the Northeast Georgia Citizen's Quality Growth Task Force, led by J. W. Fanning, retired vice-president for services at the University of Georgia, organized to lobby for a merger of city and county governments—this time calling the merger "unification." The city, the county, and the task force each appointed five members to the new Athens–Clarke County Unification Commission to create a new charter for a single government and present this unification plan to the local legislative delegation before the end of 1989 for introduction to the 1990 session of the General Assembly. The charter commission placed a high priority on educating citizens about the issues and held numerous town meetings in various residential areas and in Winterville to elicit citizens' response. A broad cross-section of people approached the task, aided by the Institute of Government and the Institute of Community and Area Development at the University of Georgia.

The Clarke County courthouse, in use since 1913, underwent a major transformation in the 1980s. The original Neoclassical building on Washington Street was restored, and a new annex for administrative offices was built behind it.

The charter commission argued that a single government seemed best suited to serve the needs of the geographically small, largely urban county. The challenge was to convince the voters and to fashion a proposed charter that would serve the county well.

In both city and county, change was the order of the day. By the end of the 1980s Clarke County had solved some of its growing pains. A 1983 grand jury report on county-owned property read, "If the present Clarke County Courthouse is to be retained and used . . . then serious study must be given to the allocation of space and building maintenance. Both the interior and the exterior of the building are in poor repair. Both the heating and cooling plants need work and stabilization."

Much of the damage to the original structure stemmed from neglect; the "old lady" had grown shabby in her eighth decade. On June 25, 1985, county voters passed a sales-tax referendum to fund a transformation of the county courthouse. Tax revenues over a

four-year period coupled with the income from the sale of some unused county properties paid for the renovation of the 1913 Neoclassical courthouse and the construction of a five-floor, contemporary-style annex connected to the parent building by an atrium and abutted by a three-level parking deck that consumed the corner of Thomas and Washington streets. Altogether the project cost $5.58 million. The old courthouse with its central stairwell and skylights restored to their former glory now housed only courts and judicial facilities, while the annex provided the multitude of administrative offices necessary to modern county government.

One block away, Athens City Hall employed its own share of construction workers. At a time when little federal funding was available to municipalities, Mayor Lauren Coile had nonetheless secured a grant from the U.S. Department of Transportation to build the Athens Transit Mall. Like College Square, the new outdoor mall widened walkways and bus stops, inserting such amenities as turn-of-the-century lampposts, recessed bus shelters, and significant greenspaces with flower beds and ash, red maple, and scarlet oak trees.

MALLS, MINIMALLS, AND DOWNTOWN ATHENS

Clarke County got its first mall in 1981, and buildings in downtown Athens emptied as "anchor" department stores—Davison's (later Macy's), J. C. Penney, and Belk—moved to the 850,000-square-foot, $20 million Georgia Square Mall on the Atlanta Highway. Downtown for a time seemed decimated. Beechwood Shopping Center felt the blow as well, when Sears too made the move to the mall. The new mall drew shoppers from all over northeast Georgia, many bypassing downtown on the newly completed perimeter around the city. A proliferation of satellite minimalls and office parks followed throughout the decade. The "exurbs" of Atlanta seemed on the move through Gwinnett and Barrow counties toward Clarke. Or, some might ask, is Athens moving ever closer to Atlanta?

Downtown Athens countered these centrifugal trends with College Square, a creative redesign of one block of College Avenue (from Broad to Clayton Street) financed by the city's sale of a

Outdoor festivals are popular events for the citizens of Clarke County. One of the most popular is a festival held in the spring. College Avenue is blocked off, and craftspeople display their wares on College Square while jazz musicians and sidewalk artists entertain the public.

defunct parking deck on Broad Street. The high-rise parking garage became a condominium complex (University Towers), and College Square—with its broad walkways, turn-of-the-century lampposts and benches, flower beds, shade trees, and sidewalk cafes—became a genuine town center and community gathering place. College Square proved worth the investment. More than an amenity, it helped attract new businesses, office development, and customers back to a more lively downtown.

The city, low on public funding but high on its citizens' propensity to propagate and replenish the urban forest, established the Athens Tree Commission in 1980. The commission's role was to spearhead a citizen-financed program of tree planting and tree preservation and to help replace the city's old trees when they died. By the end of the decade the commission was working with city council toward the establishment of a tree ordinance to protect some of the urban forest resources.

Athens had been developing a downtown revitalization process for eight years before it became a Main Street City in 1980. Athens was one of five cities in Georgia (and one of the original thirty cities in the nation) selected by the National Trust for its new Main Street Program for downtown renewal, designed specifically to address the problems of small, historic city centers. The national program stressed organization, promotion, design, and economic restructuring. Downtown Athens soon became a model for other Main Street towns and cities across the nation.

Concerts on College Square and downtown festivals such as the Golden Ginkgo Jamboree and Springfest became popular annual events and gave new life to old spaces. For two days in May thousands of spectators watched teams of international professional bicyclists compete in "preams" (races) around blocked-off downtown streets during the Twilight Criterium. For several years the popular Upstairs Downtown Tour displayed new uses for upstairs spaces—apartments, artists' lofts, design studios, and more.

A new 25 percent federal tax credit for renovation of certified historic structures and the availability of low interest loans made possible the Athens downtown renaissance of the early 1980s. In 1983 alone ADDA authorized over $3.7 million through its Conduit Loan Program for new retail businesses, offices, and building renovations.

In 1986 renovators of the Franklin House received the Georgia Trust for Historic Preservation's award as the outstanding restoration for adaptive use in the state. A brokerage firm—Johnson, Lane, Space, Smith and Company—was the first tenant to move into the newly renovated landmark, one of the few surviving antebellum hotels in the state and the oldest commercial building in Athens. This $2.5 million project (facilitated by ADDA) carried tax credits of approximately $350,000 for its developers, Broad Street Associates. The saga of the saving of the Franklin House was a long but highly successful venture for preservationists, developers, tenants, and visitors to the Classic City.

The venerable Southern Mutual Company moved from its downtown building to new offices on West Lake Drive. The old landmark on College Avenue, however, soon had a facelift and new tenants, including a new bank with an old name: Georgia National. Across the street demolition of the Palace Theater began; the city eventually bought the hole from developers to build a parking garage.

The most famous local band to emerge from the nationally celebrated Athens rock-music scene is R.E.M. Bill Berry, Michael Stipe, Peter Buck, and Mike Mills (left to right) formed the band in 1980 and two years later, after playing at local clubs, recorded their first album. Their unique sound caught fire, and fame and fortune followed.

The landmark Georgian Hotel underwent a conversion, reopening in 1986 as the Georgian, a luxury condominium complex with dining, entertainment, and office space on the ground floor. The popular singer Kenny Rogers considered buying and restoring the Georgian Hotel; instead he bought and redesigned for office space an Art Deco building across the street.

There were other famous investors in downtown in the 1980s. R.E.M., a group of local musicians destined to become the top rock band in the nation, applied to ADDA in 1986 for a one-hundred-thousand-dollar low-interest loan for the purchase and renovation of a building on West Clayton Street that then housed the Classic City Copy Center. Their building—two doors down from the former location of the 40 Watt Club, where they sometimes performed—became offices and rehearsal space for the band.

The B-52's, University of Georgia students turned rock musicians, became stars in the early eighties, but as their records moved up the charts, they moved out of Athens and on to New York and Warner Records. Small music clubs—the 40 Watt, Tyrone's, Uptown, the Mad Hatter, the Rockfish Palace, and others—were legends in their own time. Many clubs came and went about as regularly as college students advanced from freshmen to seniors.

R.E.M. (an acronym for rapid eye movement, a condition encountered in sleep associated with dreams) would remain in Athens. The band formed in April 1980 when four young men—Michael Stipe, Peter Buck, Mike Mills, and Bill Berry—found themselves and each other in Athens primarily because of the University of Georgia. As their popularity rose, they left school to join the emerging Athens music scene full-time. In December 1987 *Rolling Stone* magazine dubbed the group "America's Best Rock & Roll Band." Their albums became best sellers; their "dream logic" songs became themes for a generation; and the "hometown" boys became, (according to the *Atlanta Constitution* critic Bo Emerson) "reticently emerging megastars." Despite international fame and celebrity status, the band remained Athenian. All four band members lived in restored historic houses in Cobbham or the Boulevard Historic District. They became ardent supporters of environmental causes—especially Greenpeace—and donated generously to historic preservation. Before a forty-day tour in 1987, according to Emerson, "band members gathered enough ginkgo leaves from a particular tree in Athens to include one in every packet sent out to fan-club members. . . . But there probably aren't enough ginkgo leaves in Clarke County for the expanded circle of customers." Regardless, band members remained drop-ins at local music clubs (particularly the 40 Watt) throughout the 1980s, and they frequently joined other performers on stage in spontaneous celebration at home.

Athens grew as an artists' and writers' colony as well. Philip Lee Williams, former editor of the *Athens Observer,* emerged in 1984 as a major southern novelist with the publication of the highly acclaimed *Heart of a Distant Forest,* followed closely by three other novels during the decade, including *Song of Daniel,* a fictional tale of a caretaker of the Oconee Hill Cemetery in Athens.

AGRIBUSINESS

In 1983 there were still 101 farms on eighty thousand acres of Clarke County soil. In addition, pastures and dairy barns and various agricultural experiment stations related to university research and teaching dotted the countyscape. Despite the urban nature of a far greater proportion of the county, Clarke remained a key location for all types of agriculture, including forestry. As the traditional family farm declined in size and numbers, agribusiness became big business. Commercial nurseries and greenhouses constituted the fastest growing segment of the local agrieconomy in the 1980s. More than half the households in the county had some type of garden.

The incorporated town of Winterville (with a 1986 population of 830) still took pride in its "country town" agrarian role, capitalizing annually on that image with the Marigold Festival. Winterville designated the marigold its official flower, planted dozens of beds of the annual around town, and began in 1971 to hold every June a festival to celebrate the "friendship flower" and raise funds to restore and improve the town. Festival profits built a fountain for Town Square, renovated the old depot-turned-town-hall into offices and a dining hall, helped establish a Winterville branch office of the Athens Regional Library, and purchased playground equipment for the town park. A small museum memorializing country doctors served as a reminder of Winterville's distinctly agrarian origins.

In 1986 Clarke County ranked fifth in the state in turkey growing. Shealy Farms raised in excess of 250,000 turkeys per year in the county. Local cash crops included grain, sorghum, wheat, and soybeans. And a number of small cattle farms survived in the county as well.

Among the agriculture-related businesses were two agricultural chemical wholesalers, irrigation companies, tractor dealerships, the Clarke County Milling Company (a feedmill operation), and the State Farmers Market. In addition, within Clarke County were the State Botanical Garden and state and federal agencies for agricultural research and soil conservation. The U.S. Forest Service and the Georgia Forestry Commission had offices in Athens. Research done within the county affected the state, the nation, and the world. Thus in a real sense the county, once world-ranked as a producer of cotton and its products, now exercised enormous agricultural influence well beyond local and state boundaries.

HISTORIC PRESERVATION LEGISLATION

Following the earlier lead of twenty-three other Georgia communities (among them Savannah, Augusta, Macon, Columbus, Albany, and Monroe) the mayor and council adopted a historic preservation ordinance for the city of Athens on November 4, 1986. With a treasure trove of historic resources and the services of preservation professionals in the historic preservation program at the university's School of Environmental Design, it seems ironic that Athens was so late in passing a preservation ordinance. Perhaps because Athens had so many significant historic buildings at hand, many locals (especially native Athenians) took their architectural heritage for granted until they realized—almost too late—that one by one those landmarks were vanishing. Ofttimes the preservation movement was led by relative newcomers, people attracted to Athens in part by the town's historic ambiance and eager for legislation that would protect the unique sense of time and place they found here. Although preservationists and developers sometimes were at odds regarding the merits of the design restrictions the legislation could impose on designated historic properties, the majority of residents favored the ordinance which city council in the end passed unanimously. The preservation ordinance provided for creation by the council of a five-member (later seven-member) commission with authority to propose historic districts and landmarks and to review new construction and exterior renovations to buildings and sites designated for protection by the council. An *Athens Daily News* editorial on February 20, 1986, urged passage of the "long-delayed" ordinance: "It is too late to do anything about fine old buildings which have been demolished, but it isn't too late to preserve many that remain."

An event that may have sealed passage of the ordinance was the loss of the historic T. R. R. Cobb House in 1985. The Greek Revival mansion, undeniably one of the most historically significant structures in the state, was taken apart and moved to Stone Mountain for eventual reconstruction as part of an "Old South" theme park. Saint Joseph's Catholic Church sold the Cobb House (once the church rectory) to make space for a new school building and a parking lot.

The citizens of Clarke County lost one of their most historic houses in 1985 when the T. R. R. Cobb House was dismantled and moved to Stone Mountain Park. The historic landmark was the home of Thomas Reade Rootes Cobb, founder of the Lucy Cobb Institute, author of the Georgia code, contributor to the Confederate constitution, and Confederate general.

No local buyers came forward, and efforts to raise money to save the house failed.

During the late 1980s city council designated four historic districts—Woodlawn, Bloomfield, Boulevard, and Cobbham—as well as many historic sites for protection under the local ordinance. The Athens-Clarke Heritage Foundation continued to play a vital role in the documentation of the city's historic sites and districts as well. By 1988 the National Trust for Historic Preservtion included hundreds of sites, listing thirteen historic districts and twenty-eight individual historic landmarks in Athens (see appendix 1). ACHF established headquarters in the city-owned Fire Hall No. 2, built in 1901. When the Athens Fire Department closed the station in 1979, the city restored the exterior and ACHF restored the interior for offices, exhibition, and meeting space.

The Chamber of Commerce began a ten-year stay in converted office spaces in old Fire Hall No. 1 in 1980; the firemen moved to a new station on Jackson Street. The chamber became involved in tourism (now big business for the state and region) when Athens became the gateway to the Antebellum Trail, a route designated by

In October 1984 the University of Georgia began a sixteen-month Bicentennial Celebration with an elaborate convocation at the Coliseum. Vice-President George Bush delivered the main address and, along with five of the university's most distinguished faculty members, received a sterling silver Bicentennial medallion. Photographed at this occasion were University Vice-President for Academic Affairs Virginia Trotter, Vice-President George Bush, and University President Fred Davison. The faculty recipients included (left to right) Glenn W. Burton, professor of agronomy; Eugene P. Odum, professor of ecology; Normal H. Giles, professor of genetics; Dean Rusk, professor of law; and Lamar Dodd, professor of art.

the state legislature to direct tourists through Athens to Watkinsville, Madison, Eatonton, Milledgeville, Old Clinton, and Macon. Despite its many losses, Athens could still offer glimpses of the Old South. Jessie Poesch, a leading authority on southern art, artifacts, and architecture, wrote in 1983, "The university town of Athens, appropriately, probably has more houses still standing in Greek Revival taste than any other town in the state."

THE TWO-HUNDRED-YEAR-OLD UNIVERSITY

The University of Georgia celebrated its two hundredth anniversary as the nation's oldest chartered state university with a full calendar of special events from July 1984 to June 1985. George Bush, then vice-president of the United States, was the Bicentennial Convocation speaker in October; A. Bartlett Giamatti, then president of Yale University, delivered the Founders' Day address in January; and the entire university became a showcase during the Bicentennial Exposition in the spring. The university commissioned two histories of the institution, a Bicentennial medallion, a symphonic suite by the Pulitzer Prize–winning composer Karel Husa, and much more. During Founders' Week the U.S. Postal Service issued a seven-cent stamp from Athens honoring Abraham Baldwin, founder and first president of the university. Among many distinguished Bicentennial speakers were former presidents of the United States Jimmy Carter and Gerald Ford.

More than five thousand students received undergraduate, graduate, and professional degrees in June 1985. They had attended classes as part of a student body of twenty-four thousand from all fifty states and one hundred foreign countries. By the Bicentennial year, foreign students composed 5 percent of the student body.

The Georgia General Assembly designated the university's botanical garden the State Botanical Garden of Georgia in 1984. A "high-tech"-style Visitors Center–Conservatory (a $3 million gift from the Callaway Foundation) opened on June 30, 1985. Similarly, the legislature adopted the Georgia Museum of Art as the official state art museum in 1983, passing a resolution in 1985 favoring the match of state funds to private donations for the construction of a

new museum; but by the end of the decade plans for a new building by the well-known architect Edward Larabee Barnes remained on the drawing board, and many of the museum's total holdings (in excess of five thousand objects) were still crated in the cramped basement of the small but well-respected North Campus museum.

On March 13, 1989, headlines in the *Athens Banner-Herald* read, "New Life for a Venerable Athens Lady: Renovation of the Historic Lucy Cobb Institute Is Underway." Construction had begun to adapt the historic Milledge Avenue campus for the University of Georgia's Carl Vinson Institute of Government. For decades the university had badly neglected this property, which it had received in trust from the trustees of Lucy Cobb Institute in the early 1950s. By 1954 the main building was so badly deteriorated that it became necessary to remove the fourth floor. "I Love Lucy" bumper stickers started appearing around town as Friends of Lucy Cobb and Seney-Stovall, a group dedicated to saving the historic structures, rallied support for preservation of the historic compound. A successful fundraising campaign netted a $3.5 million federal grant in 1984, and a supplemental $1 million appropriation was approved in 1987. By the end of the decade, extensive restoration was still in progress, and plans were afoot to restore the Seney-Stovall Chapel as well.

Another university institute gave historic preservation a boost when the Institute of Continuing Legal Education moved from the School of Law on campus to the Joseph Henry Lumpkin House in 1986. The Woman's Club of Athens had maintained this landmark from 1919 to 1975, then transferred the deed to the newly formed Joseph Henry Lumpkin Foundation. This citizens group (led by Dean J. Ralph Beaird of the School of Law) secured grants and raised private funds for restoration of the home of the first chief justice of the Georgia Supreme Court (for whom the university's law school was named). The foundation began restoration of the house and in turn transferred the deed in 1986 to the Law School Asso-

In 1986 the university's Institute of Continuing Legal Education moved into the historic Joseph Henry Lumpkin House on Prince Avenue. Under Dean J. Ralph Beaird's leadership the School of Law secured funds to renovate the exterior and interior of this fine antebellum Greek Revival mansion. It is an excellent example of rehabilitation of an older building.

In September 1985 the University of Georgia honored four outstanding players by retiring their jerseys. Tailback Frank Sinkwich (21) captained the 1942 SEC championship team and that same year won the Heisman Trophy. Captain of the 1946 Sugar Bowl–winning team, Charley Trippi (62) was one of the greatest all-around backs in southern football history and an All-Pro with the Chicago Cardinals. Theron Sapp (40), who played fullback and linebacker in 1957, led Georgia to its first victory over Georgia Tech in eight years. Herschel Walker (34) led Georgia to its first national championship in his freshman year, 1980.

ciation. The completed renovation included offices and meeting spaces, with the principal rooms furnished as memorials to the first justices of the Georgia Supreme Court.

Another university-related building project in the 1980s involved Sanford Stadium. The independent Athletic Association pumped over $13 million into Sanford Stadium, which now could seat eighty-two thousand. Demands for football tickets reached a zenith in 1980 when fans flocked to see Herschel Walker, a freshman running back from Wrightsville, Georgia, in action. Walker won the Heisman Trophy and led the Bulldogs to the national championship with a victory over Notre Dame in the Sugar Bowl on New Year's Day 1981. By 1980 Coach Dooley held a 130-56-6 record over an eighteen-year tenure.

With the east end of the stadium enclosed, spectators no longer could watch the game from the railroad tracks. Soon, however, the "New Age" architecture of the towering Butts-Mehre Building, constructed by the independent Athletic Association and opened in

Coach Dan Magill is one of the University of Georgia's best-loved figures. An Athens native and university graduate, Magill served as head varsity coach of the men's tennis teams from 1955 to 1988, with 706 match victories. A promoter extraordinaire, he attracted the prestigious NCAA College Championship Tournament to Athens.

1987, afforded fans and coaches a princely perspective of playing and practice fields. The polished red granite and black glass memorial to two Georgia coaches became sports headquarters. Heritage Hall, featuring a collection of memorabilia from UGA's legendary sports history, quickly became a mecca for Bulldog fans.

Coach Vince Dooley, named athletic director in 1981, assumed those duties full-time in 1988. After a quarter-century as head football coach, Dooley turned over the reins to Ray Goff, a former Bulldog quarterback and assistant coach.

Marianne and Kenny Rogers endowed an Intercollegiate Tennis Hall of Fame adjacent to Coach Dan Magill's empire of indoor and outdoor courts. Here Magill, the "winningest coach in college tennis," played Athens host to the NCAA tennis tournaments from which Jimmy Conners, John McEnroe and other tennis luminaries launched their professional careers with collegiate championships.

Women's intercollegiate teams in basketball, track, golf, swimming, tennis, volleyball, and gymnastics rose to prominence in the 1980s. The women's basketball team consistently ranked in the top twenty (and more often in the top ten) nationally; the women's track team produced two gold medalists in the Olympics; and the gymnastics team won the national championship in 1987.

The men's basketball team won its first SEC title in 1983. Coach Hugh Durham produced consistently powerful teams and packed the Coliseum for home games. Baseball powerhouse teams were in the making as well.

The frenzy of fans and the enormous profits engendered by intercollegiate athletics contributed to excesses nationwide. Exploitation of college athletes became an issue at the University of Georgia in the mid-1980s when Jan Kemp, a developmental studies instructor, charged the administration with wrongfully firing her for protesting special treatment for student athletes. The Kemp lawsuit and subsequent trial led to reforms in the academic requirements for student athletes at the University of Georgia and hastened the departure of President Fred Davison and other academic administrators as well.

Under Davison's twenty-year leadership, the university had attained national stature as a major research institution: research

In 1989, before an Athens crowd, the University of Georgia's women's gymnastics team won the NCAA championship. At that meet Corrinne Wright became the first Georgia gymnast to capture the national all-around title. A four-time All-American, Wright is pictured on the uneven bars.

budgets tripled, and graduate enrollment doubled. In 1980 the land-grant institution gained sea-grant status as well. Davison helped establish the Center for Global Studies in 1980. He emphasized computer science and biotechnology and launched the largest single project in the history of the university system—the construction of the $32 million–plus Bioscience Complex, an ambitious genetics and biochemistry research facility under construction when Davison stepped down from the presidency in 1986. A year later Charles Knapp, a native of Iowa, became the twentieth president of the University of Georgia.

COMING ATTRACTIONS

Clarke County voters passed a local option sales tax on November 3, 1987, to finance seven special projects within the county. Revenues over a four-year period would provide $34 million for a civic center, a new library, renovation of the historic Morton Theater, expansion of the county jail, a new mental health facility, expansion and relocation of the sanitary landfill, and park and road construction.

By far the biggest slice of this budgetary pie ($22 million) would

The 1987 local option sales tax included funding for a new Athens Regional Library. The Baxter Street building, shown in this working drawing, will be nearly three times the size of its predecessor and will include a separate children's room, a young adult area with audiovisual services and computer terminals, a talking book center, and a heritage room.

go to the convention–performing arts Civic Center. The General Assembly passed a bill in March 1988 to create the Civic Center Authority, a five-member board to oversee the project. Original plans called for the library and Civic Center to be located in the Historic Warehouse District between Thomas and Foundry streets. The county considered numerous alternatives but finally selected the Thomas Street site for the Civic Center and the playing fields of Clarke Middle School at Dudley Drive and Baxter Street as the location for the library.

In a local version of the board game "Monopoly," the county gave Athens Regional Library's property to the city in exchange for city-owned Foundry Street property, three fire stations, and the Hill Street police-department building. The Thomas Street Holding Company bought the Flea Market in January 1988; the county acquired the Flea Market property through condemnation and purchased it from the holding company in December 1988.

Preliminary plans for the complex were soon under way, with architects and the Civic Center Authority encouraging citizen participation through an "Urban Design Symposium" the authority sponsored with the Athens Downtown Development Authority at the Athens Country Club; a National Trust for Historic Preservation design symposium held downtown and funded by a five-thousand-dollar grant from R.E.M.; and numerous other public

One historic structure to benefit from the four-year local option sales tax is the historic Morton Theater. Built in 1909–10 by Monroe "Pink" Morton, this four-story structure at Washington and Hull Streets served as a cultural center for members of Clarke County's black community. The nonprofit Morton Theater Corporation, established in 1981, borrowed against future county funds to repair the parapet, roof, and substructure. The restoration was scheduled for completion in 1992.

hearings and presentations as well. It would come as a surprise to many that old Fire Hall No. 1 was fast becoming endangered.

If the Civic Center was certain to transform the east end of Washington Street, another Thomas Street project already had given a visual jolt to the eastern terminus of Clayton Street. Here the Athens Newspapers had demolished their longtime headquarters at 1 Press Place. While that vacant high ground commanded a startlingly unobstructed view down to the river, on the drawing boards were plans for a huge new $20 million newspaper plant, a veritable print-media empire anchored by porticos with massive columns and pediments and consuming an area roughly equivalent in acreage to the property set aside for the Civic Center. For in a quest to add to its original property, Athens Newspapers had bought and demolished half a block of turn-of-the-century townscape along the north side of lower Broad Street from Thomas to Foundry streets.

The Morton Theater, one of only four black vaudeville theaters remaining in the United States, went on the National Register of Historic Places in 1979 and came under local protection as one of the first sites designated under the Athens Historic Preservation Ordinance. The struggle to save the Morton had been a long labor of love among its supporters, and now the prospect of a performing arts center in the historically significant building offered an exciting opportunity for the community. The Morton Theatre Corporation purchased the deteriorating building in September 1981. A design study funded by the National Endowment for the Arts, a $27,000 grant from the Georgia Department of Natural Resources, and a matching grant from Community Development Block Grant allocations and the city of Athens had helped the project along the way. But financial backing for theater renovation was slow in coming before the referendum that allocated $1.3 million to Morton renovation.

A school bond referendum passed in 1988 offered further coming attractions. Parents, students, and teachers could look forward to needed additions at Timothy Road, Winterville, Whitehead, Alps Road, Patti Hilsman, and Clarke Middle schools; three new elementary schools; and new buildings at Barnett Shoals, Barrow, Chase Street, and Gaines schools.

THE OCONEE RIVER FACTOR: ECOLOGY AND SERENITY

The importance of the Oconee River to Clarke County never diminished, but awareness of the river's value underwent a renaissance as concern for the environment turned citizens back to their river origins as a source of beauty, relaxation, and sustenance. The river remained the county's lifeline and most important natural resource. The Oconee supplied the public water system, removed public waste, and helped keep the environment cool and green.

The Oconee Rivers Greenway Committee, led by Walter Cook, a forestry professor and a tireless volunteer, explored setting aside a greenspace corridor, an "unbroken stretch of natural vegetation along the riverfront to serve as a recreational hub and valuable wildlife habitat." Its stated goals were "to protect corridors along the Oconee rivers and their major tributaries from undesirable development or alteration" and "to maintain and improve water quality; and to provide appropriate public access to the river corridors for recreation and aesthetic enjoyment."

Development had had a harsh effect on the small tributaries that feed the river. In an interview with the *Athens Observer,* Charles Aguar, a University of Georgia professor of landscape architecture and urban design and a member of the Greenway Committee, explained the impact of parking lots, commercial and residential development, and the building of Sanford Stadium (over Tanyard Creek) on the historic springs and creeks in the county: "Infill is creating development on land that was left vacant in the past because it was difficult to build on. It is filling in ravines and stream beds once left natural, that provided trees and plant life and homes for birds and raccoons and a sponge area to absorb runoff." Aguar and other environmentalists stressed the importance of maintaining some open spaces to insure quality of human and animal life.

The city, the county, and the state already owned much of the river corridor. In 1981 Sandy Creek Nature Center (established in 1977) and Sandy Creek Park came under the auspices of the county's newly created parks and recreation department. Sandy Creek originated as a two-hundred-acre nature center along the Oconee, a private, nonprofit enterprise financed by county, city, and school-district revenue sharing. By 1981 the fledgling county parks department controlled sixteen hundred acres of riverfront property.

Among the city-owned parks was the North Oconee River Park, a beautiful stretch along the river between North Avenue and East Broad Street. The State Botanical Garden offered miles of river trails. Foresters and environmentalists proposed that the university set aside a River Road walking trail connecting university land to riverfront city parks.

The Oconee Rivers Greenway Committee worked toward an unbroken stretch of natural vegetation that would combine these parks and gardens, woods and campus, while by the end of the decade a river corridor protection bill (HB 1133) was making its way to a vote before the Georgia General Assembly. This bill, inspired by the ecologist and emeritus professor Eugene Odum, would, according to proponents, "restrict floodplain development, reduce property loss from floods and preserve essential wildlife" in a buffer where animals and people would migrate.

The Athens Sierra Club initiated a cleanup of Ben Burton Park; Students for Environmental Awareness lobbied for the river's protection; and the City Clean and Beautiful campaign got into full swing.

1990: A PIVOTAL YEAR

The year 1990 brought some setbacks in the preservation movement in Athens. By March all but the steeple of Saint Mary's Church on Oconee Street was demolished for a condominium development, "Steeplechase," which took its name from the now-forlorn and naked appendage of the once-lovely little Gothic Episcopal chapel Robert Bloomfield had built in 1871 for his mill workers. The deconsecrated chapel had, in essence, suffered demolition by neglect long before the wrecking ball destroyed the sanctuary.

Also in March, Athens mayor and council voted to deny designation of a Hull Street Historic District, thereby clearing the way for the Christian College of Georgia to demolish the historic Hull-Snelling House and denude the property trustees wanted to sell to the neighboring Holiday Inn for a parking lot. The historic district was to include not only the Hull-Snelling House but several Gothic Revival cottages and the Greek Revival Wray-Nicholson mansion as well. All but one of these properties, the last remaining vestiges of Athens's oldest standing downtown neighborhood, belonged to the college; most were rental properties, acquired over a period of decades, that generated income for the Christian (Disciples of Christ) education program for a small number of students. After heated public debate in a series of hearings before the historic preservation commission and city council, Mayor Dwain Chambers broke the council's tie vote to defeat the designation. Hurried efforts to find a sympathetic buyer who would save and preserve the house failed. On Wednesday, May 23, 1990, a bulldozer leveled the 150-year-old Greek Revival landmark, one of the oldest houses remaining in Athens and once the home of Asbury Hull, Speaker of the Georgia house and state senator, and later the residence of University of Georgia president Charles Snelling. Preservationists and environmentalists alike were shocked when the college carried out its threat

The Greek Revival Hull-Morton-Snelling House was built circa 1842. It once served as the president's house for the University of Georgia. Here Herbert Hoover once dined with President Charles Snelling before delivering a commencement address at the university. The house became a fraternity house and then a restaurant (Magnolia Manor) before its purchase by the Christian College of Georgia in 1961. In 1990 the college had the house demolished for a parking lot.

to demolish most of the trees on the lot, including a noble magnolia estimated to be 116 years old. Still the way was not clear for the four-hundred-thousand-dollar sale, which by the end of the year remained contingent on the outcome of an appeal for rezoning to allow for a one-hundred-car parking lot the Holiday Inn wanted.

Later in 1990 preservationists lost another round. In January the Chamber of Commerce sold the 1912 Fire Hall No. 1 to the Clarke County Board of Commissioners for $650,000. With the purchase of the old brick structure whose solid, sturdy tower had long anchored downtown's east end at Hancock and Thomas streets, county commissioners completed land acquisitions for the new Civic Center site and gave the New York architectural firm of James Stewart Polshek and Partners an "open palette" in utilizing the property bounded by Hancock, Foundry, Thomas, and Press Place.

The fate of the fire hall hung in the balance. There followed a public outcry to save the structure, either by leaving it as a free-standing visitor and information center with the Civic Center wrapped around it or by incorporating the fire hall as an entry into the Civic Center's great hall designers had envisioned. The commissioners, who had through the Civic Center Authority invited public participation in the urban design, seemed now to resent and reject the wishes of a broad cross-section of the community that favored retention of the fire hall. When the architects came back with final plans that did not incorporate the fire hall, the county commission voted to accept those plans and try to move the fire hall somewhere else. They named an ad hoc committee to relocate and recycle the landmark for some future public purpose. At the year's end the chamber moved out of Fire Hall No. 1 and into the old Southern Mutual Building, soon to be renamed the Commerce Building.

Meanwhile the unification process moved forward. In the summer of 1990, voters elected to do business a new way by adopting unification. In order to pass, the referendum had to carry both city and county. But this time, in contrast to past votes on consolidation, city votes would, in effect, count twice—once in the city decision and once in the county referendum. On August 9, 1990, city voters agreed to forfeit their charter; Athens and Clarke County voters passed the referendum to establish a unified government by a vote of 7,954 to 5,486. The voters would return to the polls in November to elect a CEO (chief elected officer) and ten commissioners to lead the new government. Athens-Clarke would become the second city-county consolidated government in Georgia and only the twenty-eighth in the nation.

Candidates running for office in the new government swung into lively and often hotly contested campaigns in newly defined districts (including two "super districts") throughout late summer and fall 1990. In late November Gwen O'Looney narrowly defeated E. H. Culpepper (a popular attorney, banker, and chairman of the Civic Center Authority) in a runoff for CEO. Although a veteran city councilwoman, O'Looney, a social work professional, represented a strong departure from former mayors and the county commission chairmen (in recent decades all businessmen, bankers, or lawyers). With support from blacks, environmentalists, preservationists, and others, O'Looney defeated her opponents, including the chairman of the Clarke County Board of Commissioners, Jim Holland. She had won largely on quality-of-life issues; Clarke County voters had changed the rules.

As the year 1990 drew to a close, environmentalists gathered on December 8 for the dedication of the Sandy Creek Greenway, a 4.1-

In this watercolor painting Alan Campbell, an Athens artist, depicts downtown Broad Street on a winter evening in 1986. To the left is old North Campus with the Academic Building in the background. On the center median in the distance is the Confederate Monument. With its restaurants and small, locally owned shops, Broad Street remains much as it was nearly two hundred years ago, the hub of Athens and Clarke County, Georgia.

mile walking trail that followed the creek from Clarke County's Sandy Creek Park to the Sandy Creek Nature Center. With five bridges and two boardwalks crossing Big Beaver Swamp, Georgia's first official greenway was the culmination of years of planning and work. Walter Cook reminded local journalists, "A greenway is a way to experience a natural place and still stay close to home. It helps wildlife have a route of travel, from the rural area through the city." Indeed, the same may be said for what the greenway provides for humans in Clarke County—a natural link to that which is rural. By water's edge Clarke County and Georgia joined the national mainstream in planning a nature preserve for an urban area.

Meanwhile students socialized on the decks of O'Malley's, a 140-year-old renovated mill building not far from the site of Daniel Easley's eighteenth-century mill on the Oconee. They watched the leaves lazily float downriver to the dam that once harnessed power for the textile mill. Atop the hill urban designers and newly elected officials looked to the river, hoping to juxtapose the old and the new. Given the vagaries of time, their search to recapture the gifts of the river and to make a whole new public center and fashion a new government on the high ground might not be altogether different from the dreams and aspirations of a committee on horseback that came upon this river place and looked to the high ground as a site for the first public university in the nation, the "seat of the muses."

Appendix 1

National Register of Historic Places, Clarke County Listings

Congress created the National Trust in 1949 to encourage public participation in the preservation of historic buildings. The National Historic Preservation Act of 1966 established an expanded National Register of Historic Places to include districts, sites, buildings, structures, and objects of national, state, or local significance. Athens's first inclusion on the list came in 1970.

In the following list of designations and dates of entry, "HABS" denotes buildings that were included in the Historic American Buildings Survey authorized by Congress in 1933. HABS was part of President Franklin Roosevelt's New Deal plan to get people back to work—in this case architects. By the time the survey reached Athens, initial funds were dwindling, so only a few Athens landmarks were documented at that time.

Wilkins House, 385 South Milledge Avenue. May 19, 1970.

Old North Campus, University of Georgia. March 16, 1972. HABS.

Benjamin Hill House (President's House, University of Georgia), 570 Prince Avenue. March 16, 1972. HABS.

Lucy Cobb Institute campus, 200 North Milledge Avenue. March 16, 1972. HABS.

Bishop House, Jackson Street, University of Georgia campus. March 16, 1972.

Governor Wilson Lumpkin House (Rock House), Cedar Street, South Campus, University of Georgia. March 16, 1972.

Garden Club of Georgia Museum–Headquarters House and Founders' Memorial Garden, Lumpkin Street, University of Georgia campus. April 26, 1972.

Franklin-Upson House, 1922 Prince Avenue. November 15, 1973. HABS.

James A. Sledge House, 749 Cobb Street. February 12, 1974.

Albon Chase House, 185 North Hull Street. August 19, 1974. HABS.

Franklin House, 464–80 East Broad Street. December 11, 1974. HABS.

Church-Waddel-Brumby House, 280 East Dougherty Street. February 20, 1975.

Joseph Henry Lumpkin House, 248 Prince Avenue. June 27, 1975. HABS.

T. R. R. Cobb House, 194 Prince Avenue. June 30, 1975. Now removed.

Camak House, 279 Meigs Street. July 7, 1975.

Dearing Street Historic District (including Dearing and Finley streets and Henderson Avenue). September 5, 1975.

Carnegie Library Building, 1401 Prince Avenue. November 11, 1975.

Ware-Lyndon House, 293 East Broad Street. March 15, 1976.

Taylor-Grady House, 634 Prince Avenue. May 11, 1976. HABS. National Historic Landmark.

Athens Savings Bank, later Parrot Insurance Building, 283 East Broad Street. October 7, 1977.

Downtown Athens Historic District (roughly bounded by Hancock Avenue and Foundry, Mitchell, Broad, and Lumpkin streets). August 10, 1978.

Cobbham Historic District (roughly bounded by Prince Avenue, Hill, Reese, and Pope streets). August 24, 1978.

Albin P. Dearing House, 338 South Milledge Avenue. May 8, 1979. HABS.

James S. Hamilton House, 150 Milledge Avenue. April 24, 1979.

Thomas-Carithers House, 530 Milledge Avenue. May 8, 1979.

Cobb-Treanor House, 1234 South Lumpkin Street. May 8, 1979.

White Hall, Whitehall and Simonton Bridge roads. June 18, 1979.

Ross Crane House, 247 Pulaski Street. June 18, 1979.

Morton Building, 199 West Washington Street. October 22, 1979.

First African Methodist Episcopal Church, 521 North Hull Street. March 10, 1980.

Clarke County Jail, behind 419 Pope Street on old Courthouse Square. May 29, 1980.

Athens Factory, Baldwin and Williams streets. July 31, 1980.

Calvin W. Parr House, 227 Bloomfield Street. September 9, 1982.

Chestnut Grove School, Epps Bridge Road. June 28, 1984.

Boulevard Historic District. April 18, 1985.

Bloomfield Historic District. April 18, 1985.
Milledge Avenue Historic District. April 18, 1985.
Milledge Circle Historic District. April 18, 1985.
Stevens Thomas House, 345 West Hancock Avenue. May 15, 1985.
YWCA building, 347 West Hancock Avenue. May 15, 1985.
Woodlawn Avenue Historic District. October 23, 1987.
Oglethorpe Avenue Historic District. November 11, 1987.
Reese Street Historic District. November 10, 1987.
Warehouse Historic District. October 20, 1988.
West Hancock Avenue Historic District. March 30, 1988.

Appendix 2

Chief Administrative Officers, City of Athens

It is impossible to provide a complete list of the chief executive officers of Athens, because no minutes survive from the time Athens was granted her charter as a town in 1806 until 1847, when local government changed from five elected officials (who selected one of their number chairman) to the intendant-warden system with an intendant elected at large and two wardens elected from each of four wards. The January 1, 1847, minutes of the committee record the election of Leonard Franklin as chairman. He held the office for only eight days. E. L. Newton succeeded him as the last to hold the title of chairman. Dr. E. R. Ware was elected the first intendant, serving from 1848 to 1852. Albon Chase succeeded Ware, serving from 1852 to 1853.

The town of Athens became the city of Athens under a new charter granted in 1872, and the intendant, Captain Henry Beusse (CSA), became the first to hold the title of mayor of Athens. With the passage of unification of Athens and Clarke County, Mayor Dwain Chambers was the last to hold the title of mayor of the city of Athens, for the city gave up its charter and the mayor-and-council form of government on January 14, 1991.

Cincinnatus Peeples, 1853–55
William Gerdine, 1856
William L. Bass, 1857
Dr. Robert L. Smith, 1858–59
James R. Lyle, 1860
F. W. Adams, 1861
S. C. Reese, 1863–65
E. P. Lumpkin, 1866
James D. Pittard, 1867–68 and 1873
Jerry E. Ritch, 1869 and 1870
Capt. Henry Beusse, 1871–72 and 1881
Dr. William King, 1874–75
Capt. Clovis G. Talmadge, 1876–77 and 1880
Capt. J. H. Rucker, 1878–79 and 1882
Capt. W. D. O'Farrell, 1883–84 and 1895
J. H. Dorsey, 1884–85
R. K. Reaves, 1886
A. H. Hodgson, 1887–88
Dr. John A. Hunnicutt, 1889
E. T. Brown, 1890–91
H. C. Tuck, 1892–93

Capt. J. C. McMahan, 1896–97
E. I. Smith, 1898 and 1901
J. F. Rhodes, 1902 and 1905
W. F. Dorsey, 1906, 1909, and 1914
H. J. Rowe, 1910 and 1913
R. O. Arnold, 1916
O. R. Dobbs (filled out term of predecessor)
A. C. Erwin, 1918 and 1920
G. C. Thomas, 1922
O. H. Arnold, 1924–25
A. G. Dudley, 1926–35 and 1938–39
T. S. Mell, 1936–37
Robert L. McWhorter, 1940–47
Jack R. Wells, 1948–51, 1957, 1962
Ralph Snow, 1958–61
Julius Bishop, 1963–74
Upshaw Bentley, 1975–79
Lauren Coile, 1980–88
Dwain Chambers, 1989–91

On January 14, 1991, Gwen O'Looney, a former city council member, was sworn in as the chief elected officer of the new unified Athens–Clarke County government.

Bibliographic Notes: A History of the Histories

In 1906 when Augustus Longstreet Hull published *Annals of Athens, Georgia, 1801–1901*, he included introductory sketches by his father, Professor Henry Hull. Henry Hull's sketches, based on his personal observations of Athens from 1801 to 1825, had first appeared in 1879 in the *Southern Watchman*. The son continued his father's anecdotal style with his own version of Athens history (almost five hundred pages long) to the turn of the century.

Among the "strolls and reminiscences" literature of Athens are Sylvanus Morris's *Strolls About Athens During the Early Seventies* and Edward Baker Mell's *Reminiscences of Athens About 1880–1900*. Morris, a university alumnus and dean of the School of Law (1900–1927), exhibited his abilities as a storyteller with his accounts of individuals and families, the location of buildings, and present and past structures on identified town lots. Mell wrote his boyhood memories late in life. In his introduction to this slim volume he wrote of his desire "to give some 'chatty' information about places and events and people that are vivid in the memory of the writer, a citizen for more than eighty-three years."

Charles Morton Strahan, professor of civil engineering at the University of Georgia and surveyor of Clarke County, undertook a more serious local history when he wrote and published *Clarke County, Georgia, and the City of Athens* in 1893. His ninety-page volume (which sold for one dollar) included maps of the city and county as well as numerous illustrations. According to the author, his purpose was threefold: "to place on record the main facts of the history, development, and present status of the county and all its interests; to direct the attention of visitors and settlers to the manifest advantages which the county affords for capital and residence; and to indicate to other counties, by example, the means of making known in complete and permanent form their several advantages."

In 1900 Albin Hajos published *Hajos' Athens Georgia: Photo-Gravures*. His photographs vividly depict Athens in the late nineteenth century.

H. J. Rowe, a former mayor of Athens, published *A History of Athens and Clarke County* in 1923. This comprehensive, 180-page bound volume included a history of Athens and Clarke County (1801–60) by Sylvanus Morris; a chronology of the chief executives of the city of Athens by John William Barnett, who served as city engineer for forty-one years; a history of the University of Georgia by Chancellor David C. Barrow; a history of Georgia State College of Agriculture by its president, Andrew M. Soule; a history of the State Normal School by E. S. Sell; a sketch of the Lucy Cobb Institute by its principal, Mildred Lewis Rutherford (who also contributed a chapter on her own personal history); histories of Emmanuel Church (doubtless contributed by Strahan, who was a vestryman), First Baptist Church of Athens (from remarks by Judge Andrew J. Cobb), the Presbyterian church (by the Reverend Arthur F. Bishop), Athens Christian Church, and Saint Joseph's Catholic Church; a history of newspapers in Athens by T. L. Gannt; industries of Athens and Clarke County by E. W. Carroll, secretary of the Chamber of Commerce; an overview of the legal community by Frank A. Holden and a detailed analysis of the medical profession by William A. Carlton; and a section devoted to personality sketches and photographs of Athens's leading male citizens.

Historian E. Merton Coulter joined the faculty of the University of Georgia in 1919 and retired as emeritus professor in 1958. During his long and prolific career as teacher, writer, editor, and storyteller, he published forty books on southern and Georgian history and more than one hundred articles. In 1924 he became editor of the *Georgia Historical Quarterly*, a position he held for fifty years. In 1928 Coulter published *College Life in the Old South*. Reprinted by the University of Georgia Press in 1951 (for the university's sesquicentennial) and 1983, it remains unsurpassed as a valuable resource on the antebellum university and life in the college town of Athens. The files of the *Georgia Historical Quarterly* contain many entries of his articles on the early years of the University of Georgia and Athens.

In 1951 Mayor Jack R. Wells and the city council of Athens published a slick sesquicentennial booklet entitled *Athens, Georgia: Home of the University of Georgia 1801–1951*, which they distributed to all city taxpayers. The eighty-five-page book contained photographs and illustrations and an overview of the city past and present. It included financial charts of the city's income and expenditures in 1950 and photographs of most of the city's chief executive officers from 1853 through mayor and council, 1951.

With the centennial of the American Civil War the University of Georgia Press published two local histories by local authors: *These Men She Gave* (1964) by the Athens physician and historian John F. Stegeman and *Confederate Athens* (1967) by Kenneth Coleman, professor of history at the University of Georgia. Together these histories provide a vivid account of the war years at home and the men who left home to join the Confederate States Army.

In 1974 Ernest C. Hynds, a University of Georgia journalism professor, published an excellent scholarly chronicle of sixty years of change, *Antebellum Athens and Clarke County.* His meticulous local history includes appendices listing public officials, professional men and planters, and businessmen of the antebellum era.

In 1978 the Observer Press published *Strolls Around Athens,* a compilation of recollections written for the *Athens Observer* by Dean William Tate. From the perspective of a fifty-year association with the University of Georgia and Athens, Tate based his "strolls" mainly on memories of his undergraduate days (1920–24).

The Clarke County School District in 1978 published *A Story Untold: Black Men and Women in Athens History,* by Michael L. Thurmond. This remarkable volume remains the only published book to date devoted exclusively to the neglected field of black history in Athens and Clarke County.

James Reap, an attorney and preservation planner, published *Athens: A Pictorial History* in 1982. This "coffee-table volume" contains a lively narrative of town and gown and scores of historic photographs with copious descriptive captions.

The bicentennial of the University of Georgia occasioned the publication of two excellent histories of the university: *The University of Georgia: A Bicentennial History, 1785–1985* by Thomas G. Dyer, professor of history and chairman of the Bicentennial Celebration, and *A Pictorial History of the University of Georgia* by F. N. Boney, professor of history at the university. The former is a scholarly study of the university and its role in the history of higher education, while the latter is a collection of historic photographs accompanied by colorful descriptions and general narrative. Dyer's bibliographic notes offer a definitive reference for primary and secondary resources in the history of the university.

The 1987 publication by the Athens Historical Society of *Historic*

Houses of Athens by Charlotte Thomas Marshall adds greatly to the documentation of Athens's architectural landmarks and the people who lived in them. The Athens Historical Society published two volumes of papers given to the society in 1963 and 1979. Unfortunately, they did not continue to publish this series in succeeding years.

Among recent publications that define Athens and Clarke County within the context of the state and region is *The Atlas of Georgia,* a University of Georgia Bicentennial publication of the Institute of Community and Area Development written by Thomas W. Hodler and Howard A. Schretter. This mammoth volume replete with maps, charts, and overlays offers a comparative study of culture, history, and current economic and demographic trends among Georgia's towns, cities, counties, and regions.

Two catalogues of art and objects include much about the material culture of Athens and Clarke County. The Atlanta Historical Society's publication *Neat Pieces* catalogues Plain style furniture, art, and objects in Georgia exhibited at the society's galleries in 1983; Jane Webb Smith's *Georgia's Legacy: History Charted Through the Arts* documents the Georgia Museum of Art's Bicentennial (1985) exhibition, which included many entries from Athens and Clarke County.

Two other basic references for the study of local history are Kenneth Coleman and Charles Stephen Gurr's two-volume *Dictionary of Georgia Biography* (which includes many biographies of Athenians and Clarke countians) and John Linley's *Georgia Catalogue: Historic American Buildings Survey,* an excellent guide to the architecture of the state, which documents many Athens and Clarke County landmarks.

Bibliography

Athens, Ga., The Classic City: Tradition with Progress. Athens: Athens Area Chamber of Commerce, 1965.

Athens, Georgia. Athens: Athens Chamber of Commerce, 1962.

Athens, Georgia: Home of the University of Georgia, 1801–1951. Athens: Mayor and Council of the City of Athens, 1951.

Barrow, Phyllis Jenkins. *A History of Lucy Cobb Institute.* Master's thesis, University of Georgia, 1951.

Bartley, Numan V. *The Creation of Modern Georgia.* Athens: University of Georgia Press, 1983.

Beaumont, Charles. *The Windows of Emmanuel Church, Athens, Georgia.* Athens: Emmanuel Episcopal Church, 1979.

Boney, F. N. *A Pictorial History of the University of Georgia.* Athens: University of Georgia Press, 1984.

———. *A Walking Tour of the University of Georgia.* Athens: University of Georgia Press, 1989.

Bonner, James C. *A History of Georgia Agriculture, 1732–1860.* Athens: University of Georgia Press, 1964.

Brockman, Charles J., Jr. "The Confederate Armory of Cook and Brother." *Papers of the Athens Historical Society* 2 (1979): 76–87.

Brooks, Robert Preston. *History of Georgia.* Atlanta: Atkinson, Mentzer, 1913.

Calhoun, Ferdinand Phinizy. *The Phinizy Family in America.* Atlanta: Johnson-Dallis, 1925.

The Classic City. Athens: Heery and Heery, Architects, Engineers and Planners for the Athens Area Chamber of Commerce, 1965.

Coleman, Kenneth. *Confederate Athens.* Athens: University of Georgia Press, 1967.

———. *Georgia History in Outline.* Athens: University of Georgia Press, 1978.

———, ed. *A History of Georgia.* Athens: University of Georgia Press, 1977.

Coleman, Kenneth, and Charles Stephen Gurr, eds. *Dictionary of Georgia Biography.* 2 vols. Athens: University of Georgia Press, 1984.

Cooney, Loraine, comp., and Hattie C. Rainwater, ed. *Garden History of Georgia, 1733–1933*. Atlanta: Garden Club of Georgia, 1976.

Cooper, Patricia Irvin. "Athens Houses of the 1820s." *Papers of the Athens Historical Society* 2 (1979): 24–38.

Cooper, Patricia Irvin, and Glen McAninch. "Map and Historical Sketch of the Old Athens Cemetery." Athens: Old Athens Cemetery Foundation, 1983.

Coulter, Ellis Merton. "A Birth of a University, a Town, and a County." *Georgia Historical Quaterly* 46 (March 1962): 113–50.

———. *College Life in the Old South*. Athens: University of Georgia Press, 1951.

———. "Franklin College as a Name for the University of Georgia." *Georgia Historical Quarterly* 34 (September 1950): 189–94.

———. *James Monroe Smith, Georgia Planter, Before Death and After*. Athens: University of Georgia Press, 1961.

———. "The Politics of Dividing a Georgia County: Oconee from Clarke." *Georgia Historical Quarterly* 57, no. 4 (Winter 1979): 475–92.

———. "Slavery and Freedom in Athens, Georgia, 1860–1866," *Georgia Historical Quarterly* 49 (September 1965): 264–93.

———. *The Toombs Oak and Other Stories*. Athens: University of Georgia Press, 1966.

Dalton, Clarence Thomas, comp. *Highlights and Families of Yesteryears: Oconee County, Georgia*. Watkinsville, Ga.: Dalton, 1985.

DeVorsey, Louis, Jr. "Early Water-powered Industries in Athens and Clarke County." *Papers of the Athens Historical Society* 2 (1979): 39–51.

DeVorsey, Louis, Jr., Marion J. Rice, Elmer Williams, and Bonnie London. *A Panorama of Georgia*. Marceline, Mo.: Walsworth, 1987.

Dyer, Thomas G. *The University of Georgia: A Bicentennial History, 1785–1985*. Athens: University of Georgia Press, 1985.

Early Georgia Portraits, 1715–1870. Compiled by the Historical Activities Committee, Marion Converse Bright, chairman, Society of Colonial Dames of America in the State of Georgia. Athens: University of Georgia Press, 1975.

English, John W., and Rob Williams. *When Men Were Boys: An Informal Portrait of Dean William Tate*. Lakemont, Ga.: Copple House Books, 1984.

Federal Writers' Project, Works Progress Administration, comp. *Georgia: A Guide to Its Towns and Countryside*. Athens: University of Georgia Press, 1940.

Franklin County Historical Society. *History of Franklin County, Georgia*. Roswell, Ga.: W. H. Wolfe Associates, 1986.

Fry, Gladys-Marie. "Harriett Powers: Portrait of an African American Quilter." In *Missing Pieces: Georgia Folk Art 1770–1976*. Atlanta: Georgia Council for the Arts and Humanities, 1976.

Gamble, Robert S. "Athens: The Study of a Georgia Town During Reconstruction, 1865–1872." Master's thesis, University of Georgia, 1967.

Georgia Historical Review: Featuring Clarke County. Montgomery, Ala.: Business Review Editions, n.d.

Glickman, Sara Orton. "Historic Resources in African-American Neighborhoods of Piedmont Georgia." Master's thesis, University of Georgia, 1986.

Griffith, A. E. *History of the Southern Mutual Insurance Company, Athens, Georgia, 1848–1923*. 1923. Rev. ed. Athens: McGregor, 1931.

Hajos, Albin. *Hajos' Athens, Georgia: Photo-Gravures*. Athens: The author, 1900.

Hale, Elizabeth Grace. "'In Terms of Paint': The Biography of Lucy Stanton." Master's thesis, University of Georgia, 1991.

Hester, Conoly. "Sandy Creek Trail Project Fruition of Thirty-Year Effort." *Athens Observer*, December 6, 1990, pp. 1, 20A.

Hodler, Thomas W., and Howard A. Schretter. *The Atlas of Georgia*. Athens: Institute of Community and Area Development, University of Georgia, 1986.

Hudson, Karen E. *Athens High and Industrial School*. Athens: City of Athens, 1984.

Huffman, Frank J., Jr. "Town and Country in the South, 1850–1880: A Comparison of Urban and Rural Social Structures." *South Atlantic Quarterly* 76 (Summer 1977): 366–81.

Hull, Augustus Longstreet. *Annals of Athens, Georgia*. 1906. Reprint, with index. Danielsville, Ga.: Heritage Papers, 1978.

———. *A Historical Sketch of the University of Georgia*. Atlanta: Foote and Davies, 1894.

Hynds, Ernest C. *Antebellum Athens and Clarke County*. Athens: University of Georgia Press, 1974.

Jones, James Allison. "A History of the First Presbyterian Church of Athens, Georgia." Master's thesis, University of Georgia, 1949.

Knight, Virginia Deane. "The New Opera House of Athens, Georgia, 1887–1932." Master's thesis, University of Georgia, 1970.

Koch, Mary Levin. "Advocate for Art: Alfred H. Holbrook and the Georgia Museum of Art." *Bulletin of the Georgia Museum of Art* 13, no. 2 (Winter 1988).

Lane, Mills B., ed. *The Rambler in Georgia: Travelers' Accounts of Frontier Georgia.* Savannah, Ga.: Beehive Press, 1973.

Linley, John. *The Georgia Catalog Historic American Buildings Survey: A Guide to the Architecture of the State.* Athens: University of Georgia Press, 1982.

Local History and Townscape Conservation: Opportunities for Georgia's Communities. N.p.: Georgia Downtown Development Association with Assistance from the Department of Community Affairs, 1981.

McCash, William B. *Thomas R. R. Cobb (1823–1862): The Making of a Southern Nationalist.* Macon, Ga.: Mercer University Press, 1983.

McCommons, Pete. "What a Difference a Decade Makes." *Athens Magazine,* December 1989, 18–25.

Marsh, Blanche, and Kenneth F. Marsh. *Athens: Georgia's Columned City.* Asheville, N.C.: Biltmore Press, 1964.

Marshall, Charlotte Thomas. *Historic Houses of Athens.* Athens: Athens Historical Society, 1987.

———, ed. *Oconee Hill Cemetery: Tombstone Inscriptions for That Part of the Cemetery West of the Oconee River and Index to Record of Interments.* Athens: Athens Historical Society, 1971.

Martin, Van Jones, and William Robert Mitchell, Jr. *Landmark Homes of Georgia, 1733–1983.* Savannah: Golden Coast, 1982.

Mell, Edward Baker. *Reminiscences of Athens, Georgia, About 1889 to 1890.* Edited by Jones M. Drewry. Athens: N.p., 1964.

———. *A Short History of Athens Baptist Church, Now the First Baptist Church of Athens.* Athens: Privately published, 1954.

Merritt, Carole. *Historic Black Resources: A Handbook for the Identification, Documentation, and Evaluation of Historic African-American Properties in Georgia.* Atlanta: Historic Preservation Section, Georgia Department of Natural Resources, 1984.

Mohr, Clarence L. *On the Threshold of Freedom: Masters and Slaves in Civil War Georgia.* Athens: University of Georgia Press, 1986.

Montgomery, Horace G. "Howell Cobb and the Secessionist Movement in Georgia." *Papers of the Athens Historical Society* 1 (1963): 35–40.

Morris, Sylvanus. *Strolls About Athens in the Early Seventies.* 1912. Facsimile reprint. Athens: Athens Historical Society, 1969.

Muir, John. *A Thousand Mile Walk to the Gulf.* New York: Houghton Mifflin, 1916.

Neat Pieces: The Plain-Style Furniture of Nineteenth Century Georgia. Atlanta: Atlanta Historical Society, 1983.

Nicholson, Mrs. Madison G. "Ladies' Garden Club, Athens, Georgia: America' First Garden Club." Pamphlet lithoprint. Athens: University of Georgia Printing Department, 1954.

Nix, Harold L., and H. Max Miller. *Changing Classic Community: Athens–Clarke County.* Community Social Analysis Series, no. 13. Athens: Institute of Community and Area Development and the Department of Sociology, University of Georgia, 1979.

One Hundred Years of Life: Emmanuel Episcopal Church, Athens, Georgia, 1843–1943. Athens: Wardens and Vestry, Emmanuel Parish, 1943.

The Past Is Ever Present . . . in Athens, Georgia. Athens: Athens-Clarke Heritage Foundation in cooperation with the Athens Historical Society and the Clarke County School District, 1970.

Poesch, Jessie. *The Art of the Old South: Painting, Sculpture, Architecture, and the Products of Craftsmen, 1560–1860.* New York: Alfred A. Knopf, 1983.

Pound, Merritt B. *Benjamin Hawkins, Indian Agent.* Athens: University of Georgia Press, 1951.

Reap, James K. *Athens: A Pictorial History.* Norfolk, Va.: Donning, 1982.

Redwine, Morgan. "Controversy Swirled Around Wells." *Athens Observer,* January 3, 1991.

———. "Remembering Mayors Dudley, Mell," *Athens Observer,* December 13, 1990.

———. "When Wells Defeated McWhorter," *Athens Observer,* December 20, 1990.

Reiter, Beth Lattimore. *A Plan for Cobbham's Future.* Study for Historic Cobbham Foundation, Inc., funded by the National Trust for Historic Preservation and the City of Athens, March 25, 1978. Photocopy.

Rowe, H. J., ed. *History of Athens and Clarke County.* Athens: McGregor, 1923.

Schinkel, Peter. "The Negro in Athens and Clarke County, 1872–1900." Master's thesis, University of Georgia, 1971.

Sears, Joan Niles. *The First One Hundred Years of Town Planning in Georgia.* Atlanta: Cherokee, 1979.

Sell, Edward Scott. *History of the State Normal School, Athens, Georgia.* Athens: N.p., 1923.

Smith, Jane Webb. *Georgia's Legacy: History Charted Through the Arts.* Edited by Marianne Doezema. Athens: Georgia Museum of Art, 1985.

Spalding, Phinizy. "Neighborhood Conservation, or Getting It All Together in Cobbham." *Georgia Historical Quarterly* 63 (Spring 1979): 90–99.

Stegeman, John F. *The Ghosts of Herty Field: Early Days on a Southern Gridiron.* Athens: University of Georgia Press, 1966.

———. *These Men She Gave.* Athens: University of Georgia Press, 1964.

———. "Tom Cobb at the Montgomery Convention." *Papers of the Athens Historical Society* 1 (1963): 41–49.

Stephens, Lester D. *Joseph LeConte: Gentle Prophet.* Baton Rouge: Louisiana State University Press, 1982.

Strahan, Charles Morton. *Clarke County, Georgia, and the City of Athens.* Athens: N.p., 1893.

"Survey of Athens and Clarke County, Georgia: Part 1, Human and Natural Resources." Institute for the Study of Georgia Problems, Monograph no. 4. *Bulletin of the University of Georgia* 44, no. 3 (March 1944).

Tate, William. *Strolls Around Athens.* Athens: Observer Press, 1975.

Thomas, Emory M. *The Confederate Nation, 1861–1865.* New York: Harper and Row, 1979.

Thomas, Fran. "The Bicentennial Class of 1985 Commences." *Georgia Alumni Record,* Summer 1985, 15–18.

———. "Downtown Athens: A Community Renaissance." *Georgia Journal,* August–September 1984, pp. 4–7.

Thurmond, Michael L. *A Story Untold: Black Men and Women in Athens History.* Athens: Clarke County School District, 1978.

Tree Registry: Athens and Clarke County, Georgia. Athens: Junior Ladies Garden Club, 1978.

Vanishing Georgia. Athens: University of Georgia Press, 1982.

Warren, Mary Bondurant. "Athens: Its Earliest History." *Papers of the Athens Historical Society* 1 (1963): 7–12.

Waters, John C. *Maintaining a Sense of Place: A Citizen's Guide to Community Preservation*. Athens: Institute of Community and Area Development, University of Georgia, 1983.

White, George. *Statistics of the State of Georgia*. Savannah: W. Thorpe Williams, 1849.

Wilson, Robert C. "Methodism in Athens: A Historical Sketch, 1801–1953." In *First Methodist Church Directory*. Athens: First Methodist Church, 1953.

Wood, Maude Talmage. *Once Apunce a Time*. Athens: Classic Press, 1977.

Illustration Credits

Page 2
1868 Map of Clarke County. Courtesy Georgia Department of Archives and History.

Page 3
Tobacco Pipe. Photograph by David Hally. Courtesy Laboratory of Archaeology, Department of Anthropology and Linguistics, University of Georgia.

Page 4
Clay Pot. Photograph by David Hally. Courtesy Laboratory of Archaeology, Department of Anthropology and Linguistics, University of Georgia.

Page 7
Old Athens Cemetery. Photograph by Mary Levin Koch.

Page 9
Laurie de Buys Pannell, *Vernacular Country House,* ca. 1973–75, graphite on paper. Courtesy Laurie de Buys Pannell.

Page 10
Albert Rosenthal, *William Few,* 1881, etching on paper. Courtesy Hargrett Rare Book and Manuscript Library, University of Georgia Libraries.

Page 11
Albert Rosenthal, *Abraham Baldwin,* 1888, etching on paper. Courtesy Hargrett Rare Book and Manuscript Library, University of Georgia Libraries.

Page 12
Robert Field, *John Milledge,* 1802, oil on canvas. Courtesy Georgia College Library Foundation, Old Governor's Mansion.

Page 13
Unknown, *Portrait of Josiah Meigs,* ca. 1824, oil on canvas. Courtesy Hargrett Rare Book and Manuscript Library, University of Georgia Libraries. Gift of Mrs. Catherine E. Graham.

Page 15
Old College. Photograph by Albin Hajos. Courtesy Hargrett Rare Book and Manuscript Library, University of Georgia Libraries.

Page 16
1805 Plan of Athens, Georgia. Courtesy University of Georgia Archives.

Page 19
Unknown, *Portrait of General Elijah Clarke,* ca. 1800, oil on canvas. Bequest of Mrs. Francis Pickens Bacon, 1982. Permanent collection of the High Museum of Art, Atlanta, Georgia.

Page 21
Unknown, *Corner Cupboard,* ca. 1800, walnut and southern yellow pine with maple inlay. Gift of Frances and Emory L. Cocke, 1976. Permanent collection of the High Museum of Art, Atlanta, Georgia.

Page 22
Unknown, *Cellaret,* ca. 1800, walnut. Courtesy Mr. and Mrs. Henry D. Green.

Page 23
Old Stagecoach Road. Courtesy Hargrett Rare Book and Manuscript Library, University of Georgia Libraries.

Page 24
William A. and Cynthia Carr House. Courtesy Athens-Clarke Heritage Foundation.

Page 25
Unknown, *Writing Desk,* ca. 1800, walnut. Photograph by Kenneth Kay. Courtesy Mr. and Mrs. Milton Leathers.

Page 26
Pleasant Grove. Courtesy Marguerite Thomas Hodgson.

Page 27
Church-Waddel-Brumby House. Courtesy Athens-Clarke Heritage Foundation.

Page 28
Hoyt House. Photograph by Charles Rowland. Courtesy Hargrett Rare Book and Manuscript Library, University of Georgia Libraries.

Page 29
Doorway of the Cobb-Jackson-Ward-Erwin-McFeely House. Photograph by Van Jones Martin. Courtesy Hargrett Rare Book and Manuscript Library, University of Georgia Libraries.

Page 31
Unknown, *Franklin College,* ca. 1844, color wood engraving on paper. Photograph by Michael McKelvey. Courtesy Georgia Museum of Art, The University of Georgia. Gift of Laura Blackshear.

Page 32
Gardens at the President's House. Courtesy Georgia Department of Archives and History: P. Thornton Marye Drawings, ac. 52-101.

Page 34
Conger-Woods House. Photograph by Mary Levin Koch. Courtesy Mr. and Mrs. A. Y. Woods.

Page 34
Old McRee-Crawford Mill. Photograph by Patricia Irvin Cooper. Courtesy Patricia Irvin Cooper.

Page 35
Eagle Tavern. Courtesy Hargrett Rare Book and Manuscript Library, University of Georgia Libraries. Historic American Buildings Survey.

Page 37
O'Brian Inman, *Alonzo Church,* oil on canvas. Courtesy Georgia Museum of Art, The University of Georgia Portrait Collection.

Page 38
Demosthenian Hall. Courtesy Hargrett Rare Book and Manuscript Library, University of Georgia Libraries. Historic American Buildings Survey.

Page 38
Phi Kappa Hall. Courtesy Hargrett Rare Book and Manuscript Library, University of Georgia Libraries. Historic American Buildings Survey.

Page 39
Chapel. Courtesy Hargrett Rare Book and Manuscript Library, University of Georgia Libraries.

Page 41
Taylor-Grady House. Courtesy Hargrett Rare Book and Manuscript Library, University of Georgia Libraries.

Page 41
Pigeon Cote, Taylor-Grady House. Photograph by Doug Brown. Courtesy Athens-Clarke Heritage Foundation.

Page 43
Asaph King Childs, *Teapot,* ca. 1856, silver and ivory. Photograph by Michael McKelvey. Courtesy Athens-Clarke Heritage Foundation.

Page 44
John Held, Jr., *Chancellor's House,* ca. 1940–41, ink, wash, and traces of graphite on paper. Courtesy Georgia Museum of Art, The University of Georgia. Gift of the Estate of Mrs. John Held, Jr., and University Purchase through the Bequest of Edith L. Stallings.

Page 46
Unknown, *John A. Cobb,* oil on paper. Photograph by Dan McClure. Courtesy Mr. and Mrs. Milton Leathers.

Page 47
Unknown, *Sarah Rootes Cobb,* oil on paper. Photograph by Dan McClure. Courtesy Mr. and Mrs. Milton Leathers.

Page 48
John White. Courtesy Marguerite Thomas Hodgson.

Page 49
Laurie de Buys Pannell, *Princeton Factory,* ca. 1973–75, graphite on paper. Courtesy Laurie de Buys Pannell.

Page 50
Bobbin Mill. Photograph by David L. Earnest. Courtesy Hargrett Rare Book and Manuscript Library, University of Georgia Libraries. Gift of Charles Brockman, Jr.

Page 51
Unknown, *James Camak,* oil on canvas. Courtesy Hargrett Rare Book and Manuscript Library, University of Georgia Libraries.

Page 53
Stock certificate. Courtesy Charles Brockman, Jr.

Pages 54–55
George Cooke, *View of Athens from Carr's Hill,* 1845, oil on canvas. Photograph by Michael McKelvey. Courtesy Hargrett Rare Book and Manuscript Library, University of Georgia Libraries. Gift of the Moss Family.

Page 57
Franklin House. Courtesy Hargrett Rare Book and Manuscript Library, University of Georgia Libraries. Historic American Buildings Survey.

Page 59
Wilson Lumpkin House. Courtesy Hargrett Rare Book and Manuscript Library, University of Georgia Libraries.

Page 59
Unknown, *Sideboard,* ca. 1847, mahogany. Photograph by Mary Levin Koch. Courtesy Mr. and Mrs. Milton Leathers.

Page 61
John Maier, *Joseph Henry Lumpkin,* 1860, oil on canvas. Courtesy Joseph Henry Lumpkin Foundation, Incorporated.

Page 65
Lucy Cobb Institute. Courtesy Hargrett Rare Book and Manuscript Library, University of Georgia Libraries.

Page 67
Unknown, *The Rev. Nathan Hoyt,* ca. 1847, daguerreotype. Courtesy Hargrett Rare Book and Manuscript Library, University of Georgia Libraries, M.S. 828 Dr. George Baber Atkisson Collection.

Page 68
Oconee Hill Cemetery. Photograph by Mary Levin Koch.

Page 71
Ironwork at the Hamilton-Hodgson House. Photograph by Charlie Register. Courtesy Charlie Register.

Page 72
Law office of Joseph H. Lumpkin, Thomas R. R. Cobb, and William H. Hull. Courtesy Hargrett Rare Book and Manuscript Library, University of Georgia Libraries.

Page 73
Thomas Reade Rootes Cobb. Courtesy Hargrett Rare Book and Manuscript Library, University of Georgia Libraries.

Page 74
Unknown, *Howell Cobb,* ca. 1858, oil on paper on canvas. Photograph by Dan McClure. Courtesy Mr. and Mrs. Milton Leathers.

Page 76
Secession Ordinance. Courtesy Hargrett Rare Book and Manuscript Library, University of Georgia Libraries.

Page 77
Unknown, *Confederate Musician,* ca. 1861–65, daguerreotype. Courtesy Hargrett Rare Book and Manuscript Library, University of Georgia Libraries.

Page 78
Pearl-studded brooch. Courtesy Hargrett Rare Book and Manuscript Library, University of Georgia Libraries, M.S. 567 Eleanor Tschudi Papers.

Page 79
God Save the South. Courtesy Hargrett Rare Book and Manuscript Library, University of Georgia Libraries.

Page 80
Unknown, *Rufus Reaves,* ca. 1861–65, daguerreotype. Courtesy Rufus Reaves Paine, Sr.

Page 82
Confederate bond. Courtesy Charles Brockman, Jr.

Page 84
Patrick Hues Mell. Courtesy Hargrett Rare Book and Manuscript Library, University of Georgia Libraries.

Page 85
Honorable discharge from West Point. Courtesy Judge and Mrs. James Barrow.

Page 87
Grave marker. Photograph by Mary Levin Koch.

Page 88
Sledge-Cobb-Spalding House. Courtesy Hargrett Rare Book and Manuscript Library, University of Georgia Libraries.

Page 89
Unknown, *Mary Ann Lamar Cobb,* ca. 1858, oil on paper on canvas. Photograph by Dan McClure. Courtesy Mr. and Mrs. Milton Leathers.

Page 90
Banknote. Courtesy Gary L. Doster.

Page 91
Unknown, *Andrew Lipscomb,* oil on canvas on board. Courtesy Hargrett Rare Book and Manuscript Library, University of Georgia Libraries.

Page 92
Enfield-model rifle. Courtesy Charles Brockman, Jr.

Page 93
Double-barreled cannon. Courtesy Hargrett Rare Book and Manuscript Library, University of Georgia Libraries, M.S. 1590 Earnest Photo Collection.

Page 95
Slave bill of sale. Private collection.

Page 97
Augustus Thompson. Photograph from Edward R. Carter, *The Black Side* (Atlanta, 1894). Courtesy Hargrett Rare Book and Manuscript Library, University of Georgia Libraries.

Page 98
Rural houses. Courtesy Hargrett Rare Book and Manuscript Library, University of Georgia Libraries.

Page 100
Confederate monument. Courtesy Hargrett Rare Book and Manuscript Library, University of Georgia Libraries.

Page 102
Unknown, *Athens, Georgia,* 1866, watercolor on paper. Courtesy Hargrett Rare Book and Manuscript Library, University of Georgia Libraries.

Page 104
John Richards White. Courtesy Marguerite Thomas Hodgson.

Page 105
White Hall. Courtesy Marguerite Thomas Hodgson.

Page 106
Southern Mutual Insurance Company. Courtesy Southern Mutual Insurance Company.

Page 107
Map of Athens Manufacturing Company. Courtesy Map Collection, University of Georgia Libraries.

Page 108
University High School receipt. Courtesy Charles Brockman, Jr.

Page 109
Brothers of Sigma Alpha Epsilon. Photograph by C. W. Davis. Courtesy Hargrett Rare Book and Manuscript Library, University of Georgia Libraries.

Page 111
University quadrangle with Moore College. Courtesy Hargrett Rare Book and Manuscript Library, University of Georgia Libraries.

Page 112
Knox School. Courtesy Hargrett Rare Book and Manuscript Library, University of Georgia Libraries.

Page 113
Chestnut Grove School. Photograph by James R. Lockhart. Courtesy James R. Lockhart for Georgia Department of Natural Resources, Historic Preservation Section.

Page 113
Laurie de Buys Pannell, *African Methodist Episcopal Church,* ca. 1975, graphite on paper. Courtesy Laurie de Buys Pannell.

Page 114
Henry Woodfin Grady. Courtesy Hargrett Rare Book and Manuscript Library, University of Georgia Libraries.

Page 115
J. C. Buttre, *Benjamin H. Hill,* engraving on paper. Courtesy Hargrett Rare Book and Manuscript Library, University of Georgia Libraries.

Page 116
Map of Clarke County. Courtesy Hargrett Rare Book and Manuscript Library, University of Georgia Libraries.

Page 119
Clarke County Courthouse. Courtesy Hargrett Rare Book and Manuscript Library, University of Georgia Libraries.

Page 120
William W. Puryear's mill. Courtesy Mrs. Hilda Puryear Phillips.

Page 123
Robert L. Bloomfield. Courtesy Hargrett Rare Book and Manuscript Library, University of Georgia Libraries.

Page 124
J. J. Nevitt, *Interior of Emmanuel Church,* ca. 1867, graphite on paper. Courtesy Hargrett Rare Book and Manuscript Library, University of Georgia Libraries. Gift of Emmanuel Church, Athens, Georgia.

Page 125
John A. Hunnicutt House. Courtesy Gary L. Doster.

Page 126
Broad Street. Courtesy Hargrett Rare Book and Manuscript Library, University of Georgia Libraries.

Page 127
Volunteer firemen. Courtesy Hargrett Rare Book and Manuscript Library, University of Georgia Libraries.

Page 128
Map of Athens. Courtesy Map Collection, University of Georgia Libraries.

Page 130
Mildred Rutherford. Courtesy Hargrett Rare Book and Manuscript Library, University of Georgia Libraries. Gift of Hattie Elder.

Page 131
Seney-Stovall Chapel. Courtesy Hargrett Rare Book and Manuscript Library, University of Georgia Libraries.

Pages 132–33
Girls at Lucy Cobb Institute. Courtesy Georgia and Richard Patterson.

Page 134
Students at Washington Street School. Courtesy Charles Brockman, Jr.

Page 135
Closing Exercises at the Grove School. Courtesy Paul Hodgson.

Page 136
Spanish-American War Soldiers' Encampment. Courtesy Roy T. Ward, William M. White Collection.

Page 137
Spanish-American War Volunteers. Courtesy Roy T. Ward, William M. White Collection.

Page 138
Tent on Hill Street. Courtesy Roy T. Ward, William M. White Collection.

Page 140
Laurie de Buys Pannell, *Seaboard Air Line Station,* ca. 1975, graphite on paper. Courtesy Laurie de Buys Pannell.

Page 141
Winterville Train Station. Photograph by Hal Brooks. Courtesy Athens Newspapers, Inc.

Page 144
Streetcar. Courtesy Gary L. Doster.

Page 145
Streetcar on Prince Avenue. Courtesy Gary L. Doster.

Page 146
William W. Thomas. Courtesy Georgia and Richard Patterson.

Page 147
Interior, William W. Thomas House. Photograph by Albin Hajos. Courtesy Georgia and Richard Patterson.

Page 148
Billups Phinizy House. Courtesy Hargrett Rare Book and Manuscript Library, University of Georgia Libraries, M.S. 1482 The National Society of the Colonial Dames of America, Athens Chapter.

Page 148
Hamilton McWhorter House. Courtesy Hargrett Rare Book and Manuscript Library, University of Georgia Libraries. Gift of Patricia Orr.

Page 150
Lucy Stanton. Courtesy Hargrett Rare Book and Manuscript Library, University of Georgia Libraries, M.S. 392 Lucy Stanton Scrapbook.

Page 151
Harriet Powers, *Bible Quilt,* ca. 1886, appliqué and pieced work, cotton top and lining. Courtesy Smithsonian Institution. Photograph 69039.

Page 152
Ann Olivia Newton Cobb. Courtesy Eleanor Sledge Burke.

Page 153
Calvert Smith, *Establishing the First Garden Club,* 1934. Photograph from *New York Herald Tribune,* March 18, 1934. Courtesy Junior Ladies Garden Club.

Page 155
Map of State Normal School. Courtesy Map Collection, University of Georgia Libraries.

Page 156
Barnett Shoals Dam and Power Plant. Courtesy Gary L. Doster.

Page 157
Woodlawn Avenue real estate advertisement. Courtesy Gary L. Doster.

Page 159
Monroe B. Morton. Courtesy Hargrett Rare Book and Manuscript Library, University of Georgia Libraries.

Page 161
Knox Institute football team. Courtesy Hargrett Rare Book and Manuscript Library, University of Georgia Libraries.

Page 162
Interior of E. D. Harris Drugstore. Courtesy Hargrett Rare Book and Manuscript Library, University of Georgia Libraries.

Page 163
Morton Theater Handbill. Courtesy Cultural Services Division, Clarke County Parks Department.

Page 164
City Hall and water tower. Courtesy Jeanné M. Downs.

Page 165
Clayton Street. Courtesy Gary L. Doster.

Page 166
Georgian Hotel. Photograph by Clifton. Courtesy Gary L. Doster.

Page 167
Bludwine delivery wagon. Courtesy Hargrett Rare Book and Manuscript Library, University of Georgia Libraries. Gift of Joseph Costa, Jr.

Page 168
Ben Epps and his airplane. Courtesy Hargrett Rare Book and Manuscript Library, University of Georgia Libraries.

Page 171
Moses and Simon Michael houses. Courtesy Hargrett Rare Book and Manuscript Library, University of Georgia Libraries.

Page 172
Young women of Athens. Courtesy Georgia and Richard Patterson.

Page 174
Cotton Market. Courtesy Gary L. Doster.

Page 175
Tenant farmers. Courtesy Hargrett Rare Book and Manuscript Library, University of Georgia Libraries, M.S. 392 Lucy Stanton Scrapbook.

Page 176
David C. Barrow. Courtesy Hargrett Rare Book and Manuscript Library, University of Georgia Libraries.

Page 178
Sanford Stadium and Memorial Hall. Courtesy Gary L. Doster.

Page 181
Franklin D. Roosevelt with Steadman V. Sanford. Courtesy Hargrett Rare Book and Manuscript Library, University of Georgia Libraries.

Page 183
William W. Thomas, *Architectural Rendering for the William W. Thomas House,* ca. 1896, graphite on paper. Courtesy Georgia and Richard Patterson.

Page 186
Rose Bowl, 1943. Courtesy Hargrett Rare Book and Manuscript Library, University of Georgia Libraries.

Page 188
Navy Preflight School. Courtesy Gary L. Doster.

Pages 190–91
Lamar Dodd, *Winter Valley,* 1944, oil on canvas. Courtesy National Gallery of Art, Washington. Anonymous gift.

Page 192
John Held, Jr., *Another Part of the Garden at L.A.,* 1940–41, ink, wash, and traces of graphite on paper. Courtesy Georgia Museum of Art, The University of Georgia. Gift of the Estate of Mrs. John Held, Jr., and University Purchase through the Bequest of Edith L. Stallings.

Page 193
President's House (Grant-Hill-White House). Courtesy Office of Public Information, University of Georgia.

Page 194
Lamar Dodd, *Portrait of Alfred H. Holbrook,* ca. 1948–49, oil on canvas. Photograph by Michael McKelvey. Courtesy Georgia Museum of Art, The University of Georgia. Gift of Mary and Lamar Dodd.

Page 195
John Held, Jr., *Untitled* [Lucas House], ca. 1940–41, ink and graphite on paper. Courtesy Georgia Museum of Art, The University of Georgia. Gift of the Estate of Mrs. John Held, Jr., and University Purchase through the Bequest of Edith L. Stallings.

Page 196
Lamar Dodd, *On the Campus,* 1939, oil on canvas. Photograph by W. Robert Nix. Courtesy Lamar Dodd.

Page 198
Hugh Hodgson. Photograph from *The Lightning Bug,* vol. 1, no. 1. Courtesy Friends of Lucy Cobb.

Page 201
Dean Tate. Courtesy Hargrett Rare Book and Manuscript Library, University of Georgia Libraries. Gift of Mrs. Susan F. Tate.

Page 203
Hamilton Holmes and Charlayne Hunter-Gault with Fred C. Davison. Photograph by Walker Montgomery. Courtesy Office of Public Information, University of Georgia.

Page 204
Susan Medical Center. Courtesy Michael Thurmond.

Page 205
Michael Thurmond. Courtesy Michael Thurmond.

Page 207
Lawton Stephens and Robert Stephens, Jr. Photograph by Patrick Smith. Courtesy University of Georgia School of Law.

Page 208
Athens Regional Medical Center. Photograph by Ellen Fitzgerald. Courtesy Athens Newspapers, Inc.

Page 209
Saint Mary's Hospital. Photograph by Walker Montgomery. Courtesy Saint Mary's Hospital.

Page 210
Restoration on Prince Avenue. Photograph by Karekin Goekjian.

Page 211
First American Bank and Trust Company. Photograph by Mary Levin Koch.

Page 213
Ware-Lyndon House. Courtesy Moselle Burke Hodgson.

Page 214
Church-Waddel-Brumby House. Photograph by Mary Levin Koch.

Page 215
Parlor of the Church-Waddel-Brumby House. Photograph by Richard Fowlkes. Courtesy Athens-Clarke Heritage Foundation.

Page 216
Franklin House. Photograph by Mary Levin Koch.

Page 217
Planting the Tree That Owns Itself, 1946. Courtesy Junior Ladies Garden Club.

Page 219
Franklin-Upson House. Photograph by Dan McClure. Courtesy Trust Company Bank of Northeast Georgia.

Page 221
Laurie de Buys Pannell, *City Hall*, ca. 1975, graphite on paper. Courtesy Laurie de Buys Pannell.

Page 223
Vince Dooley. Photograph by Fred Bennett. Courtesy Sports Information, University of Georgia.

Page 225
Jimmy Carter and Dean Rusk. Photograph by Walker Montgomery. Courtesy Office of Public Information, University of Georgia.

Page 226
Francis Chapin, *University of Georgia Arch*, 1952, lithograph on wove paper. Courtesy Georgia Museum of Art, The University of Georgia. Patrons Fund Purchase.

Page 229
Athens City Limits Evolution. Courtesy *The Atlas of Georgia*, The University of Georgia.

Page 231
Four Mayors at Night in Old Athens. Photograph by Randy Miller. Courtesy Randy Miller.

Page 233
Clarke County Courthouse. Photograph by Mary Levin Koch.

Page 235
College Square Festival. Photograph by Paul Efland. Courtesy Athens Newspapers, Inc.

Page 237
R.E.M. Photograph by Michael Tighe. Courtesy Michael Tighe.

Page 241
Thomas Reade Rootes Cobb House. Photograph by Thomas Waterman. Courtesy Hargrett Rare Book and Manuscript Library, University of Georgia Libraries. Historic American Buildings Survey.

Page 243
George Bush with honorees, University of Georgia Bicentennial Convocation. Photograph by Walker Montgomery. Courtesy Office of Public Information, University of Georgia.

Page 244
Joseph Henry Lumpkin House. Photograph by Frances Taliaferro Thomas. Courtesy University of Georgia School of Law.

Page 245
Football Players Retiring Their Jerseys. Photograph by Paul Efland. Courtesy Athens Newspapers, Inc.

Page 246
Dan Magill. Photograph by Richard Fowlkes. Courtesy Sports Information, University of Georgia.

Page 247
Corrinne Wright. Photograph by Wingate Downs. Courtesy Athens Newspapers, Inc.

Page 248
Athens Regional Library. Courtesy Nix Mann Viehman Architects.

Page 249
Morton Building. Photograph by Mary Levin Koch.

Page 253
Demolition of Hull-Snelling House. Photograph by Don Nelson. Courtesy *Athens Observer.*

Page 255
Alan Campbell, *Winter Lights, Athens,* 1986, watercolor on paper. Courtesy Alan Campbell.

Index

Academic Building, 39, 66, 140, 176, 224, 227
Adams (Union colonel), 92, 93
Adams, F. W., 261
Adams, John Quincy, 48
Aderhold, Omer Clyde, 193–94, 200, 223
African Methodist Episcopal (AME) Church, 112, 113, 158, 170, 258
Agricultural Hall, 176, 177
Agriculture, 5, 24–26, 29, 33, 90, 119–22, 175, 184, 238–39
Aguar, Charles, 251
Air-conditioning, 199
Albany, Ga., 240
Allentown, Ga., 139
Alligator Bridge, 17
Alpha Delta Pi sorority, 71, 183
Alpha Gamma Delta sorority, 183
Alumni Hall, 188
Alumni Society, 45
American Missionary Association, 111
American Revolution, 6, 9, 17
American State Bank, 173
Anderson, Henry C., 166
Annals of Athens, Georgia (Hull), 53, 62, 64, 140, 263
Antebellum Athens and Clarke County (Hynds), 66, 265
Antebellum Trail, 241–42
Antietam, Battle of, 83
Apartment houses, 157
Archaic Indians, 1
Architecture, 8, 57, 176, 198–99, 240; Plain style, 8; Greek Revival, 33, 37, 39–40, 61, 84, 193, 195, 218, 220, 240, 242, 244, 252, 253; Federal, 37, 38, 52, 212; Georgian, 37; Italianate, 40, 71, 212, 218; Gothic Revival, 89, 163, 218, 252; slave homes, 98; Victorian Romanesque, 105, 147, 176; Second Empire, 111; Queen Anne, 146, 149, 218; Craftsman, 157, 162; Beaux Arts, 164, 168, 176, 183; Commercial, 165; Renaissance Revival, 165, 169; skyscrapers, 165, 167; Neoclassical, 168, 170, 171, 176, 185, 217
Armory Battalion Cavalry, 94
Armstrong, Louis, 163
Armstrong and Dobbs company, 182
Army of Northern Virginia, 86
Army Signal Corps, 187, 188–89
Army Specialized Training Program, 187
Arnall, Ellis G., 187
Arnold, O. H., 262
Arnold, R. O., 262
Athens, Ga., 3, 5, 7–8, 9–10, *map* 107, *map* 128; founding of, 10, 16–17; University and growth of, 12–13, 14–16, 29, 30, 36, 45, 184; roads and bridges, 22, 23, 33, 35, 48, 64, 126, 139, 174; churches, 24, 39, 65–67, 98–99, 122–23, 170; slaves in, 26, 31–33, 69, 95, 96, 99; population, 26, 46, 70, 117, 118, 145, 185, 206, 228–30; railroads, 30, 51, 52–56, 118, 124, 138, 139, 140, 150, 174, 182; cotton economy, 30, 120, 173–74, 175, 182, 185; rivalry with Watkinsville, 35–36, 118; architecture, 39–40, 57, 64, 140, 146–47, 165, 167, 170, 198–99, 218, 220, 240, 242; parks, 42, 191, 251–52; suburbs, 46, 58, 138, 146, 157, 199; businesses in, 46–47, 56, 104–5, 117, 137–38, 173, 191; investment in, 47, 48, 51, 70, 143; manufacturing in, 47–51, 118, 122, 174, 181, 189–91; schools, 63, 64, 111–12, 127–29, 131, 135, 154, 162, 204–5, 206, 207, 250; secessionists in, 70–71, 75, 77; in Civil War, 78–80, 81–82, 87–88, 90–91, 92–94; Federal occupation of, 94–95, 100, 101–2, 114; slave ordinances, 96, 97–98, 99; John Muir's praise for, 106; freedmen in, 110, 121; during Reconstruction, 114; newspapers, 115–17, 222–23, 249; as seat of Clarke County, 117, 118–19, 124; agriculture in, 121–22, 175; building booms, 124–25, 164–66; streetcar lines, 126, 144, 145–46, 154, 157; municipal services, 126–27, 152–54, 156, 169, 182; in Spanish-American War, 136–37, 138; land annexation and city limits growth, 146, 208, 228, 229; city budget, 149; black neighborhoods, 158, 160–61, 162–63; theaters, 163, 170–71, 173, 188, 249–50; fire of 1921, 169; hospitals, 174, 207–8; in Great Depression, 175, 181–82, 184; housing, 182–84, 199, 212; urban renewal, 183–84, 210–15; historic preservation, 184, 213–14, 217–19, 240–42, 249–50, 252–54, 257; in World War II, 185, 188–89, 191; flood of 1964, 216; tornadoes of 1973, 216–17; downtown revitalization, 220–22, 234–37; unified government with

Athens, Ga. (*cont.*)
county, 232–33, 254, 262; administrative officers, 261–62
Athens: A Pictorial History (Reap), 265
"Athens: The Study of a Georgia Town During Reconstruction" (Gamble), 120
Athens, Georgia: Home of the University of Georgia 1801–1951 (Wells), 264–65
Athens Academy, 131, 206
Athens Area Chamber of Commerce, 206, 220, 228, 241, 253
Athens Art Association, 151
Athens Banner-Herald, 172, 173, 243
Athens Baptist Church, 47
Athens Blade, 115–17
Athens Board of Health, 126
Athens Boiler and Machine Shop, 212
Athens Chamber of Commerce, 164–65, 169–70, 174, 197
Athens Christian School, 207
Athens City Council, 97–98, 99, 110, 124, 126–27, 154, 188–89, 206
Athens-Clarke County Planning Commission, 228
Athens-Clarke County Unification Commission, 232–33
Athens-Clarke Heritage Foundation (ACHF), 213, 214, 218, 220, 241
Athens Clipper, 117
Athens Coca-Cola Bottling Company, 222
Athens Cotton and Wool Factory, 48
Athens Country Club, 149, 248
Athens Daily News, 212, 240
Athens Department of Recreation and Parks, 221–22
Athens Downtown Council, 220
Athens Downtown Development Authority (ADDA), 220–21, 236, 237, 248
Athens Electric Railway Company, 157
Athens Factory, 24, 122, 123, 126, 258
Athens Federal Savings Bank, 207
Athens Federal Savings and Loan Association, 218
Athens Fire Company No. 1, 88
Athens Fire Department, 241
Athens Flour Mill, 122
Athens Foundry and Machine Works, 92, 104, 105, 121
Athens Gas Light Company, 64
Athens General Hospital, 174, 182, 207–8
Athens Guards, 81–82, 134
Athens Hardware Company, 56, 105, 214, 216
Athens High and Industrial School, 162, 204
Athens High School, 119, 204, 205
Athens Historical Society, 266
Athens Historic Preservation Ordinance, 240–42, 249–50
Athens Industrial Development Corporation, 209
Athens Insurance Company, 123
Athens Junior Assembly, 191, 219
Athens Junior League, 191
Athens Lodge, Order of Elks, 183
Athens Lumber Company, 182, 212
Athens Magazine, 229
Athens Manufacturing Company, 47–48, 50, 104–5, 106, 149, 189
Athens Montessori School, 207
Athens Municipal Airport–Ben Epps Field, 169, 188
Athens Newspapers, 249
Athens Observer, 149, 222–23, 238, 251, 265
Athens Park and Improvement Company, 145–46
Athens Police Department, 200
Athens Public Housing Authority, 212
Athens Railway and Electric Company, 106, 156, 157, 165
Athens Regional Library, 239, 248
Athens Regional Medical Center, 208
Athens Savings Bank, 169–70, 173, 218, 258
Athens Sierra Club, 252
Athens Steam Company, 56
Athens Street Railway Company, 126
Athens Transit Mall, 234
Athens Transit System, 221
Athens Tree Commission, 235
Athens Typographical Union, 169
Athens Wheat Club, 120
Athletic Association, 245–46
Atkinson, Fannie, 106
Atlanta, Ga., 60, 140, 169, 182, 229, 234
Atlanta Constitution, 103, 114, 192, 200
Atlas of Georgia (Hodler and Schretter), 266
Augusta, Ga., 4, 18, 52, 53, 228–29, 240
Augusta Chronicle, 8, 13
Automobiles, 138, 139, 146, 157, 166, 182, 198–99

Bacon, Mary, 131
Baldwin, Abraham, 10–11, 12, 13, 242
Baldwin, Catherine, 28
Baldwin Hall, 188
Baldwin Street, 64
Bank of Athens, 56, 90, 103–4
Banks, 43, 48, 52, 53, 56, 90, 103–4, 167, 173, 191, 207, 211, 212, 218, 219, 258
Banks County Guards, 81
Bankston, Daniel, 20
Bannerman, William T., 108
Baptists, 24, 65, 66–67, 68
Barber's Creek, 23, 65
Barber Street, 144
Barbersville, Ga., 139
Barnes, Edward Larabee, 243
Barnesville, Ga., 181
Barnett, Amanda, 3
Barnett, John William, 264
Barnett Shoals, 50, 65, 156
Barnett Shoals Elementary School, 206
Barnett Shoals Road, 215
Barrow, Clara, 108
Barrow, David Crenshaw (university chancellor), 157, 176, 179, 264
Barrow, David Crenshaw, Sr. (landholder), 81, 120

Barrow, James (Confederate soldier), 84, 86, 176
Barrow, James (Superior Court judge), 205
Barrow, Pope, 78, 81
Barrow, Tom, 78
Barrow County, 234
Barrow Elementary School, 157
Bartley, Numan V., 142
Bartow, Francis, 77
Bass, William L., 261
Baxter Street, 210
Baxter Street School, 129
Beacham, "Captain Jack," 149, 173
Beaird, J. Ralph, 244
Beatty, Rev. Troy, 123
Beaux Arts architecture, 183
Beaverdam Creek, 141
"Beaverdam Farm," 144
Beechwood Shopping Center, 234
Beechwood subdivision, 198–99
Belk department store, 234
Bell, John, 70–71
Bell, Wallace, 146
Bell Telephone, 126
Ben Burton Park, 252
Benjamin Hill House, 257
Benson's Bakery, 222
Bentley, Upshaw, 221, 231, 262
Bernhardt, Sarah, 171
Berry, Bill, 237, 238
Bethel Homes, 212
Beusse, Henry, 124, 261
B-52's, 237
Big Beaver Swamp, 255
Big Spring, 20
Billups, Richard, 26
Billups, William, 26
Billups Grove Church, 112
Bing, Micaiga, 20
Bioscience Complex, 247
Birth of a Nation (Griffith), 172
Bishop, Rev. Arthur F., 264
Bishop, Julius, 210, 211, 231, 262
Bishop House, 257
"Blackfriars," 110
Black Patti Musical Company, 163
Blacks, 69; population, 30, 70, 117, 184; freedmen, 31, 95, 96, 100, 101, 110; churches, 67–68, 98–99, 112–14, 158, 170; violence against, 99, 114–15, 200–202, 205; schools, 111–12, 127, 129, 161, 162, 163, 204; voting rights, 114; legislative representatives, 114, 115, 205; segregation and, 114, 163; newspapers, 115–17; agricultural labor, 119, 121; culture and social life, 151, 152, 163; neighborhoods, 158, 160–61, 162, 183; school desegregation, 199–205; athletes, 223–24. *See also* Slaves
Blackshear, Laura, 151
Bleckley, Logan, 60
Blind Tom, 99
Bloomfield, Robert L., 78–80, 122–23, 146, 252
Bloomfield Historic District, 123, 241, 258
Bloomfield suburb, 146, 199
Bobbin Mill, 50
Boll weevil blight, 163, 175
Boney, F. N., 83, 176, 177, 265
Bonnell, Rev. John M., 67
Boston Museum of Fine Arts, 152
Botanical Garden, 40–42, 226, 239, 242, 251
Boulevard, 144, 145, 146, 199, 216
Boulevard Historic District, 241, 258
Bowdre, Harriet Hays, 103
Bowstum, R. W., 210
Bradley Foundation, 193
Branch Bank of the State of Georgia, 52
Brand, Charles H., 168
Breckinridge, John, 70–71
Bridges, 23, 48, 126
Broadacres Homes, 183
Broad Street, 15, 19, 64, 87, 120, 126, 173, 174, 227, 255
Broad Street Association, 236
Brooks, Robert Preston, 45
Brooks Hall, 176
Brown, A. Ten Eyck, 165–66, 168
Brown, E. T., 261
Brown, John, 71
Brown v. *Board of Education* (1954), 204
Brumby, Ann Wallis, 177–78
Brumby's Drugstore, 156
Bryan, W. T., 157
Buchanan, James, 74, 75
Buck, Peter, 237, 238
Buckingham, James Silk, 49, 56–58
Budwine, 166
Buena Vista, 146
Buesse, J. H., 134
Bullock, Rufus B., 115
Burnett, Joe, 221
Burney, Mrs. A. H., 204
Burney-Harris High School, 204, 205
Burton, Glenn W., 242
Bush, George, 242
Butterbeans and Susie, 163
Butts, Wallace, 185, 189
Butts-Mehre Building, 245–46

Cabaniss, Harvey W., Sr., 206
Caldwell, Harmon W., 180
Callaway Foundation, 226, 242
Call Creek, 20
Calloway, Cab, 163
Camak, James, 49, 51–52, 69, 71
Camak, Thomas U., 83
Camak House, 258
Camak Manufacturing Company, 48–49
Campbell, Alan, 255
Camp Sumter, 94
Camp Wilkins, 177
Candler Hall, 188
Capron, Horace, 92, 93, 94
Carithers, Hershel, 134
Carithers, James Y., 157, 183
Carlton, Henry H., 81
Carlton, James R., 39
Carlton, William A., 264
Carnegie Library Building, 258
Carnes, Thomas Peter, 20, 22, 45
Carnesville, Ga., 20
Carr, Cynthia Walker, 23, 24
Carr, Florida, 24

Carr, William A., 23, 24
Carroll, E. W., 174, 264
Carr's Hill, 52–56, 92, 126
Carter, Jimmy, 214, 227, 242
Cedar Shoals, 7–8, 10, 12, 13, 48
Cedar Shoals High School, 206
Center for Global Studies, 247
Central of Georgia Railroad, 140
Central Hotel, 56
Chambers, Dwain, 231, 252, 261, 262
Chapel Hill, N.C., 14
Chapin, Francis, 227
Charbonnier, Leon Henri, 108, 111, 119
Charleston, S.C., 52, 78
Chase, Albon, 56, 261
Chase House, 258
Chatham County, 51
Check Factory, 189
Cherokees, 5–6, 14, 17, 18, 28, 58–60
Chestnut Grove Church, 112
Chestnut Grove School, 113, 258
Chicago Cardinals, 245
Chicopee Mills, 189
Childs, Asagh King, 105
Childs, Asaph K., 43
Christian College of Georgia, 252, 253
Christy, John, 70, 77–78, 95, 99, 108, 115
Church, Alonzo: as university president, 36, 37, 42, 43, 44; slaveholding, 96; home of, 157, 212–13, 214
Church, Thomas, 197
Churches, 24, 65–69, 98–99, 112, 113, 122–23, 158, 170
Church-Waddel-Brumby House, 27, 212–14, 215, 258
Citizens and Southern Bank, 66, 167, 191
City Hall, 92, 100, 212; new building of 1904, 164–65; restoration in 1980s, 221–22, 234
City planning, 64, 228
Civic Center, 247–48, 249, 253
Civilian Pilot Training Service, 187
Civil Rights Act (1875), 115
Civil War, 30, 77, 78–80, 103, 122; refugees, 14, 87–88; Clarke County units, 80–87, 101; Clarke County battles, 92–95, 101; slaves in, 98, 99–100
Clarke, Elijah, 17–19
Clarke, Hannah Arrington, 17
Clarke Central High School, 205
Clarke County, *map* 2, 27–28, *map* 116; Native Americans in, 1, 3, 5, 28; manufacturing in, 5, 47–51, 52, 120, 184; creation of, 6, 10, 11–12, 16–17, 20; land area, 6, 17, 119, 180, 230; churches, 6, 24, 65–66, 112; roads, 10, 22–24, 33, 35, 139, 174; Watkinsville as seat of, 20, 23, 33, 35–36, 117–18; slaves in, 24–26, 29, 30, 46, 95, 99; agriculture in, 24–26, 30–31, 120–22, 184, 238–39; population, 24–26, 30, 70, 95, 117, 145, 184, 185, 206, 209, 228; freedmen in, 31, 100, 110, 121; railroads, 52–53, 138, 140–41; schools, 63, 111, 127, 206; and secession, 71, 75; in Civil War, 80, 82, 87, 88–90, 92–94, 101; racial violence in, 99, 114–15; legislative representatives, 114, 115; Athens as seat of, 117, 118–19, 124; convict labor, 143; in Great Depression, 175; Board of Commissioners, 230–31, 253; unified government with city, 231–33, 254, 262; sales-tax referendum, 231, 233–34, 247; historic buildings, 257–59
Clarke County, Georgia, and the City of Athens (Strahan), 263
Clarke County Bank, 173
Clarke County Courthouse, 20, 140, 168–69, 233–34
Clarke County Grand Jury, 126
Clarke County Inferior Court, 105
Clarke County Jail, 258
Clarke County Milling Company, 239
Clarke County School District, 206, 265
Clarke County Superior Court, 20
Clarke County Tuberculosis Sanitarium, 174
Clarke Institute, 161
Clarke Middle School, 248
Clarke Rifles, 83
Classic City Street Railway Company, 145
Clayton, Augustin S., 45, 47, 48
Clayton, Julia Carnes, 45
Clayton, Ga., 124
Clayton Street, 64, 120, 165, 169, 220, 249
Climax Hosiery Mill, 149
"Cloverhurst," 122, 147, 149
Cloverhurst Avenue, 147, 210
Cloverhurst Country Club, 147–49
Cobb, Andrew J., 264
Cobb, Ann Olivia Newton, 89, 152
Cobb, Howell, 46, 47, 82, 89; and secession, 70, 74, 75, 78; U.S. government positions, 74, 75; in Confederate Congress, 78, 86; in Civil War, 86, 99–100, 149
Cobb, Howell, Jr., 78, 82
Cobb, John A. (son of Howell Cobb), 86
Cobb, John Addison (father of Howell and T. R. R. Cobb), 20, 46, 58
Cobb, John B., 218
Cobb, Lamar, 86, 89
Cobb, Laura, 46. *See also* Rutherford, Laura Cobb
Cobb, Lucy, 64, 71
Cobb, Marion Lumpkin, 61, 62, 64, 78, 83, 124
Cobb, Mary Ann Lamar, 75, 87, 89, 94, 95–96
Cobb, Mary Willis, 62
Cobb, Mildred, 46
Cobb, Sarah Robinson Rootes, 46, 47, 62, 64, 86
Cobb, Thomas Reade Rootes (T. R. R.), 46, 47, 61, 69, 170, 241; and education, 61, 64, 65; and secession, 71–73, 75, 76, 77, 78; in Civil War,

73, 81, 83, 86–87; slaveholding, 96; home of, 170, 240–41, 258
Cobbham, 46, 58, 64, 103, 119, 149, 150, 152, 211
Cobbham Garden Club, 152
Cobbham Historic District, 241, 258
Cobb House, 170, 240–41, 258
Cobb-Jackson-Ward-Erwin-McFeely House, 29
Cobb-Treanor House, 258
Cocking, Walter D., 187
Coile, Lauren, 231, 234, 262
Coile, W. R., 141
Coleman, Kenneth, 87–88, 90, 265, 266
College Avenue, 100, 136–37, 140, 211, 234–35
College Life in the Old South (Coulter), 12, 28–29, 71, 264
College Square, 234–35, 236
College Station Road, 214–15
College Street, 64
Colonial Theater, 170–73
Colonial wars, 5
Columbia, S.C., 129
Columbus, Ga., 240
Commencement Week, 45
Commerce Building, 254
Commercial Bank of Athens, 173
Community Development Block Grants, 215, 250
Compromise of 1850, 74
Compton, Martha, 60
Compton's Gap, Battle of, 83
Confederate Athens (Coleman), 87–88, 265
Confederate Congress, 81
Confederate Monument, 100, 125–26, 255
Confederate Southern Memorial Association, 130
Confederate States of America, 78, 90, 91, 103
Confederate States Army, 80–86, 92, 94, 100, 104–5; veterans, 101, 105–6, 108, 110, 172
Conger, Abijah, 34
Conger, David, 34
Congregation Children of Israel, 123, 170
Congressional Record, 130
Connecticut, 42
Conner Act (1903), 176
Conner Hall, 176
Conners, Jimmy, 246
Conscription Act (1862), 81
Convict labor, 143–44, 179
Cook, Ferdinand, 91, 92, 94
Cook, Francis, 91, 92
Cook, Walter, 250, 255
Cook and Brother Armory, 91–92, 96, 97, 105, 122
Cooke, George, 54
Costa, Joseph, 166
Cotton production, 180–81; farming, 1, 33, 90, 120–21, 163, 182; manufacturing, 30, 31–33, 47–50, 104–5, 120, 122, 173–74, 175, 184, 185, 189–91
Cottonseed oil industry, 181–82
Cotton States and International Exposition (1895), 152
Coulter, E. Merton, 12, 14, 28–29, 38, 42, 71, 117–18, 143, 264
Crane, Ross, 39, 40, 67, 71, 125, 183, 258
Crater, Battle of, 86
Crawford, E. A., 131
Crawford, John, 98
Crawford, William H., 40–42
Crawfordville, Ga., 52
Cree, Alfred B., 94
Creek people, 4, 5–6, 7, 8, 17, 18, 19, 24, 28
Creswell, Mary, 178
Cuba, 134, 137
Culpepper, E. H., 254

Dairy Pak, 198
Daughters of the American Revolution, 19, 154
Davis, Jefferson, 78, 94, 99–100
Davis, Madison, 114, 115, 160
Davis, Varina Howell, 78, 154
Davis Memorial Hall, 154
Davison, Fred C., 202, 224, 226, 242, 246–47
Davison's department store, 234
Dearing, Albin P., 102, 157
Dearing, Millie, 151
Dearing, William P., 47, 48, 52, 126
Dearing Garden Apartments, 218
Dearing (Albin P.) House, 183, 258
Dearing (William) House, 218
Dearing Street, 29, 218
Dearing Street Historic District, 258
Declaration of Independence, 12
Deloney, Rosa, 83
Deloney, William G., 82–83
Democratic party, 75, 89, 115
Demosthenian Hall, 31, 37, 38
Demosthenian Literary Society, 38, 108
Denney Towers, 212
Denny Motor Company, 169
Derricotte, Ike, 110
Derricotte, Henry, 160
Desegregation, 199–205
De Soto, Hernando, 3
d'Estaing, Count Charles Henri, 142
Deupree, Lewis J., 125
"Deupree Block," 169
Deupree Hall, 125, 126
Dictionary of Georgia Biography (Coleman and Gurr), 266
Disciples of Christ, 65, 252
Dobbs, O. R., 262
Dr. Poullain's Bridge, 52
Dodd, Lamar, 190, 194–95, 197, 242
Dooley, Vince, 223, 245, 246
Dorsey, J. H., 261
Dorsey, W. F., 262
Dougherty Street, 212, 213
Douglas, Stephen A., 70–71
Downtown Athens Historic District, 220, 258
Dudley, A. G. ("Lon"), 149, 191, 262
Dudley, Patsy, 217
Dunlap Library, 45

Dupree, LaGrange Trussell, 186–87
Durham, Hugh, 246
Durham, M. S., 75
Dyer, Thomas G., 199, 202, 224, 225, 265

E. R. Hodgson and Brothers, 56
Eagle Tavern, 35, 56
Easley, Daniel, 10, 12, 13–14, 26, 48, 255
Easley, Richard, 17
Easley, Roderick, 20, 26
East Hancock Avenue, 27
Ebenezer Baptist Church, 160
Edison Electric Illuminating Company, 156
Education. *See* Schools
Elbert, Samuel, 9–10
Elberton, Ga., 9–10
Elder, T. J., 160
Elections: of 1860, 70–72; of 1868, 114; county sales-tax referendum, 231, 233–34, 247; city-county unification referendums, 232, 254
Electrification, 156
Elijah Clarke State Park, 19
Elite Theater, 173
Ellington, Duke, 163
Elliot, Stephen, 66
Emancipation Proclamation (1863), 99, 163
Emerson, Bo, 238
Emmanuel Church, 66, 122–23, 124, 140, 167, 170
Empire State Chemical Company, 181
English, John W., 200, 202, 211
Episcopalians, 66, 68
Epps, Ben, 166–67, 169
Epps Bridge Road, 113
Erwin, A. C., 262
Espey, James, 6
European explorers, 3, 5

Fairywestward, 142
Fanning, J. W., 232
Farmer's Hardware, 174
Farrar, Geraldine, 171
Federal Building, 165
Federal troops, 138; occupation of Athens, 94, 100, 101–2, 154
Few, William, 9–10
Fifteenth Pennsylvania Regiment, 136
Fifth New York Regiment, 136, 137
Fine Arts Building, 180
Finley, Robert, 51–52, 66
Finley Street, 29, 210
Fire companies, 126, 169
Fire Hall No. 1, 169, 241, 249, 253–54
Fire Hall No. 2, 152–54, 169, 241
First American Bank and Trust Company, 191, 211, 212
First Baptist Church, 65, 163, 170
First Christian Church, 170
First Methodist Church, 170
First National Bank of Athens, 218, 219
First Presbyterian Church, 6, 40, 66, 67, 87, 170
Five Points, 157, 158
Flanigan, C. D., 157
Flanigen, Jean, 151
Flea Market, 248
Fleming, Joseph H., 146, 149
Florida, 5
Ford, Gerald R., 242
Forest Heights, 216
Fort Stoddard, 23
Fort Sumter, 78, 81
40 Watt Club, 237, 238
Founders Memorial Garden, 192
Foundry Street, 15, 113, 173, 248
Fowler, Hugh, 214
France, 5
Franklin, Benjamin, 6
Franklin, Leonard, 261
Franklin, Mary, 151
Franklin College of Arts and Sciences, 13, 14, 26–27, 31, 36–37, 46, 90, 134
Franklin County, 6, 10
Franklin House, 56, 214, 216, 236, 258
Franklin-Upson House, 217–18, 219, 257
Fraternities, 40, 108, 182–83
Freedman's Bureau, 95, 108–10, 111
Friends of Lucy Cobb and Seney-Stovall, 244
Front (Broad) Street, 15
Fry, Gladys-Marie, 152
Fullilove, Henry M., 209
Fulton, M. C., 120

Gainesville, Ga., 52, 56, 58, 182
Gainesville Midland Railroad, 140
Gamble, Robert S., 120, 121
Gannt, T. L., 264
Garden Club of America, 152
Garden Club of Georgia, 191–93, 257
Garroway, Dave, 202
Gazetteer of Georgia, 70
General Electric Company, 156
General Time, 198
George, Walter F., 181
George II (king of England), 4
George III (king of England), 5
Georgia: Native Americans in, 1–3, 5, 6, 7, 18, 58–60; colonial charter, 4; white settlement of, 4–5, 6–8, 23, 28; Indian land cessions to, 5–6, 58–60; in American Revolution, 6, 17–18; land grants, 6–7, 8–10, 18, 142; codified law, 60, 71; state constitution of 1869, 62; slave codes, 63, 99; secession convention of 1861, 75–78; Confederate Army units, 80–81, 83, 86, 88, 94; Civil War damage, 101; Freedman's Bureau, 110; constitutional convention of 1867, 114; convict labor, 143–44; public school desegregation, 199, 204; population, 206
Georgia, Carolina, and Northern Railroad, 140
Georgia Catalogue: Historic American Buildings Survey (Linley), 266
Georgia Center for Continuing Education, 197
Georgia Department of Natural Resources, 214, 250
Georgia Development Company, 157
Georgia Factory, 47–48, 50

Georgia Forestry Commission, 239
Georgia General Assembly: and University of Georgia, 10–12, 42, 242–43; and Clarke County, 17, 230, 232; and banking, 52; creation of supreme court, 60; and secession, 72; blacks in, 114, 205; establishment of Oconee County, 119; and Winterville, 141; and Athens, 146, 241–42, 248, 251; and education, 154
Georgia Highway Department, 139
Georgia Historical Quarterly, 264
Georgia Historical Society, 66
Georgia Journal, 51–52
Georgia Legion, 86
Georgia Military District 3, 114
Georgia Museum of Art, 176, 195, 242–43
"Georgia Nankeens," 49
Georgia National Bank, 173, 236
Georgian Hotel, 129, 165–66, 167, 237
Georgian Theater, 173
Georgia Peace Society, 151
Georgia Power Company, 156, 157
Georgia Railroad, 51, 52, 54, 56, 126, 140, 141, 142
Georgia Railroad and Banking Company, 52, 53
Georgia Railroad Depot, 24
Georgia Rehabilitation Corporation, 180
Georgia's Legacy: History Charted Through the Arts (Smith), 266
Georgia Square Mall, 234
Georgia State Botanical Garden, 226, 239, 242, 251
Georgia State Patrol, 201
Georgia State Teachers College, 156
Georgia Supreme Court, 60, 61, 72, 245
Georgia Troopers, 83, 88
Georgia Trust for Historic Preservation, 227, 236
Georgia Volunteers, 134
Gerdine, William, 261
Gerdine House, 218
Giamatti, A. Bartlett, 242
GI Bill, 189
Giles, Norman H., 242
Gilleland, John, 92
Gilmer, George R., 154
Gilmer Hall, 154
Gleason's Pictorial Magazine, 31
Glickman, Sara, 158, 160
Goff, Ray, 246
Golden Ginkgo Jamboree, 236
Gold Kist, 198
Goodrich, L. F., 221
Good Roads School, 139
Goodwin, Sally, 151
Gouvain, Madame, 142
Gouvain, Michael, 142
Grady, Henry Woodfin, 84, 86, 114, 219
Grady, William Sammons, 71, 84–86
Granger, Gideon, 23
Grant, Daniel, 49
Grant, John T., 33, 102
Grant, Ulysses S., 94
Grant-Hill-White House, 170, 171, 193
Great Britain, 5–6, 17–18
Great Depression, 163, 175, 180, 181, 182, 184
Great Seal of Georgia, 42
Greek Revival architecture, 33, 39, 40, 220, 242
Green, Agnes, 204
Green, Donarell R., 204
Green, Margie, 204
Green, Wilucia, 204
Greene County, 3, 6
Greenpeace, 238
Greensboro, Ga., 52
Grieve, Callender Cunningham, 60
Griffith, D. W., 172
Grove School, 131, 135
Gurr, Charles Stephen, 266
Gwinnett County, 234

Hajos, Albin, 264
Hajos' Athens Georgia: Photo-Gravures (Hajos), 264
Hall, Charles Cuthbert, 152
Halsey, Lucius Henry, 158
Hamburg, S.C., 52
Hamilton, James S., 49, 71
Hamilton House, 258
Hamilton-Hodgson House, 183
Hampton, Bonnie, 204
Hampton Street, 157
Hancock Avenue, 64, 185, 212–13, 259
Hardeman, Benjamin F., 214
Harris, E. G., 145–46
Harris, Samuel F., 204
Harris, Sarah H., 214
Harris, W. H., 162
Harris, Young L. G., 56, 69, 104
Harris Drug Store, 162
Harrison, William Henry, 48
Harrison Freshet (1840), 48
Hart, John, 20
Hawkins, Benjamin, 23–24
Hayes, Hiram, 149
Haynes, Charles, 161
"Headright" system, 8–9
Heard, J. Thomas, 162
Heard, W. H., 115
Heart of a Distant Forest (Williams), 238
Heery, Wilmer, 197
Heery and Heery, 220
Held, John, Jr., 45, 192
Henderson, Matthew H., 124
Henrietta Apartments, 157
Heritage Hall, 246
Herty Field, 179
Highland Guard, 84, 86
High Museum (Atlanta), 195
Hill, A. A. Franklin, 78, 81
Hill, Benjamin H., 77, 115
Hill, Isaac, 20
Hill, Walter B., 176
Hill First Baptist Church, 112
Hill Street, 211
Hilsman, Patty, 157
Hilsman Middle School, 206
Hiram, Ida Mae, 161–62
Hiram, Lace, 161–62

Hirsch Hall, 180
Historic American Buildings Survey, 257
Historic Houses of Athens (Marshall), 266
Historic preservation, 182–93, 210–19, 220–21, 227, 228, 233–34 236–37, 240–44, 247–50, 252–53
Historic Warehouse District, 189–91, 248, 259
History of Athens and Clarke County (Rowe), 264
History Village, 212
Hitler, Adolf, 185, 227
Hodgson, A. H., 261
Hodgson, Ann, 53–56
Hodgson, Edward Reginald, 56, 71, 114
Hodgson, Elizabeth, 53–56
Hodgson, Harry, 178
Hodgson, Hugh, 198
Hodgson, Paul, 180–81, 182, 210
Hodgson, Robert, 56
Hodgson, William, 56
Hodler, Thomas W., 266
Hogue, Ronnie, 223
Holbrook, Alfred Heber, 194–95, 197
Holbrook, Eva Underhill, 195
Holden, Frank A., 264
Holiday Estates, 216
Holiday Inn, 252, 253
Holland, James, 230, 254
Holman, W. S., 157, 167
Holman Hotel Building, 140, 167
Holmes, Hamilton, 199, 202, 203
Holmes-Hunter Lecture Series, 204
Home School, 129
"Homewood," 157
Hoover, Herbert C., 253
Hope Fire Company, 126
Hopkins, William, 20
Hospital Authority of Clarke County, 207
Hospitals, 174, 207–8
"Hot Corner," 163
Hotels, 35, 56, 165–66, 167
Housing, 182–84, 212; segregation, 158, 160
Hoyt, Rev. Nathan, 28, 67, 87, 212
Hoyt House, 28, 212
Hubert, J. H., 191
Hubert State Bank, 191
Hull, Asbury, 49, 52, 75, 76, 252
Hull, Augustus Longstreet, 53, 62–63, 64, 65, 67, 104, 114, 115, 122, 129, 136–37, 140–41, 263
Hull, Henry, 263
Hull, Rev. Hope, 13, 14–15, 16, 66
Hull, William Hope, 61, 72
Hull-Snelling House, 252–53
Hull Street, 113, 210
Hull Street Historic District, 252
Hunnicutt, John Atkinson, 125, 157, 261
Hunnicutt, Mary Deupree, 125
Hunter, Charlayne (Hunter-Gault), 199, 200, 201–2, 203
Hunting, 3
Husa, Karel, 242
Hynds, Ernest C., 31, 66, 68, 69, 265

Ilah Dunlap Little Memorial Library, 195
Illiteracy, 63, 69
Indians. *See* Native Americans
Industrial parks, 222
Industrial Revolution, 48
Institute of Continuing Legal Education, 244
Insurance companies, 56, 104, 106, 123, 165, 191, 236
Intercollegiate Tennis Hall of Fame, 246
Italianate architecture, 40, 64, 71
Ivey, Marion, 206
Ivy Building, 31, 37–39, 140

J. C. Penney, 234
Jack's Creek, Battle of, 18
Jackson, Walter E., 168–69
Jackson, William, 217
Jackson County, 6, 10, 11–12, 17, 228, 229
Jackson Street, 69
James Stewart Polshek and Partners, 253
Jefferson, Thomas, 12, 23, 26
Jefferson, Ga., 58
Jefferson County, 46
Jennings, Jefferson, 75, 76
Jeruel Academy, 111
Jewish Country Club, 149
Jewish people, 123
Jim Crow laws, 163
John, Jewel, 230
Johnson, Andrew, 114
Johnson, Herschel V., 77
Johnson, John, 47
Johnson, Lyndon B., 225
Johnson, Lane, Space, Smith and Company, 236
Johnstone, Francis E., 226
Jones, Andrew, 160, 204
Joseph Building, 169
Josephine (empress of France), 142
Jug Tavern (Watkinsville), 92, 94

Kappa Alpha fraternity, 182
Kappa Alpha Theta sorority, 183
Kellogg Foundation, 197
Kemp, Jan, 246
Kennedy, John F., 202, 225
Kennedy, Robert F., 202
Kent State University, 224
Kentucky Infantry, 94
Kettle Creek, Battle of, 17, 19
Kiker, Douglas, 200
King, Horace, 224
King, William, 261
Knapp, Charles B., 193, 247
Knox, John J., 111
Knox Institute, 111, 112, 161, 162
Knox School, 111
Koch, Mary Levin, 195
Ku Klux Klan, 114–15

L. M. Leathers Company, 222

Ladies Aid Society, 88, 89, 90
Ladies Garden Club of Athens, 89, 191–92
Ladies Memorial Association, 100, 125–26
Lamar, John B., 75
Land, 1; grants, 4, 6–7, 9–10, 142; Indian cessions, 5–6, 58–60; ownership, 8–9, 62, 121
Land-use regulations, 228
Lane, Bessie Mell, 130
Law School Association, 244–45
Lawson, Hugh, 12
League of Nations, 151
Leathers, Milton, 211
LeConte, John, 43–44
LeConte, Joseph, 43–44
Lee, Robert E., 77, 86, 87, 94
Lexington Highway, 182
Lickskillet neighborhood, 212
Lily Land Company, 157
Lincoln, Abraham, 71–72, 74, 89, 99
Lindbergh, Charles A., 157–58
Linton, John S., 56, 266
Lipscomb, Andrew Adgate, 81, 91, 102, 108, 131–34
Literacy, 98
Literary societies, 37, 38, 108
Long, Crawford W., 44–45, 218
Louisiana Purchase, 23, 197
Loyalists, 17, 18
Lucas House, 195
Lucy Cobb Institute, 43, 64, 90, 129, 131, 132, 184, 243, 257
Lumpkin, Ben, 230
Lumpkin, Charley, 87
Lumpkin, E. K., 143
Lumpkin, Mrs. E. K., 152
Lumpkin, Edward P., 81, 87, 92–94, 261
Lumpkin, Joseph Henry, 60–61, 72, 82, 102, 129
Lumpkin, William, 49
Lumpkin, Wilson W., 58, 69, 71, 177, 197
Lumpkin Foundation, 244
Lumpkin House, 81, 244, 258
Lumpkin Street, 15, 47, 56, 64, 144, 157
Lunceford, Jimmy, 163
Lyle, James R., 261
Lynchings, 99
Lyndon, Andrew Jackson, Jr., 212
Lyndon, Edward S., 212
Lyndon, Mary, 177–78
Lyndon House, 62
Lyndon Mill, 212
Lynwood Park, 103, 160

McCash, William B., 46, 62
McCommons, Pete, 222, 229
McEnroe, John, 246
McGovern, George S., 222
McGregor Company, 222
McHatton (professor), 177
Mack, Charles, 206
McKinley, William, 159
McMahan, J. C., 262
"MacNeil/Lehrer News Hour," 203
McNutt Creek, 50, 139
Macon, Ga., 240
Macon and Covington Railroad, 140
McWhorter, Hamilton, 140, 147, 149
McWhorter, Mrs. Hamilton, 25
McWhorter, Robert L. ("Bob"), 186, 217, 262
Macy's department store, 234
Madison County, 6, 142, 228, 229
Magill, Dan, 246
Magill, Elizabeth, 217
Maier, John, 61
Mail delivery, 23–24, 56, 102
Main Street Program, 235–36
Maize, 3
Malone, William, 16
Manufacturing, 1, 5, 50–51, 181; cotton-textile factories, 30, 31–33, 47–50, 104–5, 120, 122, 174–75, 184, 189–91; armaments, 91–92; employment, 184
Marigold Festival, 239
Market (Washington) Street, 15
Market Street School, 129
Marshall, Charlotte Thomas, 266
Mars Hill Church, 65
Marthasville, Ga., 60
Martin, Jack, 171
Maryland, 6
Maxeys, Ga., 120
Meeker, Christopher, 121
Meeker, John Armstrong, 121–22, 147
Mehre, Harry, 185
Meigs, Josiah, 13, 14–15, 16, 26–27
Meigs Street School, 131
Mell, Benjamin, 83
Mell, Edward Baker, 263
Mell, Patrick Hues, 83, 84, 108
Mell, T. S., 262
Mell Rifles, 83
Memorial Hall, 178–79
Memorial Park, 191
Methodists, 24, 65–66, 67, 68
Methodist School, 111
Mexico, 3
Michael, Katherine, 217
Michael, Max, 191
Michael, Moses, 169–70, 171
Michael, Simon, 169–70, 171, 191
Michael Brothers, 169, 171
Middle Cherokee Path, 5
Middle class, 146, 163
Militia units, 80
Milledge, John, 6, 12, 13, 16, 40
Milledge Avenue, 65, 121–22, 149, 162; residential architecture, 64, 71, 146; streetcars, 144, 145, 146, 157; University land purchases, 182–83; buildings demolished on, 218
Milledge Avenue Historic District, 259
Milledge Circle, 157
Milledge Circle Historic District, 259
Milledge Park, 157
Milledgeville, Ga., 35, 72, 75
Miller, Glen, 187
Mills, Mike, 237, 238
Milner, Thomas H., 219
Missionary Ridge, Battle of, 136
Mississippi Period, 3

Mississippi River, 5
Mitchell Hotel, 125
Mitchell's Bridge, 156
Mitchell's Road, 93
Mitchell Thunderbolts, 92–93, 94
Model Cities Program, 215
Mohr, Clarence L., 72–73, 98–99
Monroe, James, 40, 125, 142
Monroe, Ga., 240
Moore, Elizabeth Stockton, 66
Moore, Peyton E., 69
Moore, Richard Dudley, 66, 69, 110, 111
Moore College, 111
Morehouse College, 161
Morgan County, 33
Morrill Land Grant Act (1862), 131
Morris, Sylvanus, 58, 110, 263, 264
Morton, Charlie, 163
Morton, Joseph F., 26
Morton, Monroe B. ("Pink"), 115, 158–60, 163, 249
Morton, William M., 26
Morton Building, 162, 163, 258
Morton Theater, 163, 247, 249–50
Moss, John Dortch, 149
Moss, Julia P., 131, 135
Moss, Rufus Lafayette, 149–50
Moss, William Lorenzo, 150
Moss Manufacturing Company, 182
Movie theaters, 173, 188
Muir, John, 106, 108
Music clubs, 237

Napoleon I (emperor of France), 40
National Bank of Athens, 43, 48, 103–4, 173, 191
National Endowment for the Arts, 250
National Guard, 185
National Historic Preservation Act (1966), 257
National Recovery Administration, 181
National Register of Historic Places, 105, 113, 218, 219, 220, 227, 249–50, 257–59
National Trust for Historic Preservation, 241, 248
Native Americans, 1–3, 4, 14, 28–29; land cessions, 5–6, 7–8, 58–60; frontier battles with, 8, 17, 18, 19
Navy Supply Corps Museum, 154
Navy Supply Corps School, 3, 4, 197
"Negro in Athens and Clarke County, 1872–1900" (Schinkel), 121
Nelson, Don, 222–23
Neoclassical architecture, 40
Nevitt, J. J., 124
New Athens Opera House, 125, 170–71
New College, 39, 91, 111
New Deal, 175, 180, 181, 257
New Orleans, La., 91
New Orleans Exposition (1876), 122
"New South," 86, 103, 106, 114, 115, 182
Newspapers, 70, 115–17, 222–23
Newton, Elizur L., 49, 261
Newton, John H., 120
Newton House, 56
New York, Treaty of (1790), 18
New Yorker, 200
Nicholson, John W., 84, 102
Nicholson Reaves and Wynn, 80
Nickerson, Reuben, 105
Nisbet, Eugenius A., 60, 77
Nisbet, John, 47, 48
Normaltown, 154, 156
North Campus, 176, 197, 227, 257
North College Avenue, 140
Northeastern Railroad, 124, 150
Northeast Georgia Citizen's Quality Growth Task Force, 232
Northeast Georgia Medical Association, 204
Northeast Georgia Regional Planning and Development Commission, 228
North Hull Street, 113
North Oconee River Park, 251
Notre Dame University, 245

Oates, W. C., 136
Oconee Cavalry, 81
Oconee County, 117, 118–19, 120–21, 124, 229
Oconee Hill Cemetery, 64, 69, 87
Oconee River, 1, 4, 5, 6, 17, 30, 65, 117; bridges, 23, 126; manufacturing development on, 47; protection of, 250–51
Oconee Rivers Greenway Committee, 250–51
Oconee Street, 174
Odum, Eugene P., 227, 242, 251
O'Farrell, W. D., 261
Oglethorpe, James Edward, 4
Oglethorpe Avenue Historic District, 259
Oglethorpe County, 6, 142, 228, 229
Oglethorpe Elementary School, 216–17
Old Athens Cemetery, 6
Old College, 14, 31, 91, 188
Old Library, 140
Old McRee-Crawford's Mill, 34
"Old South" (Rutherford), 130
Olmsted, Frederick Law, 42
O'Looney, Gwen, 254
Olustee, Battle of, 84
On the Campus (Dodd), 197
On the Threshold of Freedom: Masters and Slaves in the Civil War (Mohr), 72–73
Order of the Missionary Sisters of the Sacred Heart of Jesus, 208
Ordinance of Secession, 76, 77–78
Orr, Robert C., 24
Orr Drugs, 165
Owens, Hubert B., 192, 193

Paine College, 158
Palace Theater, 173, 236
Paleo-Indians, 1
Palmer, William J., 94, 100
Paper mills, 50, 56
Parks, 42, 191, 251–52. *See also* Botanical Garden
Parkview Homes, 183

Parliament, 4
Parr House, 258
Peabody, George Foster, 154–56, 176, 179
Peabody Library, 195
Peeples, Cincinnatus, 261
Penal Code of 1833, 60
Peninsular Campaign, 86
People's Bank, 173
Perriere, Ange de la, 142
Phi Kappa Hall, 37, 38, 94
Phi Kappa Literary Society, 38, 108
Philosophical Hall, 37, 225
Phinizy, Billups, 146, 149, 157, 165
Phinizy, Ferdinand, 102, 103, 125
Phinizy, John Ferdinand, 125
Phinizy-Hodgson House, 218
Pickens Trail, 5
Pictorial History of the University of Georgia (Boney), 265
Piedmont region, 3, 4, 5, 6–7, 118, 158, 229
Pinecrest Lodge, 121
Pioneer Hook and Ladder, 126
Pioneer Paper Manufacturing Company, 56, 149–50
Pittard, James D., 261
Pittard, John, 141
Plain style architecture, 8
Plantation agriculture, 1, 5, 30, 63, 119, 142
Planters, 26, 30–31, 33, 95, 120
Planter's Hotel, 56
Pleasant Grove, 26
Pledger, W. A., 115
Poesch, Jessie, 242
Police forces, 126, 182, 232
Pope, Burwell, 81
Pope, Franklin, 81
Pope, John, 114
Post Office building, 185
Pound, Jere M., 156
Powers, Harriet, 151, 152
Presbyterian Church, 31
Presbyterians, 24, 65, 66, 68
Priestley, Joseph, 12
Prince, Noah, 48–49
Prince Avenue, 58, 64; streetcars, 144, 145, 154; residential architecture, 160, 162, 170, 171, 217–18; University land purchases on, 182–83; tornado damage on, 216
Princeton Factory, 48–49, 50, 149–50, 189
Prisoners of war, 92, 94
Private schools, 129–31, 162, 206, 207
Proctor, J. Peeble, 209
Progressive Era, 117
Provisional Congress, 86
Public schools, 127–29, 135, 204–5, 206, 250
Public Works Administration, 180
Pulaski Street, 15, 211
Puryear, William W., 121

R.E.M., 237, 238, 248
Racism, 72–73
Railroads, 30, 46, 51, 52–53, 124, 138, 139, 140–41, 143, 174
Reap, James, 129, 175, 265
Reaves, Rufus K., 80, 261
Reconstruction, 101, 114, 115, 119, 205
Reconstruction Acts (1867), 114
Red Cross, 189
Redwine, Morgan, 149
Reese, Anderson, 70
Reese, S. C., 261
Reese Street, 160, 162
Reese Street Historic District, 259
Reid, Neel, 169, 176
Relief No. 2, 115
Religion, 36, 42, 65, 68–69, 98–99. *See also* Churches
Reminiscences of Athens About 1880–1900 (Mell), 263
Republican party, 114, 115, 159
Research Road, 207
Rhodes, J. F., 262
Richardson, Alfred, 114–15
Ritch, Jerry E., 261
Rivers, 5
Roads, 10, 22, 23–24, 33, 126–27, 139, 174
Roads Extension Department, 139
Rock College, 108, 154
Rockefeller Foundation, 179
Rock House, 58, 60, 177, 257
Rogers, Dr. and Mrs. J. C., 193–94
Rogers, Kenny, 144, 237, 246
Rogers, Marianne, 144, 246
Rogers, Will, 171
Rogers, Will, Jr., 171
Rolfe, Monte, 169
Rolfe-Epps Flying Service, 167
Rolling Stone, 238
Roman Catholics, 170
Roosevelt, Franklin D., 180, 181, 257
Rose Bowl, 185, 186
Ross, Donald, 149
Rowe, H. J., 145, 166, 170, 262, 264
Rucker, J. H., 261
Rusk, Dean, 224, 225, 242
Rusk Center for International and Comparative Law, 225
Russell, Richard B., 179, 187–88, 197, 227
Russell Agricultural Research Center, 214–15
Rutherford, Johnny, 87
Rutherford, Laura Cobb, 64
Rutherford, Mildred Lewis, 125–26, 129–30, 154, 264
Rutherford, Williams, 69

Saint Joseph's Catholic Church, 61, 170, 240
Saint Joseph's Catholic School, 207
Saint Mary's Chapel, 122, 252
Saint Mary's Hospital, 174, 208
Salem, Ga., 28, 29, 30, 33, 63
Samaritan Building, 162, 163
Sams, Albert, 213, 219
Sanborn Fire Insurance Maps, 106, 129, 160
Sandy Creek, 65
Sandy Creek Greenway, 254–55

Sandy Creek Nature Center, 251, 254–55
Sandy Creek Park, 251, 254–55
Sanford, Sheldon B., 179–80
Sanford, Steadman V., 178, 181
Sanford Stadium, 69, 178, 179, 245, 251
Sapera, Leonard, 197
Sapp, Theron, 245
Savannah, Ga., 4, 51, 52, 240
Schinkel, Peter, 121
Schools, 63–64; for blacks, 111–12, 127, 129, 161, 162, 163, 204; public schools, 127–29, 135, 204–5, 206, 250; private schools, 129–31, 162, 206, 207; desegregation, 199–205
Schretter, Howard A., 266
Scotch-Irish immigrants, 8
Scott, Winfield, 77
Scott Homeplace, 157
Scudder, A. M., 131
Scull Shoals, 3, 65
Seaboard Airline Railroad, 140, 182, 211
Searcy, Chuck, 222
Sears, Roebuck & Company, 234
Secession, 70, 73, 75, 76, 77–78
Segregation, 114, 158, 160, 199
Sell, E. S., 264
Seney, George I., 130, 131
Seney-Stovall Chapel, 130, 146, 244
Settlers, 4–5, 6–8, 23, 28
Shackelford Building, 165
Shady Grove Church, 112
Sharecropping, 121
Shaw, Artie, 187
Shealy Farms, 239
Sheridan, Ann, 186
Sherwood, Adeil, 70
Shopping centers, 209, 234
Sigma Alpha Epsilon fraternity, 40, 108, 183
Simon Michael Memorial Clinic, 191
Sinkwich, Frank, 185, 186, 245
Sixteenth Georgia Cavalry, 94
Slave Code, 99
Slaveholders, 30–31, 40, 46
Slavery, 1, 4, 30–33, 69, 95–100
Slaves, 63, 66; population, 24–26, 29, 30, 95; daily life, 31–33, 49, 95–99; Southerners' fears of insurrection, 71, 72, 73; local ordinances, 96, 97–98, 99; emancipation of, 99–100, 101, 119
Sledge, James A., 70, 89
Sledge House, 257
Small Business Development Center, 189
Smallpox epidemic, 110
Smith, Bessie, 163
Smith, E. I., 262
Smith, James Monroe, 142, 143–44
Smith, Jane Webb, 266
Smith, Jennie, 151–52
Smith, John, 20
Smith, Robert L., 261
"Smithonia," 142–43, 144
Smithsonian Institution, 151, 152
Snelling, Charles, 179–80, 252, 253
Snodgrass (streetcar operator), 126, 145
Snow, Ralph, 186, 262
Song of Daniel (Williams), 238
Sororities, 71, 183, 218
Sosnowski, Caroline, 129
Sosnowski, Sophie, 129
Soule, Andrew M., 176–77, 264
South Campus, 58, 206
South Carolina, 4, 17–18, 52, 75
Southern Association of Colleges and Secondary Schools, 187
Southern Banner, 48, 52, 64, 70, 83, 89
Southern Baptist Convention, 84
Southern Cotton Oil Company, 182
Southern Cultivator, 125
Southern Manufacturing Company, 146
Southern Mutual Building, 211, 254
Southern Mutual Insurance Company, 56, 104, 106, 165, 191, 236
Southern Railroad, 140, 182
Southern Watchman, 70, 71, 77–78, 87, 95, 108, 263
Spain, 5, 8, 18, 134
Spalding, Jack, 103
Spalding, Phinizy, 149, 211
Spanish-American War, 134, 136–38
Speer, Emory, 35–36, 115
Sprague, H. B., 95
Stagecoaches, 35, 52, 56
Stanley, Marcellus, 81
Stanton, Lucy M., 150–51
Star Thread Mill, 50, 156
State College of Agriculture and Mechanical Arts, 131–34, 176, 177
State Farmers Market, 239
State Normal School, 154, 155, 156, 179, 197
Statistics of Georgia (White), 36, 68
Stegeman, Herman J., 179
Stegeman, John F., 72, 81, 82, 157, 265
Stegeman Hall, 179, 188
Stephens, Alexander Hamilton, 44, 45, 77, 78, 84
Stephens, Lawton, 207
Stephens, Robert G., Jr., 207, 212
Stern, Myer, 169–70
Stevens, William Bacon, 66
Stewart, Nathaniel, 58
Stipe, Michael, 237, 238
Stoneman Raiders, 92
Stone Mountain, 240
Story Untold: Black Men and Women in Athens History (Thurmond), 265
Stovall, Nellie, 130
Strahan, Charles Morton, 105, 117, 139, 168, 176, 263
Strand Theater, 173
Streetcars, 144, 145–46, 154, 157
"Streetcar suburbs," 138, 146, 199
Street paving, 126–27
Strolls About Athens During the Early Seventies (Morris), 263
Strolls Around Athens (Tate), 265
Strong, William, Jr., 26
Strong, William, Sr., 20, 26
Strong Street, 212
Student Army Training Corps, 178
Student Political League, 187
Students for Environmental Awareness, 252

Suburbs, 46, 58, 138, 146, 157, 199
Susan Building, 204

Taft, William Howard, 146
Tallahassee, Fla., 3
Tallassee Shoals, 156
Talmadge, Clovis G., 261
Talmadge, Eugene, 187
Tanner Lumber Company, 222
Tanyard Branch, 179
Tanyard Creek, 60, 251
Tate, William, 173, 200, 201, 202, 224–25, 265
Taxes, 96, 231, 233–34, 247
Tax Reform Act (1976), 220
Taylor, James Knox, 165
Taylor, Robert, 40, 46
Taylor-Grady House, 40, 170, 171, 217, 219, 258
Telegraph lines, 56, 78–80
Telfair, Edward, 20
Telfair Museum (Savannah), 195
Temperance Society, 68–69
Textile industry, 48–50, 52, 90, 106, 120, 175, 184, 189
Theaters, 163, 170–71, 173, 188, 249–50
These Men She Gave (Stegeman), 72, 265
Thirteenth Connecticut Volunteers, 101–2
Thirteenth Tennessee Regiment, 94
Thomas, G. C., 262
Thomas, Gertrude, 173
Thomas, Isabel, 173
Thomas, Stevens, 13, 16
Thomas, William Winstead, 130, 146, 147, 173, 183
Thomas-Carithers House, 258
Thomas (Stevens) House, 207, 259
Thomas Street, 64, 125, 212, 249
Thomas Street Holding Company, 248
Thomas-Swift-Cofer House, 218
Thomas Textiles, 189
Thompson, Augustus, 97
Thompson, Blanche, 162
Thurmond, Michael L., 205, 265
Tillson, Davis, 110
Toombs, Robert, 77, 78
Tourism, 241–42
Town Hall, 56, 75, 101–2, 114
Trail Creek Church, 65
Trans-Oconee Republic, 18
Transportation, 90–91, 173; roads, 10 22, 23–24, 33, 139, 174; railroads, 30, 46, 51, 52–53, 124, 138, 139, 140–41, 143, 174; automobiles, 138, 139, 146, 157, 166, 182, 198–99; streetcars, 144, 145–46, 154, 157; buses, 221
Trillin, Calvin, 200
Trippi, Charley, 185, 186, 245
Trotter, Virginia, 242
Troup, George M., 81
Troup Artillery, 77, 81, 82
Trussell, LaGrange, 217
Trust Company Bank of Northeast Georgia, 218, 219
Tschudi, Eleanor, 78
Tuck, H. C., 261
Tucker, C. A., 168
Tuckston, Ga., 139
Turkey growing, 239
Turner, Ed, 206
Twelfth New Jersey Regiment, 136
Twiggs, John, 12
Twilight Criterium, 236

Union Baptist Institute, 111
Union Hall, 113, 163
Union League, 114
Union party, 75
Union Point, Ga., 53, 142
United Daughters of the Confederacy, 130, 154
United States, 4, 6, 134, 151
United States Capitol, 45
United States Census, 63
United States Congress, 114, 131, 257
United States Constitution, 10, 11, 177–78
United States Department of Agriculture, 214–15
United States Department of Housing and Urban Development, 213, 215
United States Department of Transportation, 234
United States Environmental Protection Agency, 214–15
United States Forest Service, 239
United States Navy: Supply Corps School, 3, 4, 197; preflight school, 187–88
United States Postal Service, 242
United States Supreme Court, 45, 204
University of California, 43–44
University of California at Los Angeles, 185, 186
University Chapel, 24, 39, 91, 92, 94, 229
University of Georgia: land acquisitions, 6, 12–13, 60, 180, 210–11; foundation of, 10–12, 13–15, 16–17; Franklin College of Arts and Sciences, 13, 14, 26–27, 31, 36–37, 46, 90, 134; building construction, 14, 15, 24, 37–39, 140, 176, 177, 178–79, 180, 197, 206, 223, 226–27, 245–46, 247; and growth of Athens, 14–16, 29, 30, 36, 63, 184; enrollment, 26–27, 36, 91, 175, 176, 178, 180, 187, 223, 227; trustees, 27, 42, 58, 177; curriculum, 27, 43, 131–34, 176–77; temporary closures, 27, 91, 108; fraternities and sororities, 40, 71, 108, 182–83, 218; Botanical Garden, 40–42, 226, 239, 242, 251; budgets, 42, 224; students, 42–43, 44–45, 182, 185, 187, 224–25, 226; faculty, 43, 90, 176, 202, 224, 225; Joseph Henry Lumpkin School of Law, 61, 72, 180, 202, 244; donations of land to churches, 66; war veterans from, 83, 101, 108, 178, 187, 189; in Civil War, 91, 92, 94, 102; Board of Regents, 105, 187; School of Forest Resources, 105, 227; School of Engineering, 123; College of Agriculture, 123, 179; dormitories, 156,

University of Georgia (*cont.*)
211; football team, 171, 179, 185–86, 223, 245; women in, 177–78, 199; administration, 179–80, 224, 246–47; School of Forestry, 180; loss of accreditation, 187; Navy preflight school, 187–88; School of Environmental Design, 193, 227, 240; land sale to Navy, 197; desegregation, 199–204; Henry W. Grady School of Journalism and Mass Communication, 203; athletics programs, 223–24, 246; Institute of Ecology, 227; Bicentennial Celebration, 242, 265; Carl Vinson Institute of Government, 243
University of Georgia: A Bicentennial History, 1785–1985 (Dyer), 265
University of Georgia Foundation, 193
University of Georgia Press, 45
University High School, 108, 154
University of North Carolina, 12, 14
University of South Carolina, 43
University Towers, 235
University of Virginia, 12
Upstairs Downtown Tour, 236
Urban renewal, 183–84, 210–15

Vandiver, S. Ernest, 200, 202
Veterans, 101, 105–6, 108, 110, 172, 178, 187, 189
Vietnam War, 224
Vincent, Isaac S., 75, 83–84
Vinson, Carl, 187–88, 197
Virginia, 6
Vonderleith, C. A., 134

Waddel, Rev. Moses, 27, 36, 66, 67, 212–13, 214
Waddel Hall, 225
Wahroonga, 103
Walker, Abraham, 47, 48
Walker, Herschel, 245
Walton, George, 12
Ward, Malthus, 29, 40
Ware, Edward R., 62, 212, 261
Warehouse Historic District, 189–91, 248, 259
Ware-Lyndon House, 212, 258
War of 1812, 26
Warner, Hiram, 60
Washington, George, 6, 18, 42
Washington, Ga., 52
Washington County, 6
Washington Street, 15, 100, 211, 249
Washington Street School, 129, 135, 165
"Watch on the Oconee," 94
Watkins, Robert, 20
Watkinsville, Ga., 29, 30, 65, 88; as seat of Clarke County, 20, 23, 33, 35–36, 117–18; roads, 22, 33, 35; population, 28, 36; rail connections, 52; schools, 63; in Civil War, 92, 93; as seat of Oconee County, 117, 118–19
Watkinsville Hotel, 35
Watkinsville Road, 110
Welch, William Pinckney, 146, 149
Wells, Jack R., 186, 210, 262, 264–65
West, Henry S., 168
West African culture, 151, 152
Western and Atlantic Railroad, 60
Western Union Telegraph, 171
West Hancock Avenue Historic District, 160, 259
Westinghouse Electric Corporation, 198
Westlake Country Club, 149
West Lake Drive, 198
WGAU radio, 158
WGTV television, 197
"What a Difference a Decade Makes" (McCommons), 229
White, George, 14, 36, 68
White, James Richards, 49, 193
White, John, 47, 48, 103–4
White, John Richards (son of John White), 47, 104, 105, 157, 180, 227
White, William N., 79
White Hall, 105, 146, 180, 227, 258
Whitehall, Ga., 47, 50, 182, 189
Whitehall Experimental Forest, 180
Whitehall Manufacturing Company, 104
Whites, 69, 99, 121; settlement, 1, 4–5, 6–8, 33; population, 29, 30, 70, 101, 117, 184, 206; factory labor, 49–50; women, 62, 111; churches, 66–67, 68; racial tension and violence, 71, 72–73, 97, 99, 114–15, 200–202, 205; in Civil War, 81, 101; segregated schools, 127, 131, 204, 205; housing segregation, 160, 162, 183
Wilkes County, 18
Wilkes County militia, 17, 18
Wilkins, John J., 173, 177
Wilkins House, 257
Wilkins Industries, 222
Williams, Charlie, 121
Williams, Joe (dean), 202
Williams, Rev. Joseph, 98–99
Williams, Philip Lee, 238
Williams, Rob, 200, 202
Williams, William, 49
Winter, Christopher, 142
Winter, Diedrich Heinrich (Henry), 142
Winter, John, 142
Winter Valley (Dodd), 190
Winterville, Ga., 139, 141–42, 143, 144, 232, 239
Winterville Community Fair, 144
Winterville Road, 182
Witherspoon, Emily, 131
Woman's Club of Athens, 244
Women, 62–63; education, 64, 129, 156, 177–78, 199; in Civil War, 88, 90; employment, 91–92, 111, 184; women's suffrage movement, 151, 177–78; University faculty, 176; in World War II, 189; athletics programs, 224, 246
Woodburn plantation, 19
Woodland Period, 3
Woodlawn Avenue, 157
Woodlawn Avenue Historic District, 241, 259
Woodruff Hall, 173, 200

Woods, Josiah, 20
Woofter, T. J., Jr., 160
Works Progress Administration (WPA), 185
World's Columbian Exposition (1893), 183
World War I, 175, 178
World War II, 38, 175, 184, 186–87, 188–89, 191
Wray-Nicholson mansion, 252
Wright, Corrinne, 247
Wright, Sir James, 5
Wright, Wilbur and Orville, 166–67
WTFI radio, 158

Yale University, 14, 179
Yarborough, Fed, 103
Yorktown, Battle of, 6
Young Men's Christian Association, 69, 174, 207, 216
Young Women's Christian Association, 207, 259

Zeta Tau Alpha sorority, 218
Zoning regulations, 228